CITY BOUND

CITY BOUND

How States Stifle Urban Innovation

**Gerald E. Frug and
David J. Barron**

CORNELL UNIVERSITY PRESS   ITHACA AND LONDON

First published 2008 by Cornell University Press
Printed in the United States of America

Library of Congress Cataloging-in-Publication Data

Frug, Gerald E., 1939–
   City bound : how states stifle urban innovation / Gerald E. Frug and David J. Barron.
      p. cm.
   Includes bibliographical references and index.
   ISBN 978–0–8014 4514–9 (cloth : alk. paper)
   1. State–local relations—United States. 2. Municipal home rule—United States. 3. Municipal government—United States. 4. Municipal corporations—United States. 5. Urban Policy—United States. I. Barron, David J. II. Title.

   JS348.F78   2008
   320.8'50973—dc22   2008024375

Cornell University Press strives to use environmentally responsible suppliers and materials to the fullest extent possible in the publishing of its books. Such materials include vegetable-based, low-VOC inks and acid-free papers that are recycled, totally chlorine-free, or partly composed of nonwood fibers. For further information, visit our website at www.cornellpress.cornell.edu.

Cloth printing   10 9 8 7 6 5 4 3 2 1

For Stephen and Emily—Gerald Frug
For Juliette—David Barron

Contents

Preface

Traffic is terrible. Why doesn't the city do something about it? The answer, this book suggests, is simple: it may not have the power.

Cities have plenty of problems: schools, housing, crime, and global warming are just examples. Traffic congestion and inadequate mass transit are certainly on this list. Many ideas have been advanced about dealing with each of these issues. We focus in this book on the extent to which cities can implement any of them, however good they are. Only if the city has power to act can it be blamed if solutions are not implemented. This point probably seems as straightforward to you as it does to us. If so, it should seem as odd to you as it is to us that there is almost no literature analyzing in any detail how the legal system empowers and disempowers cities. We aim to fill the gap.

Let's take a closer look at the traffic problem. In April 2007, New York City's mayor, Michael Bloomberg, proposed a bold idea for dealing with traffic in mid-town and lower Manhattan: congestion charging. Under congestion charging those who want to drive to the busiest part of town during peak hours must pay to do so. Mayor Bloomberg's proposal was to charge $8 for cars that sought to enter Manhattan south of 86th Street during the workday (trucks would pay more). As the mayor recognized, congestion charging is not a new idea. Its most well-known example is in London, where the current charge is £8 (twice as much as Mayor Bloomberg proposed) to enter a large section of central London. Recently, London's affected area was enlarged, and the price of entering it was raised, due to the success of the original experiment launched in 2003. The impact of the congestion charge so far has been impressive. Traffic congestion in

London is down 20 percent, greenhouse gas emissions are down 15 percent, and bicycle trips are up 80 percent, without the loss of business in central London that merchants had feared. The money raised from the congestion charge, after paying for maintaining the system, has been allocated to mass transit improvements. Ridership on the buses—the first target for improvement, since the Underground took longer to upgrade—is up by one third, with the greatest increase among the richest part of the population. More changes are being contemplated—including barring sports utility vehicles from the area altogether (an idea that enjoys 3–1 popular support). And London is by no means the only model for New York: Stockholm, Singapore, and other cities have congestion charging too.[1]

Obviously, then, a congestion charge is a possible way to deal with traffic problems. The point we want to emphasize here is that the City of New York has no power to implement it. Only the New York state government can authorize it. In fact, London didn't have the power to install congestion charging on its own either: an act of Parliament—a very detailed act of Parliament, reserving considerable power over the issue to the national government—was required. In New York, the first level of difficulty facing the city can be found in a specific state statute—section 1604 of New York's Vehicle and Traffic law. It says quite simply: "Local authorities shall have no power to pass…any ordinance…requiring any tax, fee, license or permit for use of the public highways."

Seems pretty straightforward. But it's actually not. Sure, it's clear that New York State has prohibited the city from doing the very thing it wants to do. But what if the state hadn't enacted this statute? Could New York City then have adopted a congestion charge on its own? The issue here gets a little dicey, but the basic answer is no. We want to start, however, by emphasizing the opposite point: traffic is something New York City can do something about. Indeed, the state legislature has given every city in the state the power to install traffic signals, create one-way streets, and the like. More significantly, a special state statute that applies only to "any city having a population in excess of a million"—that is, only to New York City—gives the city very broad authority to "prohibit, restrict or regulate traffic" on its streets and, if "authorized by law," to charge tolls on its highways. Perhaps most important, the New York Constitution gives the city a degree of home rule, and, in doing so, it specifically lists the management and use of the streets as part of the city's constitutionally granted powers. Unlike many other issues that might seem outside of the city's control—taxing commuters, say, or preventing the flooding that might be caused by global warning—traffic is a local function. New York City uses its powers to deal with traffic every day, as anyone who has spent even an hour there can see.[2]

So, then, why couldn't the city implement congestion charging if the specific prohibition against doing so had not been enacted by the state legislature? The answer is that the New York courts have made it clear that the city can exercise power over its streets only in a way that benefits every one in the state, not just its own residents, and, therefore, that the state itself has ultimate control over the city's streets. On this basis, a state court in 1981 invalidated the city's effort to limit traffic on weekday mornings to cars with multiple passengers on four bridges leading into Manhattan. The problem was not that the state had prohibited this effort. The problem, the court said, was that the power to enact such a program was not expressly delegated to the city by state law. In other words, the problem was that the city had to get *specific permission* from the state to ban single-person cars. It can't just do it on its own, even if there is no state prohibition on the books. In 1988, the New York Court of Appeals relied on the same reasoning when it invalidated the city's efforts to create residential parking zones in the city. The fact that New York City has "home rule" power, in short, doesn't mean what many people seem to think it means. It does not give the city the power to control its streets on its own initiative.[3]

These rulings would make any mayor concerned that the state courts would strike down a congestion charge if the city imposed it on its own. Sure, it would apply to city residents and not just outsiders. A congestion charge is not the same thing as an entrance fee to the city. But a court might disagree. And that legal risk would make any mayor doubt whether it was worth investing time and energy in an innovative policy that rests on such shaky legal foundations.

Given this bind, Mayor Bloomberg could not simply ask the state to remove a restriction. He had no option but to go to the state legislature to get express permission for the congestion charge. He was turned down. The legislature instead agreed to set up a seventeen-member commission, with members appointed not just by the mayor and governor but also by state legislative and city council leaders, to study his proposal, among others. In addition, the legislature decided that any proposed congestion charge would have to be approved by the New York City Council, not, as the mayor had hoped, only by him and the state government. Both the statewide commission and the required city council approval quite obviously change the politics of instituting a congestion charge. Councilmembers from the outer boroughs and state legislators from the suburbs will have different reactions to the idea than the mayor. Who decides matters. And, now, who decides is very complicated indeed. As the *New York Times* somewhat elaborately put it:

> Any final plan will...need to be approved by the United States Department of Transportation, the mayor, the governor, and majorities of the new 17-member traffic mitigation commission, the 62-member State Senate, and the 150-member State Assembly.[4]

But it's actually worse than that. One of the key parts of the London congestion-charge package, as we mentioned above, is that the money raised is used for mass transit improvements. This could readily be done there because the Greater London Authority, through its mayor-appointed Transport for London, has control over mass transit, as well as over the streets, taxi regulation, bicycle permits, and other aspects of the transportation system. New York City does not have control over its mass transit operations. Instead, they are run by New York City Transit, a subdivision of a state-created and state-appointed public authority, the Metropolitan Transportation Authority. Any changes in the bus and subway system require the approval—and cooperation—of this independent authority, not just of the people mentioned in the *Times*. Worse still, we've not even mentioned the money that would be necessary to put the system in place. The mayor expected the federal government to help fund the project, and the compromise he worked out with the legislature requires that there be federal funding. So far, the federal government has agreed to provide a considerable amount of money for mass transit although not directly for implementing a congestion charge, and its participation will ultimately depend on working out the final arrangements at the state level. It's clear, given the state-imposed limits on local finance, that New York City will not be able to fund the idea—estimated to cost more than $200 million—simply on its own. Of course, all these hurdles can be overcome. Some are optimistic they will be. Yet it would be hard to defend the "compromise" worked out by the state legislature as the ideal decision-making mechanism to deal with congestion charging.

The point of this story is not to say that New York City alone should have the authority to determine whether and how to implement congestion charging. Nor is the point that New York City will never be able to implement a, perhaps modified, congestion charge. The point instead is to highlight the importance of the decision-making structure for this policy initiative—and, as this book will demonstrate, for countless others as well. This is one meaning of our title, *City Bound*. Every city in the United States has state-established legal boundaries—as well as state-established geographic boundaries—that circumscribe its powers. Although these legal boundaries differ from state to state, they exist everywhere. And there's no possibility that they all will go away. Every city will always operate under some kind of state controls. The question is what they should be. The task is to build city power in a way that can help direct it toward a sensible version of the city's future. Determining how to do so is one of topics that this book explores.

New York City, however, is not just a product of its constraints. Along with other cities on which we focus in this book, New York City is prospering in a way that was unforeseeable decades ago, when American central cities were almost given up for lost. New York City is experiencing significant economic growth and a notable increase in population. Its population in 2000, according to the census, was just over eight million, the highest ever.[5] That's why a congestion charge is being considered. People are now New York bound: it's a city with a future. The question is: What kind of future will that be? Congestion charging is now a popular way transportation experts want to deal with traffic problems, and its implementation would have a significant effect on life in New York City for decades to come. But in the 1950s and 1960s, experts had another popular idea to deal with traffic problems: highway construction. Robert Moses planned to build a series of highways across Manhattan—the Lower Manhattan Expressway (an elevated highway above Brome Street), the Mid-Manhattan Expressway (an elevated highway above 30th Street), the Cross Harlem Expressway (ground level on 125th Street), and the Trans-Manhattan Expressway (at the George Washington Bridge); only the last was in fact built. Like congestion charging, these highways were seen as a solution to traffic congestion in Manhattan, and they too would have depended on federal support and required state approvals. But they would have created a very different city than congestion charging. Hidden in the detailed issues of city power, in short, are large questions about the nature of the urban age American cities can and should promote. The kind of people who live in the city, the city's connection to its suburbs, and the impact of transportation planning on historic neighborhoods, housing affordability, and office construction—like many other urban issues—are implicated in the choices among the possible alternative legal structures that determine city power. Designing a decision-making structure is part of the process of designing America's urban future. This too will be a theme of the book that follows.

Acknowledgments

Although we did not know it at the time, the genesis of this book began in a seminar that we co-taught at Harvard Law School in 2001. With the help of a wonderful group of students, the course examined the extent of home rule in the 101 municipalities that comprise the greater Boston metropolitan area. The students undertook a thorough study of the legal powers that the state had given the region's cities and towns, and they surveyed the attitudes of local officials living and working in these communities. With the assistance of the Rappaport Institute for Greater Boston, we published the results of that research as a short book, *Dispelling the Myth of Home Rule: Local Power in Greater Boston.* That initial foray into the reality of city power in the Boston area led us to collaborate with the Boston Foundation on a project comparing the legal powers of the City of Boston itself to six other major American cities. The resulting report, *Boston Bound: A Comparison of Boston's Legal Powers with Those of Six Other Major American Cities,* laid the groundwork for this book.

Although this earlier work, along with some of our other writings on local government law, has informed this book, we have also relied on the advice and encouragement of many colleagues and friends. We owe a special debt of gratitude to Jerry Rappaport, the founder of the Rappaport Institute, as well as to its founding executive director, Charlie Euchner, and its first faculty director, the former dean of the Harvard Graduate School of Design, Alan Altshuler. They provided us with the initial support and encouragement that led us to take a close look at the nature of city power in our own backyard. We are indebted as well to the energy, enthusiasm, and insights of the president of the Boston Foundation, Paul Grogan, and to his exceptional colleagues, Mary Jo Meisner and James Rooney, as well as advisers they brought into our midst, above all, Larry DiCara, Sam Tyler, and Steve McGoldrick. All of them knew a good deal more about Boston than we did. Early in the project, we received funding from the Real Estate Academic Initiative at Harvard, led by Richard Peiser, as well from our own dean, Elena Kagan. We are very grateful to them as well. Two other people were indispensable: Kathy Goldstein and Patricia Fazzone, who helped in countless ways preparing the manuscript. Thanks to them too.

In the course of preparing *Boston Bound,* we asked six experts on local government law to prepare reports on the legal powers of the six comparison cities: Keith Aoki of the University of California-Davis (Seattle), Richard Briffault of Columbia Law School (New York), William Buzbee of Emory Law School (Atlanta), Richard Ford of Stanford Law School (San Francisco), Richard Schragger of Virginia Law School (Denver), and Laurie Reynolds of the University of Illinois College of Law (Chicago). Their reports were of enormous value to us then, and we have relied on them in this book as well, particularly in part II. We have also had the good fortune to receive research assistance from a number of excellent students, including Kate Bowers, Elizabeth Frieze, Chris Pistilli, Eli Rosenbaum, and Josh Stern. We would especially like to single out Rick Su, now an assistant professor at Buffalo Law School, for his outstanding research and many insights into local government law. His contributions were so important to us that we made explicit what to us was undeniable: he is listed as a co-author of *Dispelling the Myth of Home Rule.* Finally, in thinking about the issues we discuss in this book, we have benefited from conversations from a number of colleagues, including, in addition to those already mentioned, Archon Fung, Morton Horwitz, David Kennedy, Duncan Kennedy, David Luberoff, Wendell Pritchett, Saskia Sassen, Richard Sennett, and Todd Swanstrom.

We thank the publishers of some of our earlier articles, written either together or individually, for their permission to reprint relevant selections. These articles include "Reclaiming Home Rule," *Harvard Law Review* 116, 2255 (2003); "Beyond Regional Government," *Harvard Law Review* 115, 1763 (2002); "A Localist Critique of the New Federalism," *Duke Law Journal* 51, 377 (2001); "International Local Government Law," *Urban Lawyer* 38, 1 (2006); and "Defensive Localism," *Virginia Journal of Law and Politics* 21, 261 (2006).

David owes special thanks to his parents Jerry and Myra Barron, herself a practitioner of local government law, and to his three children, Cecilia, Leo, and Jeremiah, some of whom were not yet born when this book first began but all of whom are a joy. His greatest thanks, however, is to his wife, Juliette Kayyem, who lives the real work of state-local relations every day, and whose boundless enthusiasm, energy, commitment, and general sense of excitement exemplifies the attitude towards the future that more states should be encouraging their cities to embrace. Jerry's special thanks go to his children, Stephen and Emily, to whom this book is dedicated, and to those who helped guide him into local government law, above all Frank Michelman. But it is to the youngest generation in his life—Charlie and Maddie—that he hopes the book will have particular meaning, because thinking about their lives has helped inspire the book's call for changes in the way American cities are governed.

CITY BOUND

Part I
CITY STRUCTURES

Lewis Mumford used to ask a very basic question: "What is a city?"[1] The answer depends on one's angle of vision. For many people, the word "city" is associated with images of density, so that only parts of the city seem citylike. Residents of Queens often talk about going to "the city," meaning Manhattan, even though they already live in the City of New York. The entire metropolitan region can also be experienced as one big city. Many residents of Boston's suburbs say they live in Boston even though they don't.

These differing definitions of a city work well for some purposes. But when one is considering the powers of city governments they won't do. The residents of Manhattan can't make policy for themselves any more than the residents of Queens. Only the City of New York is a city government. Only it can pass ordinances, deliver public services, levy taxes, enforce land use plans, or issue binding regulations. Moreover, the borders between cities matter. The mayor of Cambridge, Massachusetts, cannot affect development in Boston except indirectly, just as the mayor of the City of New York does not formulate urban policy for Jersey City. Although some city governments do exercise a limited amount of extraterritorial governmental authority over neighboring areas, city power is largely limited to the area defined by the city's own borders.

When thinking about making urban policy in the United States, therefore, one should begin with the fact that American metropolitan areas are divided into a multitude, often dozens, of different local governments. These governments are the primary institutions in America that exercise power at the local level. It is also important to recognize that, even within their own territory, these local governments are not free to do whatever they want. The reason is not simply that their powers—like those of all levels of government in the United States—are limited by the federal Constitution and by federal statutes. Local power in the United States is derived from state law. Unless states authorize their local governments to do something, they have no power to do it. As John Dillon put the matter in the earliest, and most important, American treatise on the subject, the fact that local power depends on a delegation of authority from its state is *"of transcendent importance, and lie[s] at the foundation of the law of municipal corporations."*[2] (The italics are his.) In this book we take Dillon's insight seriously: we outline an understanding of local power that takes as its starting point an analysis of the extent and limits of the state-defined power of American city governments.

The importance of this starting point is regularly overlooked by analysts of city power, as well as by those who call for regional policies even though there is no regional authority empowered to adopt them. Many scholars treat cities more as markets than as governments. As a result, they give more attention to the activities of private actors than to the power of city governments to respond to what they are doing. Even those who have focused on cities as governments have tended to concentrate on the nonlegal constraints on urban policy-making. These constraints include the city's internal political dynamics, the demands of interlocal competition for private investment, and the ways in which large-scale technological developments, such as the invention of the automobile, promote broad antiurban social trends such as suburbanization. Indeed, it is not uncommon for scholars simultaneously to assert that cities have considerable local autonomy as a legal matter and that, as a practical matter, they are limited in the kinds of policies that they can actually adopt.

In what follows, we take a different path. We carefully examine the effect of local government law (our name for what Dillon calls "the law of municipal corporations") on city power. Local government law does not include all of the legal rules that affect cities. It refers simply to the portion of state law that is specifically designed to define the powers of cities. Local government law determines whether city governments are elected or appointed. It dictates whether cities can act on their own initiative or only with express approval from the state legislature. It specifies which governmental services will be provided locally and which will be provided by others. It defines cities' fiscal authority and their powers to regulate land use development within their boundaries. And it decides where those city boundaries are. Local government law, in short, determines the legal status of cities. And it is different in every state in the country.

By focusing on local government law, we are able to emphasize the importance of what we call city structures. These structures are the legal frameworks within which cities operate. They contain a mix of grants of, and restrictions on, local power that cities do not themselves define. And they have an important and largely unexamined impact on cities' capacity to control their future. Sometimes they exert this influence directly by preventing a city from using specified economic development tools, barring it from levying particular kinds of taxes, or mandating that it provide services or offer its employees benefits. But city structures also influence the exercise of city power indirectly. The state definition of the city taxing authority, for example, does more than determine how much money cities have to spend. It also provides the city an incentive to pursue a particular kind of economic development—the one that best fits with the revenue stream the state has permitted it to tap. The rules that limit local fiscal authority thus influence, even distort, city land use planning. This dynamic between the formal legal rules of local government law and the city's decision-making process operates in many contexts.

As Dillon made clear in his treatise, local government law determines the legal powers of all local governments in the United States, not just those of major cities such as Boston and New York. Every municipality—whether a city or a suburb, a town or a village—operates within a structure that has been established by state law. Our focus in this book is more limited. We concentrate on the impact of city structures on the powers of large, successful central cities. These cities represent a small fraction of the more than nineteen thousand general-purpose local governments in the United States, but they nevertheless merit special consideration. There are an increasing number of them across the county. Central cities were once thought to be dying, but many are now emerging from the difficult years of the 1950s to become diverse, vital, and economically powerful governments. These days, many American central cities are more likely to be hailed as drivers of their regional economy—even as part of a worldwide system of global cities—than to be written off as relics of the past. The cities on which we focus are often the largest single municipality in their state, sometimes by orders of magnitude, and the future of the states in which they are located is bound up with their success. As a result, they not only have an influence on state policymaking but become the special targets of legislative interest. Indeed, because of their obvious importance, large central cities are often singled out by their states for special legal treatment in ways that both empower and restrict them.

In recent years, many commentators have examined the emergence of large central cities as successful urban environments for people to live and work. But few have examined the ways that state law—through state constitutional provisions, statutes, administrative regulations, and judicial decisions—structures their powers. No one has done so in a detailed, comparative way across a number of cities in different states. As a result, there has been little consideration of the questions that are our principal concern: What state-imposed limits constrain the ability of large, relatively successful city governments to improve the lives of city residents, workers, and visitors? What are the differences in the ways that states have set up their legal structures for cities and how do these differences influence the ways cities make choices about their future? These questions are particularly urgent for large, successful cities. Because of their size and their growing market power, they potentially have the ability to make choices about their future to an extent that other municipalities do not. They therefore are more likely than smaller cities to feel the constraining impact of the kinds of legal rules that we describe in this book.

In this book, we investigate the city structures that govern seven major American cities: Boston, New York, Chicago, San Francisco, Seattle, Denver, and Atlanta. The details about these cities, as well as about our approach to comparing them, are the topic of part II. By focusing on the importance of city structures for these seven cities, we seek to open up an area for inquiry as much as to provide definitive answers to its importance. Our goal is to identify key ways in which city structures matter. By examining state-defined city authority, we investigate who is responsible for any particular urban problem and, therefore, who can implement a proposed solution.

The value of this way of thinking about urban issues is not limited to pinpointing the entity capable of carrying out reform. It also helps identify the need for revising the city structures now in place. Most states have not significantly altered their city structures for decades; for some cities, key features can be traced to decisions made nearly a century ago. Yet, as everyone knows, central cities operate in an economy—and serve a population—that has changed markedly in the past few decades. If entrenched legal structures were made more responsive to contemporary realities, cities' ability to improve the delivery of traditional city services and to assert greater control over their development could be significantly enhanced. A proper understanding of the nature of city power can therefore change the way people think about solving urban problems. By exploring the importance of the legal power of local governments, one can generate new ideas about improving the delivery of city services by modifying city power through state legislation. States could increase it in some ways and decrease it in others, thereby altering what cities do and how well they do it.

Our emphasis on the constraints imposed by the current rules of local government law should not be interpreted to suggest that cities should be allowed to do whatever they want. We are not advocates for what is often called "city autonomy." On the contrary, as we stated in the preface and develop in chapter 2, we think that every state government will and should continue to control what its cities do. Our purpose is to describe the city structures that now determine the power of major American cities and illustrate possible alternatives. By framing city power in the right way, we argue, states can do more to address urban issues, both local and regional, than is currently thought possible.

The impact of city structures can best be understood if one has some sense of the kinds of choices that a large American city might want to make about its future. The kind of powers that these cities might need over the next few decades can then become more apparent. So will the gap between their needs and their current legal authority under state law and the ways in which a state's legal structure now push them to favor certain ideas about their future over others. In order to provide this kind of context for reexamining local government law, we offer four possible futures that successful cities could pursue. The detailed investigation of these four futures will be the subject of part III.

The four futures we envision build on the work of other urban scholars. In recent years, many of them have sketched a number of alternative pathways for city development. The four city futures on which we will focus are a global city, a tourist city, a middle class city, and a regional city. A global city concentrates on developing connections to the global economy—through technology, finance, and innovative research—as the city's primary strategy for growth. A tourist city seeks to attract visitors from around the world as its major emphasis—concentrating on cultural and sports facilities, convention centers, festival marketplaces, hotels, and restaurants. A middle class city treats the provision of services for residents, above all public education, as its most important function. A regional city focuses on surrounding cities and towns in the metropolitan area, and thus is more concerned with the city's relationship to development in its suburbs than to its relationship with Shanghai. These four futures are not mutually exclusive. An effort to become a middle-class city by improving public education might also strengthen efforts to become a global one. A city focused on tourism might invest in neighborhood preservation in order to create an authentic urban feel for visitors, and, thereby, improve the fortunes of middle-class neighborhoods.

Nevertheless, these four urban futures are not necessarily mutually reinforcing. A city that is focused on its connection to the global economy may pursue policies that make it inhospitable to middle-class families with small children. It might, for example, concentrate on the development of high-end housing for part-time residents who have no kids at all. A city that is dedicated to tourism might make building tourist attractions in the downtown area a high priority at the expense of investment in neighborhoods far from the city center. A city concerned primarily with its relationship to the region might adopt transportation policies designed to serve suburban commuters rather than those directed at renovating its airport, even though the airport might do more to make the city appealing to visitors and to investment from abroad.

Not only might these futures not overlap but one can readily imagine other ideas of urban life—such as becoming an immigrant city—that we do not discuss. It is sufficient for us if these four futures represent plausible options that are sufficiently distinctive that a city that consciously chooses to focus on one of them might look and feel different from one that chooses to pursue another. It is also important to us that none of the options is obviously superior to the others. If these assumptions are right, it means successful cities have genuine alternatives from which to choose. If so, it is important to investigate whether the city structures in which they operate permit them to pursue all of the futures or, on the contrary, channel their decision making to favor some choices over others.

Of necessity, our analysis of the relationship between city structures and city futures will be both speculative and incomplete. There is no sure way to promote any of these conceptions of a city's future, let alone other goals that we do not consider. Besides, legal changes are only part of a strategy designed to further different conceptions of the city's devel-opment. Despite these complexities, it seems to us helpful to take a closer look at each of these ways in which large success-ful cities might develop and the kind of legal structures that might help them do so. Moreover, although our focus will be on the power of the central cities to plan their own futures, it should be clear that none of the cities we examine can ignore the suburbs that surround them. Here, too, state law matters. A city's ability to cooperate with nearby cities is a function of the legal powers that the state has given to (and withheld from) all of its localities. We will therefore highlight aspects of the legal structure that affect the ability of the seven cities to work with—or struggle against—neighboring cities and towns in their region.

Our conclusion, which we develop in this book, can be stated here at the outset. Current city structures frustrate cit-ies' efforts to exercise control over their future development whatever their goals are. But, as we shall develop at length in the third section of the book, current legal rules make it eas-ier for large central cities to pursue some objectives—namely, the global city and the tourist city—than others. Indeed, the difficulties that cities face if they seek to pursue being a mid-dle class city or regional cooperation themselves push cities in the direction of focusing instead on being a global city or a tourist city. The limitations on cities' ability to pursue their objectives operate in different ways for different cities. Some are worse off than others. Boston offers a particularly glaring example of the impact of an outdated city structure on city decision making. Boston's legal structure was largely prescribed in the late nineteenth century. The key changes since then took place in response to the challenges that Bos-ton faced following World War II, when the city suffered dramatic population losses in connection with nationwide economic restructuring. Many of these changes resulted in the city's ceding control over key parts of its infrastructure to entities run by the state. Although there may well have been good reasons at the time for that transfer of power, Boston is no longer a city in decline. It is now a thriving, successful city, in competition for residents and investment with other cities, such as New York, Chicago, San Francisco, Seattle, Denver, and Atlanta. Yet Boston has little capacity to chart its own future because its legal powers are unusually limited. These limitations should be of concern not only to city residents and officials but also to people who live outside the city, because Boston is the economic engine for its metropolitan area and the state as a whole.

Boston is not unique. All of the cities we examine are structured by state controls—particularly over revenues and expenditures and land-use planning—that limit their choices about future development. A comparison of the different kinds of grants and denials of authority that govern cities will demonstrate the ways in which alternative structures of city power set different directions for a city's development. Examining these different structures points the way to the kinds of changes in the legal system that can better enable cities, including many we do not discuss in this book, to develop in the twenty-first century. We hope that our focus on city structures will generate renewed interest in augmenting city power. People who live outside America's major cities can easily dismiss concerns about limited city power because they do not appear to be connected to broader structural issues that concern the state as a whole. Demands for city power often seem to be veiled pleas by the mayor to meet a municipal payroll that many already believe to be excessive. Yet the central issue concerning city power is not about the city's short-term budgetary needs, important as they are. Nor is it simply a matter of principle—that local self-government should not be unduly limited. The issue is that large central cities—even more than other municipalities in the state—now operate within a legal structure not of their own making, one that needs to be updated in light of new urban realities. As we describe in chapter 10, one of the goals of a revised city structure can be not only to promote the power of central cities but a regional approach to urban issues that is now itself frustrated by state law. A revision of city structures, in other words, can help rethink the organization of metropolitan areas as a whole.

When we turn later in the book to an examination of the local government law that structures the power of our seven cities, we will describe in detail how a state's grant of power affects specific cities. But our larger aim is to make clear how local government law affects the behavior of large central cities more generally, not just the effects of local government law on the seven cities. It thus seems important first to address the connection between law and city power at a more conceptual level. The urban studies literature has a rich tradition of investigating the exercise of city power. A useful way to understand our approach is to see how it builds on, yet deviates from, this existing literature. This requires situating our notion of city structures within urban theory, the task of the first two chapters.

CITY STRUCTURES AND URBAN THEORY

One important way that urban theorists analyze city power involves examining the relationship between structure and agency. By structure, we mean the external factors, those outside of the city's control, that affect what cities can and cannot do. By agency, we mean a city's power to make choices within that structure. H. V. Savitch and Paul Kantor provide a useful account of the conventional understanding of these terms:

> The idea of structure entails long-term, underlying, relatively fixed forces that configure decision making and make it quite difficult for human actions to overcome. Economic benefits that spring from geographic location is an example of a structural factor that cities can do little about. By contrast, the idea of agency conveys human volition, personal discretion, and freedom of action. The ability of elected leaders to adopt development strategies that solely satisfy popular preferences represents an instance of agency.[1]

Our focus on local government law's influence on city power leads us to build on this distinction, but to alter it in two key respects.

First, we break with the common assumption that nonlegal external constraints are the ones that really matter. Structural influences on city power have traditionally been understood, as Savitch and Kantor do, to take the form of "long-term, underlying, relatively fixed forces…difficult for human actions to overcome." By suggesting that local government law represents an independent and significant structural constraint on city power, we focus on a limitation that is the product of contingent political choices rather than deeply rooted social, economic, or geographical conditions. The fact that this constraint results from political choices means that it is more amenable to human action than the more conventionally understood examples of structural forces. The differences among the city structures that we examine in this book underscore this point. Our view of local government law's role is thus consistent with the recent scholarship that suggests that a city's "interest" can be changed through politics.

We also treat the concept of agency differently. We agree that legal constraints limit cities' agency only if, in their absence, cities would have the capacity to act differently. We also agree with the growing body of work that emphasizes the substantial degree of agency that cities possess. Our interest in how local government law restricts a city's range of choices, however, suggests that city agency may be both broader and narrower than others imagine. The increase in agency stems from our conviction that many of the conventional ways of framing the choices attributable to cities are too abstract to be useful. A city's options are often presented as a choice between promoting development or redistribution, exchange values or use values, growth or no growth. Viewed through the perspective of the four futures we develop in part III, it becomes apparent that these terms have a variety of possible meanings and, in fact, that many city choices cannot easily be categorized as belonging on only one side of these stark dichotomies. Our focus on local government law's impact on the four futures offers a better way of seeing the choices that the cities confront and the substantial degree of agency that they possess. But our focus on these four futures also provides a cautionary note about the extent of city agency. Cities may have more agency than some urban theorists suggest, but they are subject to state-imposed restrictions that limit their ability to take advantage of the discretion afforded them by prevailing economic and social conditions.

Although we adopt the structure/agency vocabulary in this chapter, we recognize, along with many others, that the sharp dichotomy often drawn between the two concepts is untenable. Agency can never be isolated from the structure in which it operates. And the constraining structure, in part, can be self-imposed: the agent can be constrained by a structure of its own imagination. As we shall see when we discuss the concept of "home rule" in chapter 3, some of the limits on city power are the product of the cities' internalized lack of confidence in their ability to act. The conceptual interpenetration between structure and agency raises theoretical complexities that we do not explore in this book. Even the way we have used the two terms in this paragraph is problematic: we continue to distinguish them even though we say they cannot be disentangled. Instead of pursuing these perplexities, we treat the theoretical debate as helping us to demonstrate that city power is constituted by the circular relationship between state-imposed legal rules and the cities' own actions. Despite the objections that might be made about the two terms, we invoke them as a shorthand: they allow us to compare our approach to the extensive urban literature that analyzes the ingredients that define city power.

Local Government Law and the Role of External Structure

To explore the relationship between our approach and other ways of conceptualizing structural influences on city power, we turn to a brief analysis of the important debates about city politics that have been generated by the foundational question Robert Dahl asked in his celebrated study of New Haven: "Who governs?"[2] The controversy over how this question should be answered, and whether it is even the right question to be asking, has generated a rich investigation of the relationship between structure and agency in the exercise of city power. The debate has not directly examined the role that local government law plays in shaping city policy. To be sure, on occasion, some scholars have suggested that changes in the legal structure might enable cities to expand their capacity to respond to the economic and societal forces that otherwise constrict their politics to a narrow band of options. But those who have made these suggestions have not developed them in a systematic fashion, and they have almost always focused on the need for changing federal rather than state law. It is not surprising that the legal structure has not figured more prominently in previous studies of structural constraints on urban power. The urban theorists who have been trained as economists, political scientists, historians, planners, geographers, and sociologists have been aware that law shapes the forces on which they have focused, but their primary interests have quite naturally led them to place law well in the background of their analysis. Even urban scholars who are legally trained, however, have often downplayed local government law's constraining influence. Many have argued that cities now have local legal autonomy and, therefore, that states should increase the legal restrictions on local power in order to protect central cities from ruinous suburban competition. We examine this position in detail in the next chapter.

The Community Power Debate

The issue that Dahl raised required analyzing who exercised policy-making authority within the city. Is the local population as a whole, or only an unaccountable minority of wealthy and connected people within it, in charge of city decision making? The debate that pursued this question—one that has come to be known as the community power debate—dominated urban political science in the decades following World War II. One group of analysts, the elite theorists, tended to portray cities as exclusive clubs, run by a small and relatively unaccountable oligarchy that persistently exercised local power. Another—the pluralists—responded that shifting interest groups within the city exercised power on an issue-by-issue basis. Although the pluralists did not argue that every citizen of the city had an equal voice, they rejected the view that a single "power elite" consistently dominated.[3]

The divide between those who viewed city politics as elitist and those who viewed it as pluralist was fundamental. Depending on whom one believed, cities were either legitimate democratic institutions in which the electorate had a fair chance of having its voice heard or unaccountable handmaidens to a small, elite group of wealthy residents. Of particular interest for present purposes is the fact that, at least on the surface, both sides of the debate assumed that cities possessed a great deal of agency. The disagreement over who governed a city mattered precisely because cities were thought to have the power to make a wide range of important decisions of interest to their residents. If cities lacked this authority, the attention devoted to determining who governed them would have been badly misplaced.

Given the time period in which the community debate took place, it is not hard to understand why such a strong assumption of city agency took hold. The debate began in earnest at the height of the urban renewal movement when cities were using their powers to remake themselves. Whole neighborhoods were condemned, cleared, and rebuilt at the city's command. It was not unthinkable that a city could bring about great changes in its environment because that was precisely what many cities were doing. Although it seemed clear that they had the power to make important decisions, it was not clear whether the decisions they were making were the right ones. There were sure to be winners and losers. This raised the question of whether city politics was systematically biased against some people, and, in particular, against the low-income residents who were bearing the brunt of redevelopment efforts. The community power debate was thus not just an abstract academic dispute—it had direct implications for the legitimacy of urban renewal.

Even though the community power debate rested on a strong assumption of city agency, it was not unconcerned with the potential impact of external structures. Significant economic and social forces provided the frame within which city politics took place, and urban renewal was clearly responsive to these forces. The influences that received the most consideration did not concern state-granted legal authority. They focused instead on factors such as the decline of manufacturing, the rise of suburbia, and the creation of the federal highway system. Still, there was some recognition that the rules of local government law mattered as well. Because cities were engaged in creative policymaking, they were stretching conventional understandings of the scope of their legal authority. Although Dahl's focus was on the political dynamics within New Haven, he noted that the city's vigorous pursuit of urban renewal was aided by changes in state law. To permit New Haven to take aim against "blight," he explained, state law had been altered through generous interpretations of the state-conferred power of eminent domain—interpretations that the state courts were initially very reluctant to accept. He also noted that Connecticut's decision to delegate to the city the right to establish a redevelopment authority was responsive to a requirement attached to the federal funding on which New Haven relied for most of its urban renewal projects. He concluded his study of New Haven by offering various models of pluralist urban politics—ranging from an executive-centered coalition to a more managerial model—that were clearly linked to the state legal rules that defined the city's governmental structure.

Nevertheless, the discussion of the impact of state law on city politics was a minor ingredient in the community power debate. In fact, the role that state law played in *limiting* city power—either by directly prohibiting the exercise of city power or by giving the city an incentive to pursue particular policies by making them reliant on property taxes—was hardly considered. The debate downplayed the importance of economic and social constraints as well. The real focus was on who exercised power within the city, a focus that subsequent commentators sharply challenged. As they did, the legal structure's role in shaping city power came to figure more prominently in the analysis.

City Limits

The community power debate's focus on the city's internal political dynamics was the target of an important critique by Paul Peterson in his 1980 book, *City Limits*.[4] Other critics had already complained that the debate had proceeded on the basis of a far too narrow concept of what constituted local political "choices." Even if multiple constituencies had been given a say in the policies that cities actually adopted, they argued, cities also made policy by deciding to keep many matters off the agenda. Nondecisions were decisions too. Thus it was entirely possible—perhaps even likely—that the urban agenda consistently reflected the influence of elites despite the fact that a broad range of interest groups were involved in making the city decisions that were in fact implemented.

Peterson's critique cut deeper. It applied equally to elite and pluralist theorists. Writing shortly after New York City's near bankruptcy in the 1970s, Peterson

argued that the community power debate was fundamentally misconceived because it focused on internal political struggles and thus gave undue weight to
the significance of local agency. The community power scholarship wrongly
assumed that city politics was just like national politics—that cities were fundamentally autonomous governments. True, community power theorists often
noted that cities faced constraints on their powers—including those imposed
by higher levels of government. But their focus on the internal dynamics of city
politics suggested that they did not quite believe their own qualifications. They
wrote as if the decisions that cities made were the products of the local political decision-making process. Peterson contended that, unlike higher levels of
government, cities were fundamentally limited as to what they could do. These
external limitations on their authority exerted a powerful influence on the kinds
of decisions that cities made.

It seems likely that this skepticism about city agency was fueled by the decline
in urban fortunes in the 1960s and 1970s. Although cities had once seemed
capable of doing big things, their situation indicated that they were not masters
of their own fate. Dahl wrote against the background of Richard Lee's vigorous
urban renewal efforts in New Haven. Peterson wrote with the experience of the
Lindsay administration in New York City in mind. It is not surprising, then, that
Peterson began to construct a theory of urban decision making that was pre-
mised on an assumption of limited, rather than expansive, city power. Peterson
argued that the choices cities make are powerfully influenced by the national
political economy. For that reason, both sides of the community power debate
were mistaken. Even if a small group maintained a dominant political position,
they were essentially responding to market forces that they could not control.
Similarly, pluralists wrongly concluded that participation in local politics showed
that diverse interests were well represented. In reality, issues of great importance
to city residents never became subjects of serious political debate because cities,
as a structural matter, had little power to address them.

At times Peterson seems to be suggesting that an inexorable economic logic
represents the critical limitation on city power. This is particularly evident in
Peterson's discussion of the nature of what he terms a city's "interest." The fact
that the subject of city politics was limited meant that cities inevitably developed
an interest in improving their position within the larger structure in which they
were embedded. A city's interest was not the aggregation of the individual interests of its residents. It was the product of the city's rational desire to enhance its
position given its limited jurisdiction within a larger nation. To be sure, cities
might have a variety of interests that they might want to pursue, ranging form
enhancing their social prestige to augmenting their political power. Peterson,
however, focused chiefly on the city's economic interest—an interest that, he

said, would lead cities, like private firms, to compete with each other to maximize their economic well-being.

Given interlocal economic competition, Peterson argued, cities were interested primarily in pursuing developmental policies that sought to attract commerce and industry, because these policies enhanced the economic position of the city. Indeed, if traditional economic analysis is correct, cities' interests were essentially the same as the interests of its export industries. Cities know that they will benefit if their export industries are thriving. To promote their export industries, cities might try to exert power over land, labor, and capital. Yet cities had little or no power to control labor and capital flows. They did, however, have some power to control land use. Yet even that ability was a two-edged sword. Although land was a factor of production that cities could control, it also defined cities' boundaries and thus made their need to compete for labor and capital investment all the more intense.

The same logic, he contended, indicated that cities could be expected to have little interest in pursuing "redistributive" policies. These policies—those that benefit low-income residents—threaten the local economy. Attempts to adopt redistributive policies can drive away the very investment that it is in the city's economic interest to retain or attract. The structure of interlocal competition, rather than the character of city politics, explains why cities have an interest in pursuing developmental policies over redistributive ones. A pluralist city could largely be expected to pursue its economic interest in the same manner as one governed by a power elite because redistribution is not—and usually cannot be—an important part of local governmental policymaking.

This aspect of Peterson's argument has engendered intense criticism. Many contend it presents an unduly deterministic view of city power. Among the problems with this view, critics argue, is that it cannot explain policy variations among different cities, even though all of them are trapped by the same structure. Some commentators lump Peterson's approach with Marxist accounts on the ground that both unduly discount the role of urban politics by wrongly assuming that there is a direct correspondence between economic structure and urban policy. Although important portions of Peterson's analysis no doubt invite this critique, we want to highlight a different dimension of his analysis. Despite Peterson's own assertions that city limits are rooted in economic and social conditions— and despite critics' assumption that Peterson argues that economic logic is the primary structural constraint on local politics—the limitations on city power that Peterson identifies in his book are products of the legal system.

Peterson notes at the outset of his analysis that cities are not like nation-states because they cannot "make war or peace; they cannot issue passports or forbid outsiders from entering their territory; they cannot issue currency; and they cannot control imports or erect tariff walls."[5] The reason that cities cannot do these things has little to do with the underlying economic system. These limits derive from the U.S. Constitution that, in combination with a number of federal statutes, reserves these powers to the federal government. Indeed, Peterson recognizes that the legal structure plays a key role in leading the city to pursue developmental rather than redistributive policies. For example, he refers to legal limitations—which he consistently characterizes as having a "constitutional" dimension—that prevent cities from regulating the flow of capital and labor. Without legal powers over capital and labor, he argues, cities have little choice but to reject redistributive policies that might discourage investment. They have to adopt developmental policies that would encourage it.

The repeated references to the constitutional status of these limitations no doubt contributed to critics' claims that Peterson thought cities were trapped in a national political economy that was all but impervious to change. Yet Peterson expressly rejected this position. At the close of his book, Peterson contended that continuance of an external structure that excludes redistributive measures from the urban agenda was unrealistic and insensitive, given the obvious interest that city residents have in considering the adoption of these kinds of policies. This did not lead him to call for revolutionary change; that course of action, he said, would be both dangerous and unnecessary. But he did argue that the structural arrangements that limit the possibility of local redistribution could be modified without overhauling the social and economic structure of the nation. By changing the background legal structure in more modest ways, cities could be empowered to pursue the kind of redistributive agenda that can open the possibility for greater equity.

To promote this reform agenda, Peterson proposed that the federal government pledge its full faith and credit behind all state and local indebtedness, thereby enabling cities to use their otherwise limited borrowing capacity to fund redistributive programs. (To avoid the problem of excessive borrowing, he proposed that cities be required to win approval from federal agencies before incurring debt.) Peterson also proposed a federal revenue-sharing plan aimed at equalizing cities' per capita fiscal resources. In this way, a city could receive increased federal funding as its economy improved, thereby giving it a surplus that could be devoted to redistributive efforts. Finally, he argued that a comprehensive revenue sharing plan would free cities from the more targeted grants-in-aid regime that dictated city spending. The federal government could impose minimum service provision requirements, but, in return, cities could be empowered to address issues that would otherwise not be in their interest to consider. Although these legal changes would not ensure greater equity, he concluded, they would enable localities to debate the trade-off between equity and productivity in a manner similar to the debates that now take place at the national level. As a result, "a new range of local policies will become possible. Even more, local political life itself may acquire a new meaning."[6]

These proposals to broaden city limits seem to run counter to what many commentators have taken to be the main theme of *City Limits*—that cities have no choice but to pursue a limited set of pro-growth policies that are prescribed by economic realities. But that makes them all the more interesting to us. They portray cities as legal creatures, and they suggest that the definition of cities' legal authority influences the kinds of choices they can make. Peterson's approach, like ours, assumes that a critical constraint on city power is the legal structure within which it is exercised. It also indicates that the substantive transformation of city power can be accomplished without fundamentally revising the economic order.

In arguing that changes to the legal structure of local power are needed to transform the substance of city decision making, Peterson focused almost exclusively on the federal government's role in defining city power. He gave no real attention to the constraining influence of local government law. In part, this is because Peterson seemed to equate the state and the city, as if each were equally limited in its powers and only the national government had the power to free them. This conflation of the city and the state is difficult to defend. States clearly have a superior legal status compared to cities. Peterson himself insists at various points that cities are distinct governmental institutions because of their peculiarly limited territorial jurisdiction. In our view, Peterson's analysis underscores the need to push his basic insight further and consider whether alterations in the body of state law that defines city authority might broaden city limits in ways that could change the substantive exercise of local power.

Regime Theory

Peterson criticized the community power debate for its internal focus. Clarence Stone pursued a different perspective some years later.[7] In setting forth what has come to be known as regime theory, Stone located the problem with the community power debate in its assumption of a "social control" model of power. The social control model imagines that groups seek to assert control over each other, so that the one with the greatest control would have the greatest power. Stone contended that this was a limited way of thinking about power in general and city power in particular. In his view, the important question about city politics concerned not who controlled whom but whether anyone within the city could exert sufficient control to get something done. As Stone put it, conceptions of urban politics should shift from a "power over" to a "power to" model. The key issue would become "how, in the face of complex and sometimes divisive forces, an effective and durable capacity to govern can be created."[8]

Looked at this way, the critical problem for city politics is that public officials need to find partners with sufficient resources to implement their policies. Cities are underresourced, highly constrained political institutions. Like Peterson, Stone was skeptical of the capacious notion of agency that undergirded the early community power debate. But while Peterson focused on the ways in which external constraints conditioned local political choices, Stone focused on the process by which cities could assert their own agency. For cities to get something done within the fragmented institutional terrain in which they were required to operate, city officials need to form governing coalitions, particularly with private business. Cities need the resources that business uniquely commands. At the same time, private business cannot accomplish what it wants without the city's help. Because of this mutuality of interests, Stone argued, private business enjoys a privileged position among the interest groups within the city—even if no elite secretly runs the city and even if a regime could emerge that business did not dominate.

Regime theorists have produced detailed case studies about specific cities, and these studies set forth a range of possible urban visions for cities to pursue. One can contrast, for example, Clarence Stone's portrayal of Atlanta's business-friendly regime, which sought to create peace across the city's racial divide, with the progressive antigrowth regime that DeLeon argues briefly held sway in San Francisco.[9] Whatever the city's goal, regime theory tends to stress the limits that cities face. As Stone emphasized in his study of Atlanta:

> Given the weakness of governmental authority and fragmentation in the nonprofit sector, the business elite are uniquely able to enhance the capacity of a local regime to govern. An imbalance in abilities to contribute to the capacity to govern is thus at the core of the Atlanta regime. Until that imbalance is corrected, biased governance and weak governance appear to be the only real alternatives. That is the lesson to be learned from a social-production model.[10]

Like Peterson, Stone's conclusion led him to seek ways of altering the external structure to minimize the policy bias he identified. His impulse to do so seems not to be based on a desire to ensure that redistributive policies get a fair hearing locally. The point Stone highlights instead is that the attraction of insider privilege will preclude a business-dominated governing regime from obtaining the benefits of social learning. Even putting concerns about equal representation to one side, Stone's account thus raises a problem with local politics. Since those who govern always have only a limited understanding of the consequences of their decisions, they need input from other sources. To obtain valuable information about the possible unintended consequences of their policies, they are dependent on the participation of affected groups.

Stone, like Peterson, looks to the federal statutory structure to bring about the transformation in urban politics that he believes is warranted. He proposes changing federal urban redevelopment programs to encourage public-private partnerships with nonprofit community development organizations rather than solely with for-profit developers, as has traditionally been the case. He recommends augmenting programs like Volunteers in Service to America (VISTA) to stimulate the production of a vibrant, nonbusiness associational life at the local level. The national legal structure, Stone argues, can be reformed to promote the emergence of civic activity within cities that can serve as a counterweight to business.

Stone's proposals for legal reform, like Peterson's, are noteworthy for being relatively brief and for focusing on the ways in which the federal legal structure might be altered to reshape urban decision making. Still, his basic instincts are similar to ours. Stone's analysis, no less than Peterson's, suggests the potential value of examining the ways in which the legal context that most directly defines city power—local government law—constrains city power and can be reformed to improve its exercise.

Our discussion of Dahl, Peterson, and Stone is not intended to suggest that law is the primary, let alone the only, external structure influencing city decision making. Nor are we arguing that the assumption of economic determinism be replaced with legal determinism, thereby making it unlikely that cities subject to the same legal regime would adopt different policies. We do contend, however, that local government law is an important structural factor, one that urban theorists have rarely explored even though the logic of their own analysis often indicates its significance. This omission is unfortunate. As long as the rules of local government law evade serious analysis, they are unlikely to be changed. Moreover, ideas for reform like Peterson's and Stone's that focus on altering the federal legal structure are unlikely to be effective if they do not take account of the constraining effect of the rules of local government law. Proposals to enhance city decision-making capacity by increasing federal aid or federal support for local bonds—such as those suggested by Peterson—cannot achieve their intended effects if state law substantially circumscribes a city's regulatory authority or borrowing power. Proposals to change federal law in order to make governing regimes more inclusive—such as those Stone advances—assume that cities can pursue a much more balanced form of development. But even an inclusive governing regime cannot promote more balanced development if state law deems the strategy off limits to cities, as it often does. City power, as John

Dillon explained more than a century ago, is ultimately a creature of state law. Reformation of the state legal structure must therefore be the primary means by which city power is enhanced.

Local Government Law and the Scope of City Agency

No one now believes, perhaps no one has ever believed, that city development policies are solely the product of local choices. The works of Stone, Peterson, and many others have made it clear that cities cannot be viewed in isolation from larger social and economic forces. But cities do have room to maneuver within the constraints under which they operate. A key issue, therefore, concerns the kinds of choices that cities can make on their own. Urban theorists have offered a number of influential frameworks to identify the choices that cities have available. Our approach shares with these theorists the criticism of deterministic models of city power. But we think that the frameworks they embrace do not offer an adequate account of city agency.

Challenging the Conventional Choices

The literature identifies three broad ways to frame the basic policy choices that cities can make. The first of these, already discussed, suggests that the key divide is between developmental and redistributive policies. This is the argument advanced in Peterson's *City Limits*. The second, derived from Marx, identifies the critical choice as between policies that promote exchange value and those that promote use value. In his *City and the Grassroots*, Manuel Castells offers a useful account of this distinction by analyzing the history of urban social movements:

> The content of this use value changed considerably from place to place....It could be decent housing provided as a public service, the preservation of a historic building, or the demand for open space. But whatever mobilization occurred, it was for improved collective consumption, in contradiction to the notion of the city for profit in which the desirability of space and urban services are distributed according to levels of income.[11]

The third framework, well articulated by Harvey Molotch in his essay "The City as a Growth Machine," presents the key divide as being between policies that are aimed at promoting growth and those that are intended to manage it or even slow it down. Molotch offers the following definition to flesh out this distinction:

> Growth is a constantly rising urban-area population—a symptom of a pattern ordinarily comprising an initial expansion of basic industries followed by an expanded labor force, a rising scale of retail and whole-sale commerce, more far-flung and increasingly intensive land development, higher population density, and increased levels of financial activity.[12]

These three frameworks are not usually presented to describe how cities *should* make policy. They more commonly explain how they *do* make policy, either because the prevailing social and economic conditions allow them no other choice or because, given the ideological disposition of urban policymakers, no alternatives can gain traction. The frameworks do not set forth ironclad rules about how cities must behave. But they do indicate, particularly in combination, that cities are powerfully attracted to a particular policymaking vision and that those who favor alternatives face an uphill battle. The usual contention is that cities are more likely to pursue policies that promote development, exchange value, and growth than those that favor redistribution, use value, and no growth. The reason for these choices is that cities have a limited jurisdiction and depend heavily on private investment to generate the revenues they need to fund their services.

Our interest in these frameworks lies in the ways in which they treat local government law as an influence on city policymaking. At first glance, they seem to suggest that the rules of local government law are of little importance. If cities are generally inclined to favor policies that promote development, exchange value, and growth, there would be little reason to delve deeply into the ways in which different states have set up cities' legal powers. The interlocal variations in the structure of local government law would be overwhelmed by the social, economic, and, perhaps, ideological forces that drive cities to make policy in certain ways. Even if cities have *some* agency over how to pursue development, the effect of the frameworks is to turn one's attention away from alternatives that cities might pursue. Those who use these frameworks often emphasize how limited city politics is or how mechanistic it tends to be: "The city as a growth *machine.*"

If one looks more closely at these distinctions, however, it becomes clear that they conceal an important range of choices that cities can make. It is these choices that local government law influences. Because there is no single way to promote development, exchange value, or growth, cities might often find that state law affects the ways in which they pursue these goals. Equally important, some cities—particularly the kind of large, successful cities we examine—are strong enough to adopt policies that would seem to be beyond a city's reach or against its interest because of their perceived antibusiness character. This might stem from the fact that businesses located within the city find themselves more tied to the city than generalizations about the hypermobility of capital indicate. If so, the city might have an ability to exercise a degree of political control over them without an excessive fear that doing so will drive them beyond its borders. Alternatively, the fact that the business community is much less rooted in any particular community than it was a generation ago may mean that its political influence is diminished. City policymakers may therefore feel freer to adopt policies that do not meet with the support of particular businesses, preferring instead to cater to other local constituencies. Either way, the range of policy options that cities might view as plausible might include many that, under the prevailing frameworks, would not seem to be options. For this reason alone, the range of choices that state law influences—either directly or indirectly—could be more important than the traditional frameworks might indicate.

But the fact that cities have the ability to pursue policies other than the standard ones that urban theory suggests raises only the first of many choices that cities must make. If a city is not locked into the pursuit of developmental policies, it must make a host of important decisions about how to implement the alternative policies it wishes to pursue. A city that wants to increase its stock of affordable housing can pursue a "redistributive" goal in a variety of ways. It could use local taxes to provide public housing that the city would own. It could require new private developers to provide below-market units in return for the right to build market-rate housing. It could provide direct cash subsidies to renters. It could increase rental opportunities by prohibiting condominium conversions. It could donate city land to subsidize private, multifamily developments. It could use the power of eminent domain to acquire the land necessary to make these donations. These different options would produce different consequences for the city. Some might attract different kinds of residents or do more to integrate them into areas where those with different income levels live. Some might facilitate private development, while others might suppress it. A narrow focus on the question of whether cities will or will not redistribute, therefore, overlooks important aspects of city policymaking and its potential impact on the urban environment. It tends to conceal the fact that state law may bias cities to choose some modes of implementation rather than others.

There is an even more fundamental conceptual problem with the conventional frameworks: the indeterminacy of the distinctions between development and redistribution, exchange value and use value, and growth and no growth. The frameworks suggest that cities confront a series of binary choices because, given the economic reality, only one outcome is in the city's interest. They further suggest that, in confronting these binary choices, cities will resolve them in predictable ways. Yet many, perhaps even most, of the policies that cities contemplate straddle these categorical divides. Is a city that increases funding for its public schools engaging in redistribution, given who is enrolled in them, or is it helping to boost property values and to induce new employers to locate within its borders? Is a city that protects its historic buildings privileging use values over exchange values, or is it helping to sell the city to tourists by maintaining a valuable commodity? Is a city that restricts office development from casting shadows on a downtown park taking a stand against growth or is it protecting an attractive amenity in order to attract new residents? These kinds of questions become even more pressing when one considers that the frameworks might well be in tension with one another. Some redistributive policies, such as those aimed at making the cost of housing more affordable, could also be justified in pro-growth terms on the ground that the city's population is shrinking due to the high cost of living. Similarly, investment in a new park could be opposed on grounds that it takes land out of the market or be defended as a means of promoting new development.

The opposing categories of policies that urban theory posits, in short, are not sharp enough to establish useful parameters. The claim that cities ordinarily cannot engage in redistribution does not reveal much about the scope of city agency, because many local policies may plausibly be described as both redistributive *and* developmental. The same can be said about the contention that cities cannot ordinarily protect use values or that they must support growth. A city policy that is criticized for falling on the wrong side of the line usually can be defended as actually falling on the right side of it. This is not to say that cities face no market-based constraints. Some policies may in fact be quite harmful to a city's future economic prospects. But it is difficult to know in advance what those policies are. For that reason, cities can be expected to treat decisions about whether to pursue a given policy as difficult in ways that the current language of urban theory fails to capture. As a result, the outcomes of city decision making are likely to be much less determined than urban theory often suggests. Because cities will often not know how to act, city decision making will be substantially affected by the direction that the rules of local government law gives to specific policies even if cities want to act in the ways urban theory indicates that they should. And there is no reason to assume that these rules will match up well with traditional models of urban decision making. Since the rules are often products of earlier eras, the legal structure also will often be inconsistent with the city's own assessment of whether the adoption of a particular policy would be in its own best interest.

Toward a New Range of Choices

A different vocabulary for assessing the scope of city agency would focus less on explaining the kinds of choices that cities cannot make and more on fleshing out the nature of the ones that they can. There are examples in the literature of the kind of vocabulary we have in mind—frameworks that present policy choices that cities can decide either way and are important enough to have real consequences for the city's future. Consider Guido Martinotti's claim that there are three different conceptions of the nature of cities around the world: a "first generation" that understands them principally as providing services to their own residents; a "second generation" that emphasizes their relationship with nonresident users, such as tourists, students, or commuters; and a third generation in which the main focus is on attracting and serving the interests of international finance and business executives with worldwide contacts.[13] Martinotti does not argue that cities are predisposed to pursue one of these alternatives to the exclusion of the others. They are all viable, even if the second- and third-generation ideas have recently become more attractive. Aspects of the current economy might push cities to organize themselves to serve some of these purposes more than others. But most cities are likely to have all of these purposes in mind in making urban policy. Inevitably, then, cities will face hard choices about which policies to adopt and which interests to emphasize.

Martinotti's choices do not track the development/redistribution, use value/exchange value, and growth/no-growth dichotomies. Although second- and third-generation cities are presumably interested in development, exchange, and growth, they must make crucial decisions about the basic character of their urban environment. Will it be organized to benefit insiders rather than outsiders? Will it privilege work or play? Is its future influenced by nearby commuters or far-off business executives? How a city answers these questions will be reflected in city policies. The city over time will therefore acquire a particular look and feel. Choices such as these go to the heart of the kind of city one values: one organized for city residents, for example, is likely to be very different from one focused on attracting visitors. As Martinotti indicates, the answers are by no means obvious even though the questions are unavoidable.

Another example of the vocabulary we have in mind is Richard Florida's argument that cities need to adopt a new approach to economic development policy.[14] Cities, Florida argues, have long scrambled to entice businesses by offering them tax abatements and other subsidies. Yet businesses are not really looking for the biggest tax break. They want instead to be where creative people are. If a city can attract this "creative class"—a stratum of society comprised of scientists, artists, computer technicians, gays and lesbians, and media people, among others—the jobs produced by the twenty-first century economy will follow. As a result, Florida says, cities should strive to make themselves the kinds of places where creative people want to live. Having a warm climate or a beautiful waterfront might help. But natural amenities are not necessary. A tolerant civic culture, a well-developed high-tech infrastructure, and a vibrant nightlife can be just as important.

Like Martinotti, Florida is not arguing that social and economic imperatives mandate that cities become what he calls "creative cities." In fact, he is discouraged by the fact that many cities are disinclined to adopt the economic development strategy that he favors. His point is that cities can choose to adopt policies of this kind and laments that too few have done so despite the fact that they would be wise to do so. The decision whether to be a creative city is thus presented as an option, one that Florida tries to convince readers is attractive and, if properly pursued, likely to bring about a successful outcome. In contrast to the traditional way of talking about the scope of city agency, which highlights the choices that cities cannot make, Florida's approach is aimed at adding to the list of ones that they can.

The urban commentator Joel Kotkin underscores the utility of this way of discussing city agency when he rejects Florida's argument.[15] He does so not because he thinks that cities will not adopt it but because he fears that they might. Kotkin shifts the discussion from an analysis of what cities will do with their agency to what they *should* do with it, a shift that he can make because his alternative option is also one he believes the prevailing social and economic conditions allow. Kotkin laments the decision made by many cities to focus on fashion, style, and trendiness rather than on retaining middle-class families and factory jobs. Although he concedes that some cities—or parts of cities—can survive by being "hip," he argues that entertainment, tourism, and other "creative" industries fail to provide upward mobility for the vast majority of city residents. Moreover, by favoring the culture industry and constructing eye-catching buildings, cities tend to neglect their basic industries, schools, and infrastructure. By following such a course, they are likely increasingly to evolve into "dual cities" made up of a cosmopolitan elite and a large class of people who service their needs, usually at low wages. To avoid this future, Kotkin urges cities to foster their specialized industries, small business, schools and neighborhoods, not just their clubs, museums, and restaurants.

The debate between Florida and Kotkin might be thought to track the conventional divide between policies that promote use values and exchange values. In fact, it is not at all clear who is on which side. Florida seems to be arguing that an emphasis on use values—making the city a tolerant and fun place—will create exchange value. Kotkin, by contrast, seems to be arguing that a focus on more traditional business development—the promotion of classic exchange value—is what will make the city a place with use value. That's because it will help create the kind of social bonds that make urban communities catalysts of social mobility and sites for appreciating people different from oneself. It is hard to know, in reading the Kotkin/Florida debate, which vision of the city is the one that most cities will or should pursue. Both seem possible. Yet the kind of city Florida promotes would have a very different look and feel from the one that Kotkin favors. The choice must be decided on the basis of a normative judgment about the kind of city one wants to create.

The choices among the four futures we described at the beginning of this book—the tourist city, the global city, the middle class city, and the regional city—are much like the choices identified by Martinotti, Florida, and Kotkin. They reflect plausible ideas of what a city could be, and they depend on the kinds of policies that cities enact. They too are controversial. There is no reason to think that, in light of existing economic and social conditions, the choice among them must be made in a certain way. The existing economic and social imperatives could be marshaled in support of the pursuit of any or all of them. That is what makes them helpful frameworks for capturing the kind of agency that cities possess.

This way of thinking about city agency, like the approaches adopted by Martinotti, Florida, and Kotkin, makes an exploration of city structures important. Once there is a way of talking about the scope of city agency that offers cities significant options, it becomes necessary to determine whether cities possess the legal power needed to implement them. Those who study cities pay too little attention to this issue. The debate between Florida and Kotkin illustrates this lack of attention. Both of them assume that cities have the ability to choose between the visions of economic development that they articulate. They make no reference to local government law. Yet, as we explain in more detail in the final four chapters of this book, the kinds of choices about the future that they describe are ones that the rules of local government law powerfully influence.

Two brief examples can serve as illustrations. Florida suggests that the creation of a tolerant atmosphere may be an important component of an effective development strategy in the current economic environment. One way that cities might signal their openness is to adopt measures expanding civil rights protections to gays and lesbians or provide a method of registering domestic partnership. Many mayors have considered adopting these measures for just this reason. As we shall see, however, it is not at all clear, under the legal doctrine of home rule, that states in general have given their cities the authority to adopt either of these measures. Kotkin suggests that cities would do better to focus on improving their infrastructure or their public education system. Yet many cities lack control over these aspects of city life; the state has vested control over these issues in public authorities or special districts over which the mayor and the city council have little influence.

The existence of alternative possible urban futures—our four futures, those that Martinotti, Florida, and Kotkin set forth, and many others—offers a corrective to the abstract, dichotomous way in which urban policy choices have too often been described. It complements the important body of work showing that cities have more agency than some urban models imagine. But it also casts doubt on an unduly robust sense of city autonomy. Even if the economic structure is not constraining city power to a limited policy domain, and even if there are divergent ideas about urbanism that cities might choose, state law—including rules adopted decades ago—might substantially impede city decision making. The recent attention to local agency implies that cities have "volition,...discretion, and freedom of action."[16] Paradoxically, this insight increases the need to examine the ways in which the rules of local government law operate as a constraint on a city's capacity for local self-government.

Although our approach assumes cities have discretion to make important decisions about their future notwithstanding the substantial nonlegal structural constraints that they confront, it foregrounds the substantive legal rules that states rely on to constitute local power. Changing the legal rules of local government law can change the kinds of futures that cities can make for themselves. To say that cities should be empowered to grapple with the contested ideas about their future, however, is not to say that cities should be given local autonomy. On the contrary, as we explain in the next chapter, debates over whether cities should be given or denied local autonomy are fundamentally misconceived. Our goal is to shift the ground of debate over urban power away from the notion of local autonomy to a very different question: whether the current structure of local government law frustrates or facilitates cities' ability to pursue an attractive vision of their future.

CITY STRUCTURES AND LOCAL AUTONOMY

Our discussion of the constraining influence of local government law might suggest that our purpose is to defend local autonomy. This chapter explains why this is not our goal. Part of the reason has to do with the complexities of defining what "local autonomy" means. Part has to do with the normative undesirability of such a goal. And part derives from our conviction that there is no escape from the city structures that this book is devoted to describing. Our position on these matters is unusual among law professors concerned with local government, and it is also not the way urban theorists generally talk about what it would mean to enhance local power. We begin, therefore, with a statement of the more common view, which applies not only to large central cities but to local governments in general.

The Notion of Local Autonomy

The Assumption of Autonomy

An unrealistically expansive idea of the amount of legal power that states have conferred on their local governments—often termed home rule or local autonomy—has been the reigning assumption in recent decades among legal scholars who study local power. This position draws heavily on urban theory, particularly on the ideas about the necessarily limited nature of local power put forth by Paul Peterson. It typically foregrounds a pair of contrasting images of the local sphere. On the one hand, it depicts a privileged suburban enclave that has been empowered to veto new development in an effort to protect the property values of its homeowners. The beleaguered central city is then presented as a contrast to this privileged suburban enclave. The central city cannot gain much from this state-delegated power to veto development because development is what it wants. But it also has no practical means to compel the development it needs. In this picture, then, both central cities and suburbs are imagined as having a broad range of formal legal powers. But, as a practical matter, the central cities, unlike the suburbs, have little choice but to resign themselves to an inevitable downward spiral, pursuing a "beggar-thy-neighbor" development strategy (often focused on downtown) in the hopes of boosting their tax base and lobbying (usually unsuccessfully) for handouts from the state or federal government. Many of those who present this picture of metropolitan America are legal scholars who are committed to aiding central cities. Given the picture they present, local autonomy appears to them to be a problem, not a solution, because the broad recognition of home rule, so advantageous to the suburbs, is one of the chief reasons that central cities are in trouble.

These contrasting images of central cities and suburbs are clearly codependent. Indeed, the legal recognition of home rule is thought to produce the divide between well-off suburbs and desperate central cities. Although these legal scholars acknowledge that some localities can and do adopt strategies that are different from those forced on them by their zero-sum competition with each other, they often dismiss the alternatives as simply a product of the same kind of self-interested, parochial decision-making process that favors the privatized, exclusionary policies favored by the stereotypical suburban jurisdiction. Local governments that act outside of the standard paradigm—whether central cities or suburbs—are seen as captives of a narrow faction that has its own special interests in mind. Their efforts too are therefore met with suspicion.

Given this analysis, there is surprisingly little support among legal scholars for increasing the legal powers of local governments—central cities included. Some argue that the best way to improve the current position of central cities would be to enlarge their boundaries, thereby enabling them to capture a larger share of the suburban tax base. But if that radical solution is unavailable, others suggest that the next best way to help central cities would be to require the state to intervene more frequently in matters that are now thought to be of local concern. The privileged position that suburbs now enjoy could then be checked in ways that would benefit the central cities, and central cities would lose little power of practical significance if more matters were decided by the state. Sheryll Cashin, for example, condemns the inequities that she sees built into the current legal structure—inequities that she astutely observes typically favor a minority of the regional population. A key part of the problem, she explains, is "society's strong cultural preference for local powers" and "our nation's ideological commitment to decentralized local governance." She concludes that "localism, or the ideological commitment to local governance, has helped to produce fragmented metropolitan regions stratified by race and income." She therefore recommends limiting the matters that states treat as fit for local resolution.[1]

The most complete statement of this position is offered by Richard Briffault, a professor at Columbia Law School.[2] In a pair of mammoth articles, he argued that it is no longer true that cities are "creatures of the state." Previously, the state creature notion sought to limit the power of local initiative by requiring specific state delegations of authority and by ensuring that, in case of a state-local conflict, state rules prevailed. This idea, he argues, has now been abandoned. Local governments empowered by home rule now have broad regulatory and spending powers. Indeed, all but two states have enacted express constitutional or statutory home-rule provisions. These measures typically cover most, although not all, of the local governments in the state, including the large central cities. These measures self-consciously reject the notion that local governments have no independent powers of their own, and they therefore overturn the rule of strict construction of local governmental powers, known as Dillon's Rule, that accompanied the once-dominant state creature idea.

Briffault and other legal scholars also point to the steps that states have taken to supplement express home-rule provisions. Legal scholars often note that the states have enacted broad statutory delegations of specific powers to central cities and suburbs—most notably, state zoning enabling acts that give many local governments important powers to regulate land uses within their boundaries. Moreover, they contend that direct state efforts to overturn local governmental decisions are relatively rare. Even though home rule provisions usually do not give rights of local immunity from conflicting state laws, localities retain important measures of control over their borders, their tax base, and their police powers. Home rule, in short, has become something more than just a specific legal doctrine established by express statutory and constitutional provisions. It has become synonymous with the "substantial legal autonomy"[3] that local governments in the United States are said to enjoy.

Given this depiction of the legal structure, Briffault argues that the sorry state of central cities cannot be attributed to their legal powerlessness. Their condition instead arises from the fact that the legal recognition of local autonomy has created a problematic structure of interlocal competition. Economic reality has made legally autonomous suburbs better competitors than legally autonomous central cities. The suburbs, especially the most prosperous suburbs, are primarily interested in controlling growth and preserving the status quo, and "local legal autonomy significantly empowers them in this quest." By contrast, central cities "may have autonomy in law, but their economic and political power in practice is shaped by private investment decisions." Thus, echoing Peterson, Briffault argues that "the principal constraint on local power is often not legal but economic: the limits of local resources and the structure of interlocal competition." A legal system that equally empowers local governments does not create a free market. It privileges the wealthiest suburbs at the expense of the poorer cities. The legal protection of localism, Briffault concludes,

> reflects territorial economic and social inequalities and reinforces them with political power. Its benefits accrue primarily to a minority of affluent localities, to the detriment of other communities and to the system of local government as a whole. Moreover, localism is primarily centered on the affirmation of private values. Localist ideology and localist political action tend not to build up public life, but rather contribute to the pervasive privatism that is the hallmark of contemporary American politics. Localism may be more of an obstacle to achieving social justice and the development of public life than a prescription for their attainment.[4]

This diagnosis suggests a remedy: reclaim the state creature idea of local power that home rule sought to displace.

Problems with the Assumption of Autonomy

There are two important problems with this conventional narrative. First, for reasons reviewed in the previous chapter, the depressing portrait of central cities' incapacity to exercise control within the existing structure of interlocal competition is overdrawn. The kinds of local governments that are the focus of this study—large, successful central cities—are not limited to begging for state or federal assistance, declaring themselves tax-free zones, or desperately trying to lay claim to the resources now found in the suburbs. Many large central cities are now much better off than inner-ring suburbs. Indeed, revenue-sharing models developed in an earlier era now sometimes make successful central cities donors and not receivers. The standard legal account—and its assumption that central cities have ample formal home-rule authority but little effective power—has its origins in the urban experience of the 1970s and 1980s, when New York City's financial troubles were perhaps the most salient urban event. Today, it is clear that the conditions of interlocal competition allow many central cities to assert their public powers. And the choices that they make in building on their current success are fundamental ones.

The conventional account is also mistaken in identifying the legal grant of local autonomy as the problem that generates central city/suburban inequality. Neither central cities nor suburbs have autonomy, despite the fact that most states have given them home rule as a formal matter. We demonstrate this point at length in part II, where we discuss home rule, land use, local fiscal authority, and education. At the moment, we will simply mention some of the ways that the conventional legal account misdescribes the prevailing legal structure. It overlooks the myriad limitations on local power that are built into home rule grants. It ignores the important ways in which states remove major parts of the local infrastructure from local control. And it fails to acknowledge the dramatic extent to which state statutory and constitutional provisions preempt contrary local judgments. These points would not be a surprise to most local officials in America. In thinking about innovative policy responses to new conditions or problems, it will be the rare local official that will not be concerned about the possibility that their preferred course of action will run into legal problems either because of a lack of authority to initiate it or the specter that existing state law conflicts with it.

There is a relation between the two problems with the standard account of local autonomy that we have identified: the overly restrictive view of central cities' agency and the overly expansive view of their legal authority. As the capacity of successful cities to assert their market power has increased, the legal restrictions on their authority that have always been in place have become more important. When central cities were desperate for whatever private investment they could attract, it may well have seemed that removing legal limitations on their regulatory authority would not make much of a difference. To be sure, as Peterson's and Stone's proposals indicate, it might have been possible to design legal reforms that could have increased the legal powers of central cities in meaningful ways. But that hardly seemed to matter. Thus, although there may have been some justification for the dismissive view of the import of legal limitations in an earlier period, such a view does not describe the present situation. The kinds of cities that Peterson and Stone had in mind—and that we focus on—now have meaningful opportunities, within the prevailing economic and social conditions, to set policy for themselves.

A better, and more relevant, way to conceptualize the extent of local legal power is necessary. It begins with recognizing that the current legal structure does not grant autonomy to any local governments. Instead, it grants them some substantive powers but denies them others. For that reason, the key feature of the current legal system is that it directs the substantive ways in which local power is exercised through the complex mix of grants and limits that it establishes. Effective reform measures should therefore not focus solely on challenging state law's solicitude for local power. This is too incomplete a way of responding to a legal system that now imposes many limits on local power. Reform involves altering both grants of and limits on local power. Moreover, the reform is likely to require that these changes be made in complementary fashion so that the resulting grants and limits reinforce each other in a way that promotes the desired substantive direction for cities to pursue.

A Different View of Home Rule

This way of thinking about local power would not be an innovation in American legal culture. In fact, it mirrors the way that the urban reformers who first struggled to win home rule in the late nineteenth century thought about the issue. The early proponents of home rule rejected the idea that home rule meant local legal autonomy. They envisioned it instead as a way for the great cities of their day to become significant actors in the promotion of whatever underlying substantive vision of government the urban reformers favored. Of course, the fact that reformers long ago had such a view of home rule does not mean that we are obliged to adopt it. Moreover, the particular goals that drove their various proposals for home rule are no longer of direct relevance. Nevertheless, the complex view of home rule that these early urban reformers developed is a better way of thinking about local power than the one provided by the notion of local autonomy.

The home rule movement in the United States was a response to the rapid urbanization of the country in the late nineteenth century. Its objective was to overturn the then-pervasive view, embraced by John Dillon, that municipal corporations were "creatures of the state." Its focus was on enhancing the independence of the newly emergent central cities that helped to define the Industrial Age. But in doing so, the early proponents of home rule did not seek simply to enhance the freedom of central cities and diminish the power of state governments. Home rule decreased some kinds of state power over cities but it increased others. The specific mix of increases and decreases depended on the vision of urban life that the hotly contested notion of home rule was designed to further.

Home rule advocates agreed on some basic points. They sought to promote principles of good government in the nation's growing urban centers, and they did so by targeting these local governments for reform. They were driven by a sense that the major cities of the time were failing to serve either their own residents or the nation as a whole. They believed that, in large part, this was because they were saddled with an outdated legal structure that had been designed in a preurban age. Early home rule advocates disagreed, however, about what "good government" was. They envisioned different kinds of cities with very different kinds of city powers, and their proposals for home rule were thus quite distinct.

One group, whom we call the old conservatives, shared a good deal with those, like John Dillon, who embraced the state creature concept of local power.[5]

Like Dillon, they sought a low-tax, low-debt, incorruptible form of local government that had limited regulatory authority over private decision making. Dillon thought that this objective could best be accomplished by strict state control of the exercise of local power. The old conservatives focused instead on the dangers of state control. State legislatures in the nineteenth century had often enacted special legislation aimed at the state's principal cities, and some of this legislation expanded the very kind of city authority that the old conservatives, like Dillon, feared. Home rule advocates favored home rule in order to immunize cities from this kind of targeted state intervention. One approach was to allow cities to adopt their own charters through a process designed to give property-owning residents a large say in their design. These charters would be made difficult to change either at the local or the state level, thereby locking in the limited view of the legitimate ends of local power that they favored. In this way, the old conservatives thought, home rule could empower cities to assume their traditional, limited role free from state intervention. The old conservatives considered the limits on what the city could do to be as important to their home rule vision as the cities' protection from state interference. The limits would derive from the fact that home rule would only authorize city legislation that affected local, not general, matters—thereby preventing excessive city intervention into the private sphere. The limits would also derive from the continued enforcement of state constitutional restrictions on local taxing and borrowing. In the old conservative version, the result of home rule would be to ensure the exercise of limited government on the local level. Old conservatives had no desire to allow cities to do whatever they wanted.

The same could be said about another strand of the home rule movement, one promoted by urban reformers who sought to foster the administration of cities by apolitical experts.[6] These advocates were less concerned than the old conservatives about city spending and regulation. They sought instead to create an administrative city—an efficient, bureaucratic form of local government. Like the old conservatives, they wanted to curtail the kind of special legislation that interfered with their version of proper city governance. But, unlike the old conservatives, they also wanted to empower cities to deal with the problems that rapid urbanization produced. At the same time, they were concerned that, left to themselves, cities might not create the kind of expert-based, apolitical bureaucratic governmental structure that they favored. Thus, like Dillon, they thought that some form of state supervision of city government was indispensable. To avoid politicizing this state control, they favored state administrative, rather than state legislative, oversight of city decision making. An expert, quasi-scientific government at the state level, they thought, could guide a similar kind of government at the local level. For them, home rule was an effort to put this structure into place.

One final group of late nineteenth-century home rule advocates deserves mention—a more radical group of urban reformers who challenged the form of limited local government that the old conservatives and Dillon favored.[7] Like those who envisioned an administrative city, these advocates sought to empower the growing cities of America. But they rejected not only the limited role of the public sector embraced by the old conservatives but also the apolitical vision of the administrative city. They saw the city as a fully political, social enterprise. They feared not local taxation or regulation but the private control of city policy. Indeed, to critics, their support for municipal ownership of transportation and utilities, as well as for city planning that dealt with land use and development, seemed to envision municipal socialism. Like other supporters of home rule, however, the advocates of the social city sought limits on city power as well as its expansion. The promotion of the social city, they thought, required restrictions on city initiatives that might privatize important local services. It also required the facilitation of the annexation of the suburbs by central cities in order to create the proper scope for municipal enterprise.

These historical examples are important not merely because they illustrate the diverse definitions of home rule at the time of its initial adoption. They help introduce what home rule continues to mean today. The three versions of home rule just described conflicted with each other, but they shared one thing in common: they envisioned home rule not simply as a way of enhancing local power but also as a way of guiding it in a particular substantive direction through the imposition of state law. Home rule, like the state creature concept that preceded it, was a way to structure city power, not simply to unleash it. It still is. Every version of home rule now adopted in the United States embraces a mixture of state decision making and local discretion similar in form to the ones proposed in the late nineteenth century. In the next four chapters, we illustrate this contemporary state-city structure by comparing the kind of home rule that Boston now enjoys with that of other major American cities. Although every city we examine has some degree of discretionary decision-making authority, the extent of that state-granted discretion, and the state-imposed rules that circumscribe it, differ a good deal.

The Complexities of Local Autonomy

This way of understanding decentralized power has implications that go well beyond the particular history of home rule in the United States. Beneath this history lies a fundamental conceptual point that applies equally to all local governments, whether large central cities, developing suburbs, or rural towns. Decentralized power always involves limits on local discretion, not just its conferral.

These limits sometimes derive from the explicit terms of the grant of the local government's authority. Its power might extend only to "local" or "municipal" matters; it might exclude specific topics (taxes or foreign affairs); it might make clear that, when a state/local conflict arises, the state will have the final say on the issue. But the limits on local power do not arise simply from these kinds of express provisions. They exist even if the grant of local authority is silent about any restrictions. The very existence of a central government armed with its own authority—and of a larger geographical territory within which the city is located—circumscribes local power.

Local autonomy is often presented as a simple idea. If we protect some aspects of local decision making from centralized power, so it is imagined, a sphere of local autonomy will be established. But local autonomy is a more complex concept than this picture allows. Immunizing local decision making from central power does not automatically promote local autonomy. It could do the opposite because a local government's ability to make effective decisions is also shaped by its relationship to other local governments and to private market forces. These relationships are structured by important, even if not visible, centrally established rules. Local decision-making authority is therefore circumscribed not just by explicit state requirements but by the way that the central government regulates interlocal relations and the relationship between public and private power. Indeed, the impact of this form of state lawmaking can cause a single-minded desire to curb state power to have a perverse result. Limiting central power can threaten local autonomy instead of protecting it.

Consider an example. The amount of money local governments need to spend on improving their own air quality depends on the approach to air quality adopted in neighboring localities. A local government that has a neighbor that is lax in policing air pollution, or that encourages its industry to locate at the city border, will have to devote resources to combating the air pollution that its neighbor generates. Imagine, then, that a state legislature is considering a law to prohibit lax air pollution policies. Would this state legislation infringe local autonomy? Clearly, the state statute would limit local autonomy in some respects. It would frustrate the policy choices of local governments with lax air pollution laws, and it would deny all local jurisdictions the freedom to adopt such a policy. At the same time, however, it would enhance the decision-making discretion of those local governments that are subjected to decreases in their own air quality because existing legal rules authorize their neighbors to generate pollution that imposes costs on them. If environmentally conscious local governments no longer had to respond to the negative effects imposed on them by their neighbors— negative effects that the existing centrally imposed legal system requires them to accept—they could allocate more resources to other priorities.

The proposed statute can thus be attacked as an infringement on local autonomy and also be defended as an enhancement of local autonomy. Local autonomy would be limited by a centrally imposed command that narrows the scope of local discretion. But local autonomy is limited as well by the centrally established legal rules that permit some localities to avoid costs and require others to bear them. The absence of a new central law that alters these existing interlocal legal relations thus itself limits local autonomy. The state legislature's decision whether to pass the legislation therefore requires it to make a policy judgment about the type of local autonomy that it wants to promote.

This argument should in some respects be familiar. It is hardly novel to contend that central lawmaking may be necessary to respond to interlocal effects or to produce interlocal redistribution. This classic argument for central power, however, is often understood as an argument for the promotion of some value—such as efficiency or equal treatment—that can be realized only by acknowledging and overcoming the pathologies that attend smaller-scale decision making. This way of understanding the function of central power is a partial one—and it has unfortunate consequences. If the successful defense of every central intervention depends on emphasizing the problems generated by local decision making, the argument inevitably invites the counterargument that central power threatens the values protected by local decision making. The calculus changes, however, once one sees that a central government intervention can itself have a pro-decentralization effect. The case for central power would no longer point inevitably towards ever-increasing centralization. The central government's action might promote local discretion even as it limits it.

Of course, the state government's choice to pass environmental legislation might not be based on a concern with local autonomy. It might stem from its own independent assessment of the state's interest in combating air pollution. If so, the legislation would not be an effort to promote local autonomy. We are not claiming that every state legislative enactment has the potential of promoting local autonomy. We are making a more limited point: local autonomy is a possible state objective, one that might be achieved through the enactment of what otherwise seems like a limit on local power. State legislators might value the fact that local jurisdictions would have more resources to devote to other governmental projects if they didn't have to pay for the costs imposed on them by their neighbors. They might also recognize that a state's effort to protect local autonomy by removing formal limits on local power might actually undermine it. Simply limiting central power, in short, is not a sufficient strategy for enhancing local power.

There are many other ways—in addition to requiring cities to accept the costs of activities engaged in by their neighbors—that local autonomy can be constrained by centrally imposed, often invisible, rules. To offer but one more example, local autonomy may also be limited by the competitive pressures that the central government allows local jurisdictions to impose on one another. If centrally imposed rules of local finance generate interlocal competition to attract private business, these rules will generate decisions by private market actors that no local government can counter on its own. As a practical matter, the effects of these finance rules can burden local autonomy as much as a newly imposed central law. A redesigned finance system could relieve these effects. Of course, it is likely to burden local autonomy as well, albeit in different ways. Any effort to protect local autonomy will be incomplete. Every central intervention interacts with a multitude of other, less visible, centrally imposed constraints and can increase and decrease local discretion at the same time.

A similar insight underlies Paul Peterson's proposals for revising the financial authority of large cities. Under his plan, they would be able to incur debt only if they received advance approval from the national government—a restriction that plainly infringes on their discretion. In return for accepting that limitation, however, they would receive the federal government's backing of the bonds they issue—a benefit that would substantially enhance their borrowing capacity. A trade of this kind cannot easily be characterized either as enhancing local autonomy or infringing it. It has to be defended in the more substantive terms that Peterson supplies: such a proposal, he suggests, would protect cities from some of the ill effects of the existing interlocal competition for private investment and thereby improve their ability to engage in redistributive programs. By doing so, this approach would permit local politics to engage with more of the important issues that cities face.

The Trouble with Local Autonomy

The view of local power just presented suggests that there is no such thing as local autonomy. Every local decision is circumscribed by the decisions made by other local governments and by the centrally imposed rules that empower them. Every local decision is equally circumscribed by the decisions made by private decision makers and the centrally imposed rules that empower these private actors. And, of course, every local decision is circumscribed by the decisions made by the central government for its own purposes, including its definition of the extent and limits of local governmental power. Central decision making is thus always implicated in the exercise of local power, and vice versa. Whenever the central government acts—or fails to act—it does so in a world in which other decision makers, both public and private, have been empowered to take action. All these locations for the exercise of power must be analyzed together in order to understand the structure of local power.

One can view this kind of complexity in state-local relations as a tragic story. Local autonomy, one might think, is desirable goal; it's too bad it's so hard to achieve. This is not our view of the matter. Not only do we think that local autonomy cannot be achieved but we do not wish it were otherwise. A grant of unsupervised local authority is likely to fuel a desire to separate city residents from those who live on the other side of the city line. Even today, especially in the prosperous suburbs, the popular, albeit false, belief in local autonomy encourages many people to think of the city line as separating "us" from "them": crime, bad schools, and inadequate resources across the city line, far from generating pressure for intercity negotiation, are dismissed as "their problem." Those who see themselves as better off can also experience the powerlessness of their neighbors as a form of self-protection. Why should we be willing to help others gain power that might ultimately threaten us? At the same time, concerns about corruption and waste have long undermined confidence in the legitimacy of large city governments. There is always a risk that they will make decisions on the basis of short-term political imperatives that undermine the long-term interests of the city. Unchecked power at any level is a matter of concern.

Given the multitude of local governments that constitute America's metropolitan areas—as well as the states and the nation as a whole—it is hard to see how a central government could justify giving its local governments autonomy. The notion of local autonomy imagines localities as able to do whatever they want as long as they stay within their sphere of delegated authority. They can act in their own self-interest, cooperate with others on their own terms, and cause harm to those who disagree with them. It should not be surprising that central governments are unwilling to give them this kind of power. No one could trust such a government to operate without some form of centralized control. It presents too much danger to outsiders and even to its own citizens. The dangers associated with the exercise of city power—ranging from control by elites to corruption to the infringement of the rights of minorities to the selfish imposition of costs on outsiders—are real. To be sure, the values of decentralization—increased participation, local accountability, generating opportunities for experimentation—are real too. Given this conflict over the value of decentralization, however, some entity other than the cities themselves must have the power to define local authority. Individual local governments cannot define the scope of their own authority. In the United States, state governments—state constitutions, state legislatures, and state courts—have been given this power. Another form of organization could be assigned this task—indeed, in chapter 10, we describe one. But some kind of decision-making power lodged in a higher government authority seems irresistible.

The same point can be restated in terms of democratic theory. The legitimacy of governmental action at every level is based on a fundamental democratic claim: we, the people, should be able to decide our own future for ourselves. As Robert Dahl observed long ago, the great question left open by this formulation is who is included in the term "we."[8] Every geographically defined unit—from the neighborhood to the city to the region to the state to the nation to the entire world—can repeat the same formula: we should be able to decide our own future for ourselves. The smaller the geographical unit, the more people will be excluded from the decision-making process. Indeed, small units will exclude people living right across the border who are affected by the local decision yet have no voice in it. Whenever a prosperous suburb votes for rules that exclude the poor, it profits from just this form of democracy. Similarly, whenever a central city gets itself into a fiscal jam that requires state financial assistance, it also benefits from a system that enables it to impose obligations on people who have no direct role in making the policies that caused the problem.

Of course, the same problem arises at the city, regional, statewide, and national level. Ultimately, only by including everyone in the world would all people affected by decisions have a voice in making them. Yet, most people agree, an all-powerful world government is a frightening prospect. How, then, does one decide who to include and exclude from any governmental decision-making process? Democratic theory, Dahl says, provides no answer to this question. This theoretical ambivalence should feel familiar, because it is reflected in the common, everyday ambivalence about where to lodge governmental power. People generally embrace local power over some issues and fear it over others. The controversy revolves around deciding which issues fall into each of these two categories. Local governments cannot be trusted to make this allocation themselves because they could make the wrong choice. But every other level of government could make the wrong choice too. Although every level of government has a legitimate claim for being the decision maker, every claim can also be illegitimate. Yet decision-making power has to be lodged *somewhere*. Not surprisingly, in the United States as well as elsewhere, governmental authority is usually allocated simultaneously to many levels of government, mixing them in ways that are so complex that they are often incomprehensible. Only rarely is the local government given the final word.

Splitting the Difference

Federalism and Subsidiarity

One possible way out of this complexity is to try to make a clear and definitive allocation of power, assigning specific kinds of tasks to different levels of government. On the national level in the United States, this kind of division of authority is associated with the term "federalism." In the European Union, the favored term is "subsidiarity." Neither federalism nor subsidiarity, however, has done much to resolve the basic problem that the complexity of the concept of local autonomy poses: there is no clean way to divide matters into discrete "local" and "central" spheres. Indeed, rather than overcoming this problem, the concepts of federalism and subsidiarity reproduce it. And they have done almost nothing to protect *local* governments. In fact, both concepts have been used to justify denying powers to localities.

Federalism envisions a division of powers between the national government and the states. From the time of the writing of the Constitution to the present day, there has been a spirited debate about the meaning of the term. Arguments have been advanced that emphasize the scope of national power (the original federalists), the limits on national power (the original antifederalists, but now often associated with the word federalism itself), and the degree of unavoidable overlap between the activities of the two levels of government. As this debate has continued, the definition of the kind of national-state relationship the Constitution has created has become one of the most perplexing issues of American constitutional interpretation.

From the perspective of local governments, the important point to note is that this debate has done little to further local autonomy. To be sure, a few Supreme Court cases have invalidated federal legislation that affected city power (although, as our earlier discussion of the complexity of local autonomy suggests, some of these cases may have done more harm than good for advocates of enhanced local power). But the most significant restrictions on local power in the United States come from state governments, not the national government. And federalism has generally been interpreted to protect the states' power to structure their local governments in whatever way they choose. The Supreme Court has made clear that there is no general federal constitutional limit on the states' ability to restrict, reallocate, or even abolish local governmental authority. It has also expressed reluctance to interpret federal statutes in a way that interferes with the state's power to structure the state-local relationship. Federalism, then, tends more to justify strict state control over local governments than to be a meaningful basis for promoting greater decentralization to the local level.[9]

One might think that the notion of subsidiarity could do more for local authority. The Treaty on European Union defines subsidiarity to mean that, except for the areas of the European Community's exclusive competence, the Community shall act "only if and in so far as the objectives of the proposed action cannot be sufficiently achieved by the Member States and can therefore, by reason of the scale or effects of the proposed action, be better achieved by the Community."[10] Subsidiarity thus "expresses a preference for governance at the most local level consistent with achieving government's stated purposes."[11] One reason offered for this preference is furthering the project of democratic self-government by locating power at the level closest to the people. As George Bermann notes, this preference for decentralized decision making distinguishes subsidiarity from federalism:

> Although federalism conveys a general sense of vertical distribution, or balance, of power, it is not generally understood as expressing a preference for any particular distribution of that power, much less dictating any particular inquiry into the implications of specific governmental action for that distribution. In this respect, federalism and subsidiarity, though of course closely related, are quite different.[12]

There is as much controversy about the meaning of subsidiarity as there is about the meaning of federalism. For local governments, the important point about this debate is that the effect of subsidiarity on local power is similar to the impact of federalism in the United States. Despite the stated preference for governance at the local level, subsidiarity has been interpreted to protect the power of national governments, not local ones. As one commentator puts it, the European Union has embraced "a 'sawn-off' form of subsidiarity. It is subsidiarity down as far as the national level but no farther."[13] Indeed, the embrace of subsidiarity "entrusts Member States with determining whether more decentralized action is preferable....Member States are free to distribute national authority as they wish."[14] To be sure, decisions of the European Union can limit local power, just as actions taken by the national government in the United States can limit it. But the European Community does not attempt to authorize local governments to take actions that are not themselves permitted by the national governments. In fact, when the European Union has sought to empower subnational authorities, its focus has been not on local governments but on regions. Its creation of a "Committee of Regions" is designed to provide a subnational voice into some aspects of Community decision making. Regions are not the equivalent of local governments. In fact, local governments need not even be represented in the organization of regional decision making.

The reluctance of both the federal government in the United States and the European Union to embrace local power should not be surprising. The decentralization envisioned by federalism and subsidiarity focuses on the states in the United States and the national governments in Europe. One of the decisions that these governments are authorized to make—one of their powers that need protection—is determining the extent of the authority that should be granted to local governments. To enhance local power over the objections of American states or the member states of the European Union would limit their power.

A decision by the United States or the European Union to enhance the power of local governments in the name of federalism or subsidiarity would thus undermine these very principles.

Two-Tier Government

The respect for state and national governments is not the only reason that federalism and subsidiarity have failed to empower local governments. Another reason derives from the peculiar difficulties involved in defining the scope of local governmental power: there are so many local governments, they are so often located next to each other, and their responsibilities and objectives so regularly overlap those of higher levels of government. The difficulties of dividing power between local and larger-than-local governments can best be illustrated by the efforts to create metropolitan wide regional governments in the United States. Long before the dramatic postwar expansion of American metropolitan areas, reformers who favored regional solutions to urban problems recognized that a single government for the entire region was not the solution to metropolitan fragmentation. They therefore sought to create a "two-tier" system of government by dividing governmental functions into those that could best be performed on a regional level and those that could properly remain local in character.

A report written in 1896 by the Metropolitan District Commission, an organization created by the Massachusetts legislature to consider the establishment of a regional government for Boston and its surrounding suburbs, provided the earliest articulation of this idea.[15] Strongly rejecting the option of annexation, the Commission offered in its place a design modeled on the notion that power can be allocated to two levels of government simultaneously. The Commission based its proposal on the assumption that the rationale for regionalism was the promotion of the area's economy and that the justification for regional performance of any particular government function lay in its ability to generate greater efficiency. From this perspective, it found that the essential metropolitan wide functions were sewerage, parks, and water supply (each of which was then the responsibility of its own metropolitan organization), with metropolitan transportation a likely future addition. The Commission argued that these regional functions could be performed by a new county covering greater Boston while "the local independence of the various municipalities would be assured" because any additions to the list of functions would require proof that the matter was of general character and that it could not adequately be undertaken by the localities.

The Metropolitan District Commission's proposal for Boston never got out of the state legislature, but its equation of two-tier regional government with a functional division of power has continued to the present day. So has its reliance on the notion that a region wide consensus could determine which functions should be performed at each of the two levels of government. The Commission's version of this consensus derived from its focus on the economy; that's what enabled it to describe the region as having "common interests and a fairly homogeneous people." The same focus also inspired efforts in the 1920s to establish two-tier regional governments in localities ranging from Alameda County (California) to Pittsburgh, Cleveland, and St. Louis. But so great was the fear of centralization that the voting rules were designed to ensure the proposal's defeat (in Pittsburgh, for example, a two-thirds vote in each of the municipalities was required for adoption).

Efforts to establish two-tier governments were revived in the late 1950s in St. Louis and Cleveland, with both proposals again going down to defeat. By this time, however, the comforting notion that there existed a consensus that could allocate functions to the two levels of government had largely disappeared. The problem was not just that the idea of "economy and efficiency" could be broadly interpreted to include virtually the whole range of local government activities, thereby making the two-tier structure simply a stepping-stone toward centralization. This difficulty had long been recognized by sophisticated two-tier proponents when they considered contentious issues such as the allocation of the power to raise taxes. Equally troubling was the growing realization that other values needed to be added to the rationale for regionalism.

This expanded vision was most carefully articulated in a series of reports issued in the 1960s and 1970s by the United States Advisory Commission on Intergovernmental Relations.[16] The Commission analyzed local government functions in terms of four different factors—economic efficiency, equity, political accountability, and administrative effectiveness—and explored the complexity involved in applying these conflicting criteria to any specific local function. The Commission insisted that an allocation of power consistent with all of these values was possible. Yet its confidence failed to mask the fundamental dilemma: every traditional city function—police, education, housing, transportation, parks, sanitation—is simultaneously a matter of local concern and of regional concern. Decisions on these issues regularly affect not only the people who live within city boundaries but those who live outside of them. As a result, the very items that are most important to local citizens can be understood as proper subjects for regional governmental action. The Commission thought that this difficulty could be overcome through expertise. It called on the states to undertake a case-by-case analysis that would strike the right balance between regional and local power, urging them to recognize that a solution would often require subdividing individual functions and apportioning their component parts to the two levels of government.

The two-tier solution to regional problems is still widely embraced. Some proponents continue to invoke arguments of efficiency and economy, but most of them now focus instead on promoting the racial and economic integration of the region's housing, designing a more equitable allocation of tax revenues, and establishing growth boundaries to curb suburban sprawl. In other words, they have made the achievement of regional equity, rather than efficiency, the essential regional function. David Rusk, who has offered the most detailed contemporary proposal for a two-tier regional government, insists: "*While it may be a beneficial result, greater efficiency is no part of [my]...argument.*"[17] This shift in emphasis, far from resolving the ambiguity that plagues two-tier proposals, has made it even harder to imagine how specific tasks would be allocated to two different levels of government. Unlike the arguments based on economy and efficiency, the emphasis on equity overtly threatens the very advantages that many proponents of local autonomy have fought so hard to retain. After all, residential segregation, unequal tax revenues, and unlimited potential for growth have benefited some suburban residents at the expense of their poorer neighbors. Even residents of the poor suburbs and central cities—the beneficiaries of the proposed exercise of regional power—are likely to realize that a regional government empowered to achieve equity could limit the aspects of local self-determination they value most. Today's two-tier advocates do little to assuage these kinds of concerns. Although they suggest that local autonomy would remain even after their regional goals have been accomplished, they have not indicated what functions of any importance local governments would continue to provide. They have concentrated solely on the achievement of their regional goals.

The demand for regional equity and the protection of local autonomy conflict with one another, and it is disingenuous to pretend otherwise. The goals of regional efficiency and regional equity can easily conflict with one another as well. These conflicts cannot be resolved by a functional division of power because the fundamental issue is political, not technical. The effort to create a functional division of power is based on the idea that there is an uncontroversial way to divide governmental functions between those that serve a parochial conception of self-interest and those that serve the greater good. But the notion that there is some neutral way of deciding which functions foster parochialism and which promote the common good is not simply illusory. The search for it has frustrated the effort to achieve regional goals. Too often, to avoid making such a controversial judgment, analysts falsely hold out hope that it is possible to allow localities to advance a parochial notion of self-interest on some issues without imposing negative consequences on outsiders. In this way, the two-tier model strengthens this narrow conception of self-interest at the expense of regionalism.

The problem with the two-tier solution, in short, is similar to the problems facing federalism and subsidiarity: the concept does not identify any topics that should be clearly reserved to only one level of government. Peterson's analysis again is instructive. He presents an account that suggests that developmental policies should be left to cities and redistributive policies should be left to the central government. But, as he recognizes, city residents are interested in making policy on the redistributive side of the line. Perhaps, then, the legal framework should be adjusted so that city residents would be able to engage in making the kinds of trade-offs that the current system reserves to national politics. If a legal framework can be devised that would permit local engagement on a matter of such great local concern, why not adopt it? The answer cannot then be that redistribution is not a local matter. The issue is whether the legal structure should be organized to make it a local matter.

Although any particular legal framework makes it easier for some policies to be decided at one level than at another, the reason for preferring any specific allocation reflects a policy choice about the content of local politics. This is the insight that animated the early home rule reformers. Cities could be empowered and limited in ways that would encourage them to pursue an agenda that protects the private sector or in ways that would make it possible for them to pursue a more ambitious policy. There is no natural order dividing topics into those that are local and those that are not.

The Value of the Decentralization of Power

But *why* should local governments generally—or even simply the kinds of large, successful central cities on which we focus in this book—be empowered to make choices about the kinds of future that they want to implement? If local autonomy is a concept that reflects the substantive preferences of the central government about how local power should be directed, why bother with entrusting the decisions to local actors at all? Why shouldn't the central government simply decide what kinds of cities that it wants and then adopt policies that are likely to bring this vision of urban life into being?

The answer to these questions depends on making an effective challenge to the assumption that a larger entity would make decisions in a preferable way. There are a number of reasons why this assumption is mistaken. First, there is an intrinsic value in local participation that would be lost if local governments ceased to be—as Tocqueville called them—schoolhouses of democracy.[18] Cities can retain their ability to enable people to learn the skills of self-government only if they are given sufficient power to make decisions that have tangible consequences for the quality of local life. If they are precluded from deciding important matters, the civic culture can be expected to whither, with detrimental effects on the expansion of human capacity that political participation entails. To be sure, the kinds of cities on which we are focusing—each of which has hundreds of thousands of residents and some of which have millions—are not small enough to permit direct, face-to-face engagement on major policy questions. Indeed, some of these cities have more people than some states. Nevertheless, these kinds of large urban centers remain important schoolhouses of democracy. They are the most diverse local governments we have in terms of income, ethnicity, and race. The kind of politics and policymaking that they engage in is not easily replicated either in the more homogeneous but smaller suburbs that surround them or in the more distant and geographically larger states that ultimately control them. For this reason, large cities can and do play a uniquely important role in promoting participation in civic life.

Another reason for favoring decentralization is the important role that major cities can play in generating innovative ideas about urban policy. No doubt, decentralization runs the risk that the local government will not make sound decisions. Still, analysts now recognize that effective, generalizable policy solutions are often best discovered through consideration of broad problems within a local context. Working out a problem in a localized setting can reveal solutions that a more abstract consideration cannot identify. The geographically confined nature of local institutions also provides an opportunity to build the kind of civic capacity that political scientists increasingly see as necessary to sustain efforts to implement proposed solutions to seemingly intractable public problems. Because discovering solutions is an important goal of institutional design, local governmental institutions are critical agents of reform.

This general observation has particular force in the United States. As we have seen, the critique of home rule rests on a rather crude distinction between central cities and suburbs. It is increasingly clear, however, that such a sharp central city/suburb divide is inaccurate. Some central cities are enjoying boom times. Their main concern is preserving affordable housing because developers already have a more-than-adequate desire to build new office developments and luxury condominiums in town. To be sure, there is a great variation among large cities in terms of their economic situation, and not all successful large cities are succeeding in the same way. But this reinforces the fact that their choices about how best to maintain their present status are likely to be influenced by their own local conditions. At the same time, many outlying suburbs are feeling the strains of rapid development on their infrastructure, making it difficult for them to sustain their current growth rates. Others are struggling not to become poorer than their neighboring central city; they need policies to prevent a self-perpetuating downward spiral. These variations among local governments suggest the need for different types of responses to the conditions that each of them faces. They also suggest a variety of sites for identifying the problems with the current pattern of development. The very fact that so many communities seem to be experiencing such disparate burdens—as well as experiencing such unanticipated benefits—makes clear the potential advantages of local governments as laboratories of democracy.

The current diversity among suburbs and central cities also highlights the potential dangers of attempting to forge a solution by assigning decisional power to greater-than-local decision makers. There is a tendency for central governments to see problems through a limited lens that bleaches out variation. This framework can result in a form of planning that saps the vitality of local lived experience. Centralization, in other words, limits opportunities for learning at the center and not just locally. Generating the kind of civic commitment necessary to sustain reform is also much more difficult on a state or national than on a local scale.

Even within the current system, there is evidence of the potential beneficial effects of permitting locally generated policy discovery. Local policies have broken with the stereotyped image of the wealthy suburb or the hapless central city. They have been spurred by a "social contagion among decision makers otherwise uncertain how to proceed"[19] and not merely in response to the isolated lobbying efforts of particular, internal interest groups. Cities "look to each other to define appropriate policies and models of governance."[20] Indeed, the appearance of an innovation in one city increases the likelihood of it appearing in another precisely because it has now become a concretely available policy option. The living wage movement has gained traction in many places through just this kind of interlocal process. Of course, the same phenomenon works in both directions. The tendency of localities to copy one another helps explain the high degree of similarity in economic development practices across cities. The point is not that the local learning process always produces optimal results. Cities will remain within state-mandated structures that direct the kind of experimentation that localities engage in.

Here, again, we can learn from the early home rule reformers. They were acutely interested in using local power to transform public decision making more generally. Indeed, the great early-twentieth-century urban reformer Frederick Howe contended that the city should be an "experiment-station" for not only the nation but the world.[21] Importantly, however, these reformers were also aware that the rules that constitute local power affect the kind of experiments local governments can undertake. The present rules established by state law cannot be taken as given. They may need to be changed in order to open up possibilities for the exercise of local power along currently foreclosed lines. For early urban reformers, as for us, the key question was not whether local autonomy should be preserved or undermined. There is no local autonomy to be protected or discarded. The key question is what kind of legal reform would enable cities to pursue a substantive agenda for the future and to engage in political debate over what that future should be.

Part II
SEVEN CITIES

The argument advanced in part I was framed in general terms: the different legal structures that define local power are a major factor in determining a large, successful city's policy and its ability to alter it. At this level of generality, the proposition may well be easy to accept. But it also is likely to be too vague to be useful. What kind of legal structures are we talking about? How exactly does a legal structure affect a city's policymaking?

In this part we address these questions of specificity. We provide a detailed examination of the power of the City of Boston, as compared to six other major cities, both as a matter of home rule and in the important substantive areas of revenue and expenditures, land use, and education. Nowhere in the literature, as far as we aware, is there a thorough examination of the different ways that states empower and disempower cities in the United States. There is a good deal of talk in general terms—using phrases like relative autonomy, subsidiarity, home rule, and the trend toward decentralization—but far too little discussion about the actual legal context in which major American cities operate. In the following chapters, we want the reader to experience the ways in which city policy is controlled by state law. And our review is by no means exhaustive, even on the topics we cover. Additional chapters on transportation, public safety, and public health could be written in the same manner. Our goal is to convey in concrete terms the role that legal reform might play in the pursuit of any or all of the four possible city futures examined in part III.

To pursue this goal, we have examined the legal structures that govern seven major American cities: Boston, New York, Chicago, San Francisco, Seattle, Denver, and Atlanta. All of these cities are large, economically influential actors within their regions and states. Each has an ethnically and racially diverse population, one that is substantially more diverse than the other communities that comprise its metropolitan region. Each is doing fairly well, as compared to other major cities in the United States. And each faces substantial but related challenges, occasioned by increasing suburban growth, significant immigration, and the persistence of concentrated poverty.

But the seven cities are also quite different from each other. They vary in the size of their populations, their diversity, the level of education of their residents, and the size of their economies. They are located in distinct regions of the country, each with its own political culture and attitudes about urbanism and local self-government. Most important, for our purposes, they have been organized by their states in very different ways, with different governmental structures and different legal limitations on their ability to guide their futures. The variety of ways in which these cities are constrained and empowered itself suggests a potential need for reform. It would be remarkable indeed if each of these structures, different as they are, is well designed to meet the needs of a large city facing today's urban problems and challenges.

We have chosen to focus primarily on Boston, using the other cities simply for comparative purposes. A detailed discussion of the legal structures governing seven different cities in seven different states would be tediously repetitive. It would be better, we thought, to explore one legal structure in detail, using the other cities to illustrate alternatives. Although any of the cities could have served as our focal point, Boston had a number of advantages. It is a very successful city—one of the American cities that has thrived after the difficult days of the 1950s. Yet, like other major cities in America, it is only a small part of its region: it is surrounded by more than one hundred other cities and towns. Focusing on Boston highlights the relationship between state limits on city power and the importance of connecting central cities to their surrounding suburbs. Boston is also the symbolic location in America for the virtues of local self-government: the cradle of the town meeting, the home of American democracy. But its powers of self-government are very limited, even more so than the six other cities that we examine. At the same time, although Boston has less power than other cities, its limitations are not unusual: on almost every specific point, at least one of our comparison cities is just as limited as Boston (sometimes more limited). What seems important is that the limits on Boston's power are substantial enough, and common enough, that readers from other cities can be alerted to the ways in which their city too might be subject to restraint.

Before we turn to a comparative analysis of legal powers of the seven cities, it seems useful to provide a brief comparative sense of the cities themselves. In land area, Boston is the second smallest of the seven cities (San Francisco is a fraction smaller). In population, Boston, with a population in 2000 of 589,141, is smaller than three of the cities (New York had eight million residents, Chicago two million, and San Francisco 776,000) and larger than three others

(Atlanta with just over four hundred thousand is the smallest). Boston is last on the list in one important respect. The population of all of the other cities—and all of the other metropolitan areas—grew faster in the 1990s than Boston and its metropolitan area, some at dramatically faster rates. (Since 2000, only New York and Atlanta have grown substantially; the other cities have been relatively stable, with Chicago and San Francisco losing population and Boston's population increasing only slightly.)

In racial and ethnic diversity, Boston is right in the middle—fourth out of the seven cities—in its percentage of African American, Asian/Pacific Islander, and Hispanic (of any race) residents. Like four of the other cities—all but Seattle and Denver—Boston is a "majority-minority" city.[1] Adopting another definition of diversity, Boston is third out of the seven cities in the percentage of foreign-born residents.[2] Finally, in all seven cities there are sizeable populations of both highly educated people and those living in poverty.[3] Boston is distinctive in one interesting way: it is first out of the seven cites in the percentage of the population enrolled in college or graduate school, with a percentage twice that of two of the other cities.

The metropolitan regions within which these cities are located are also very different. Using one well-known definition, the primary statistical metropolitan area,[4] the Boston metropolitan region is in the middle of the seven in terms of both land area and population. None of the cities has a majority of its metropolitan population. Indeed, most of them, including Boston, are home to less than a quarter of the residents in their metropolitan areas. On the other hand, except for San Francisco, the metropolitan areas themselves constitute roughly half, if not more, of their state's population. In addition, while the economies of the regions in which the seven cities are located are quite different, three—the Boston,

Chicago, and New York areas—are among the four largest in the nation. (If the Boston metropolitan area were a separate country, its economy would rank twenty-second in the world—a fraction smaller than Switzerland but larger than Belgium, Sweden, or Austria.)[5] One aspect of the metropolitan economic picture is similar for all seven cities: the city economy has fared substantially less well than the regional economy.[6]

One last way of comparing the seven cities is worth noting given the crucial importance of state decision making on city power: the cities' influence in the state legislature. Political influence is an elusive concept to measure, but some basic numbers demonstrate that there are differences among the seven cities. In Massachusetts, 11 percent of the members of the House of Representatives and 15 percent of the state Senate represent at least a portion of Boston.[7] These figures are comparable to those of Denver, Atlanta, and Seattle, although New York and Chicago have much larger delegations.[8] Another way to judge influence might be to look at the state legislative leadership. As is the case for New York, Chicago, San Francisco, and Seattle, the leader of one of the state's legislative bodies comes from Boston. Legislative delegations from Denver and Atlanta, on the other hand, are in the legislature's minority, depriving them of much of their effective power. A glance at the past, however, shows that Boston has been in a position similar to Denver and Atlanta for much of its history.[9] Finally, the state legislature meets in Boston—as it does in Denver and Atlanta—and representatives and senators from outside of Boston might therefore have a better understanding of the city and more stake in its success than if the legislature met elsewhere. Even so, Boston was weakly represented in the statehouse during the period when many of the laws defining its legal powers were passed.

In writing the following four chapters, we have relied on reports issued by city and state agencies, nonprofit organizations, and scholars. We have examined a broad range of legal materials, including state constitutional provisions conferring home rule, statewide initiatives (such as Proposition 2½ in Massachusetts, Proposition 13 in California, and the Taxpayer Bill of Rights in Colorado), and numerous state statutes that touch on virtually every aspect of local power. We have focused as well on more narrowly targeted legislative enactments that uniquely constrain (and, on occasion, empower) the cities, including laws that have shaped city charters and that have authorized public authorities, such as the Massachusetts Turnpike Authority and New York's Empire State Development Corporation, to exercise important regulatory and land use control within city limits. All of these legal materials have been considered in light of the state judicial opinions that have interpreted them, often in ways that further confined the choices the cities could make (while, on occasion, providing them with significant protection from state interference). Finally, to help us obtain an adequate understanding of the comparison cities, we consulted six prominent local-government-law scholars from across the country. Building on a mutually agreed on research design, each of these scholars performed a detailed investigation of the legal powers of one of the six comparison cities. The substantial reports they submitted to us have provided an indispensable resource for this book.

The following chapters do not present a comprehensive outline of the legal structure that organizes all seven cities. We sought instead to highlight the choices that states make when framing city power. The choices made by Massachusetts for Boston are illustrative, and their controversial nature is illuminated by seeing the different choices that other states have made for their cities. (When we talk about "other cities" we mean only the six comparison cities, not all cities in the United States.) No doubt, if we had expanded our list of cities, we would have found even more options that have been adopted somewhere. And we would have found that some cities are even more restricted by state law than Boston. Indeed, the city of most interest to the reader—one we perhaps do not discuss—might be a good focus when reading these chapters. How, one might ask, does the set-up of my city compare with that of Boston?

HOME RULE

Every major American city operates within a legal framework not of its own making. These frameworks vary substantially. One key difference is whether a state defines local powers through specific statutes or through general delegations of authority. For most of the nineteenth century, all states chose the first path. They defined local government power and offered city charters through specific legislative enactments. As local governments grew in size and complexity, most states shifted course. Rather than requiring fast-growing central cities to seek special permission from the state legislature each time they wanted to act, states granted them what is known as "home rule." Home rule gives local governments the authority to take some kinds of actions without state permission and, in a number of states, provides that some of these local decisions prevail over conflicting state laws. All seven cities we examine have been given home rule powers.

But there is significant variation across the country—and for the seven cities—about what home rule means. Although home rule is usually thought to symbolize the rejection of the kind of local legal powerlessness embraced by prior law, home rule provisions shape local power not only through a grant of power but also by imposing limitations on its scope. All states limit cities' independence, and some limit it more significantly than others. The details matter a great deal. They establish the basic rules of the game for exercising local power. By doing so, they affect not only the particular policies that cities can pursue but the confidence each city has in its ability to chart its own future free of state legislative influence. For these reasons, the differences among home rule provisions are important. We examine these differences in this chapter. All states, however, have one thing in common: nowhere does home rule give cities local autonomy.

We briefly outline below the pre-home-rule nature of local power in Boston. The city's history of state legislative oversight illustrates the detailed kinds of state interventions into city life that can take place when a city lacks home rule. We then describe Boston's home rule powers as compared to those of the other six cities. We focus on two important powers that state home rule provisions typically confer. The first is the power to establish a charter of government for the city. The second is the general home rule power: the power to act without specific statutory authorization. Boston fares no better, and often much worse, than the other cities on these key dimensions of home rule. Yet all seven cities are subject to important limitations that are built into their grants of home rule.

The textual bases for these limitations vary. Some home rule provisions expressly confine the power to initiate legislation to matters of "local" concern. This terminology leaves courts free to label matters of pressing societal interest—such as efforts to counteract discrimination in the housing or employment market—beyond the scope of the home rule power because they are thought to be of greater-than-local concern.[1] In some states, the grant of home rule only over "local" matters also leads courts to construe the scope of local initiative narrowly to avoid a possible conflict with a state statute that governs the issue; here, too, local efforts to address matters such as discrimination, housing, or the environment may run into legal obstacles.[2] In addition, some home rule provisions—including those governing some of the seven cities—expressly bar local lawmaking that touches on what are known as "private or civil affairs." This category has always been somewhat of a mystery, but it provides courts with a way to restrain local efforts to undertake a wide range of actions that might mitigate the social impacts of private development, ranging from rent control to living wage ordinances.[3] Finally, home rule provisions sometimes expressly deny local governments the power to tax. This limitation does more than simply deny them the ability to impose commuter taxes or experiment with taxes other than the property tax. It provides judges with a basis for casting doubt on the legality of a range of local attempts designed to ensure that private land use development pays its own way. The grant of home rule, in short, is always more limited than its name suggests, even when it is broader than the highly restrictive form that applies to Boston.

The Legal Powers of Boston before Home Rule

The states in which the seven cities are located adopted home rule at different times. By the time Boston finally received home rule in 1967, more than two-thirds of the states across the country had already given their cities home rule. Among the cities we examine, only Chicago received home rule later than Boston, and even Chicago enjoyed at least some protection from state interference well before Boston did. Boston's failure to win home rule earlier was not due to its lack of effort but to state opposition. Boston officials submitted home rule proposals to the state legislature on a number of occasions. Boston was eager to get out from under state control, and for good reason. The state legislature had aggressively asserted its power over Boston's affairs for hundreds of years.

For nearly two centuries—from 1630 to 1822—Boston, like other towns in Massachusetts, was run by a town meeting. As early as 1635, the state legislature carefully circumscribed the powers of towns—of which Boston was one of fewer than thirty at the time—to those matters "which concerne[d] only themselves." It also made clear that even within that sphere local governments would have no authority to make laws that were inconsistent with state law. Over time, with the exception of a brief interlude during the Revolutionary War, the legislature progressively increased its control over the towns, especially Boston. By the end of the nineteenth century, legislative power was supreme.[4]

One way to see how the state asserted power over local matters during this period is through an examination of the state legislature's role in shaping Boston's charter. In 1822, the Boston town meeting applied for, and was granted, a city charter, making Boston the first city to be incorporated in Massachusetts. The 1822 charter was enacted as special legislation—that is, it was adopted by the state legislature and could thereafter only be changed at the legislature's discretion. Over the subsequent period, the 1822 city charter has undergone a series of revisions, progressively strengthening the power of the mayor and, beginning particularly with the charter amendment of 1885, introducing greater state oversight into Boston's political structure. In 1885, the legislature enacted another important piece of special legislation—one that divested the city of all control over its police force and placed it in the hands of the governor. Both the 1885 charter amendment and the police legislation were simply enacted by the legislature—indeed, unlike for the 1822 charter, the legislature did not even provide for referendum approval by Boston voters. In 1909, again without a referendum, the state legislature amended the charter to establish a Finance Commission, appointed by the governor, to investigate the city's accounts and expenses and, at the same time, subjected mayoral appointees to the state's Civil Service Commission. Other state interventions during this period included targeted limits on the city's power to borrow funds and caps on the amount that the city could spend on its public schools. Boston was also barred from raising tax rates, or increasing assessments, without receiving express permission from the state legislature. As if to make the state's assumption of local powers crystal clear, the state legislature even played a direct role in selecting the city's mayor. Shortly before Mayor James Michael Curley was elected to a second term in 1922, a new statute made it impossible for a mayor to succeed himself in 1926.[5]

The decades immediately following World War II were difficult ones for Boston. Boston's population dropped by over 100,000 residents in the 1950s—its worst decade. It then dropped by over 50,000 in the 1960s and over 70,000 in the 1970s before rising slightly in the 1980s. (The worst decade for the other cities was the 1970s, except for Denver, when it was the 1980s.) There was little reason in those years, as the economist Ed Glaeser has put it, "to suspect that Boston would be any more successful than Rochester or Pittsburgh or St. Louis over the next few decades."[6] Dramatic action was necessary. But Boston was constrained in its ability to respond. Lacking the power to find new sources of revenue, and unable to get the state to have other entities assume burdens that hit Boston particularly hard, the city repeatedly ceded important authority to the state in return for additional access to funds or relief from burdensome costs.

Whether the bargains made during this time were wise ones is open to debate. Boston did become a national leader in redevelopment during these years, and it was aided in that effort by state measures that gave Boston additional powers in return for giving up some old ones. Nevertheless, state-created public authorities—and sometimes the state itself—took over important city assets. The mayor agreed to a state proposal to place a proposed garage underneath Boston Common under the control of a state-established Massachusetts Parking Authority run by a three-person board, two of whom would be appointed by the governor. With the support of the mayor, the state established another public authority—the Massachusetts Port Authority—to take control of the city's port, the Tobin Bridge, and Logan Airport. (Massport, managed by a seven-member board appointed by the governor, now owns nearly 10 percent of the land within the city's limits.) The state also created the Massachusetts Turnpike Authority and built (and kept control over) the Massachusetts Turnpike extension into the city. And, in 1959, a cash-strapped Boston sold the Sumner Tunnel, which the city had built in the 1930s, to the state. In important respects, Boston emerged from the era of urban renewal with considerably less legal control over key parts of its city than it had decades before.

This pattern would repeat itself in later decades. Faced with a fiscal crisis, the state would come to Boston's aid in return for Boston selling off property or transferring control over important parts of the city. During the 1980s, the city would sell off numerous municipally owned parking garages to the private sector and the state. And yet another state-controlled authority, the Massachusetts Convention Center Authority, would be established to run a major public facility in the city. There were exceptions to the pattern. Although the state was exercising more control over the city's transportation network in the 1950s, the state legislature allowed Boston to veto proposed state highway projects that would have had a dramatic impact on the city. At the city's request, the state also established the Boston Redevelopment Authority, thereby enhancing Boston's overall ability to coordinate redevelopment even as it injected a measure of state control into the process. And a 1962 statute returned control over the appointment of the Boston police commissioner to the mayor of Boston. (The statute transferring the appointment of the police commissioner to the mayor made sure that he did not have too much control over the police department: it provided that the police commissioner was to be appointed for a fixed term.) Overall, however, as Boston underwent significant economic, social, and demographic changes over the course of more than a century, state law generally barred the city from responding to these forces as it wished. Instead, as the city changed, the state shifted important control over the city from the city to the state.[7]

The State Grant of Home Rule Power

Given this history of state legislative control, the state's 1967 grant of home rule promised to mark a new phase in the legal relationship between the city and the state. The Massachusetts definition of home rule is set forth in Article 89 of the state constitution (known as the Home Rule Amendment) and spelled out further in the Home Rule Procedures Act. The preamble to the Home Rule Amendment explains that its purpose is to "grant and confirm to the people of every city and town the right of self-governance in local matters." This sweeping language is quite misleading. Boston remains to this day highly dependent on, and beholden to, the state legislature in exercising legal power. A key reason is that the Home Rule Amendment turned out to be relatively weak in terms of both of its key features: the charter power and the general home rule power.

The Charter Power

The city charter is a miniconstitution for the city. It sets forth the administrative structure of the city's government, the procedures that city agencies and officers must follow, and, often, many of the city's regulatory powers. The charter's significance makes it matter whether the city or the state writes it. The Massachusetts Home Rule Amendment gives Boston the right to establish a charter for itself, but that grant of power has not proved consequential. Like Chicago and Atlanta, Boston has not written its own home rule charter. Indeed, like only Atlanta, Boston's charter was specially written for it by the state legislature.

The fact that the state legislature has written Boston's charter does not mean that the charter is a single state law. The city's "charter" is a patchwork of laws enacted by the state legislature over the course of two hundred years.[8]

Boston's failure to write its own charter can be explained in part by the fact that the city did not obtain the home rule charter power until relatively late in its history. Boston was already a fully developed modern urban center when it got the power to draw up a governmental structure on its own. San Francisco and Seattle adopted their own charters in the nineteenth century, and Denver followed a similar course in 1904. New York City wrote its own charter in the 1930s. Even more fundamentally, however, the way Massachusetts structured the city's home rule charter power explains why Boston has not used it. Under the Home Rule Amendment, the city can bring order to the current jumble of statutes that constitute its charter only by placing the whole of its governmental structure in the hands of a separately elected charter commission. By law, that commission can pursue an unlimited reform agenda once established. It then is to submit its proposal for an up-or-down vote by city residents. This process thus puts everything on the table without any means by which city officials can structure it. As a result, it gives city officials little incentive to push for charter reform.[9]

Other state constitutional home rule provisions are not nearly so rigid. Colorado permits Denver's city council to initiate substantial charter reform efforts without establishing an independent charter commission, and California does the same for its cities. Under Washington's state constitution, cities like Seattle may present voters with an alternative to the elected charter commission's proposal. But Boston is not alone in being subjected to state control of its charter. A major charter reform occurred in the 1970s in New York City at the behest of a commission that was created and partially controlled by Governor Nelson Rockefeller. The Colorado Constitution specifically defines aspects of Denver's administrative structure, making it impossible for the city to alter them on its own initiative. And the Georgia state legislature had a major hand in writing Atlanta's charter.

Still, Boston is less in control of, and is less engaged with, its charter than the other cities we examined. In New York City, the charter has been a major focal point of local civic debate and discussion in a way that it has never been in Boston. In recent years New York City has considered charter amendments and referenda concerning the creation and modification of the city's campaign finance system, the adoption of modifications to term limits for city officials, the relocation of Yankee Stadium from the Bronx to the West Side of Manhattan, and, most recently, the adoption of nonpartisan elections for municipal offices. Denver has reformed its city charter on an almost annual basis since 1904. In the last four election cycles, voters have amended the charter to establish the Department of Community Planning and Development, modernize revenue procedures, modify initiative and referendum procedures, alter the powers of its water commission to issue bonds, change civil service rules, require the city council to create a Board of Ethics, and increase the mayor's and the city council's ability to set pay and benefits for city employees. In San Francisco, at least six charter reform committees have been established in the last forty years. In 1996, San Francisco passed a revised charter that reduced its length by more than two-thirds and altered the management structure for the city, putting the mayor in charge of day-to-day operations while allowing elected officials, rather than appointed commissions, to set policy.[10] There may be advantages to Boston's more passive approach. Charter reform can be a distraction from more substantive concerns. Nevertheless, Boston's lack of homegrown charter activity is striking. The city appears to have given up on a way of focusing civic attention on the city's future that many cities have used. The state-mandated process of charter revision has given it little incentive to do otherwise.

The General Home Rule Power

Even though Boston has not written a home rule charter, it can still exercise the general home rule power. Section 6 of the Home Rule Amendment vests home rule power in all municipalities whether or not they have written a charter for themselves. (Denver, San Francisco, and Seattle had to adopt home rule charters in order to obtain general home rule powers under their state constitutions.) Section 6 appears, at first glance, to be very broad. It authorizes any city or town to exercise "any power or function which the general court [the Massachusetts state legislature] has the power to confer…." This language is important. It provides the basis for the Massachusetts Supreme Judicial Court's conclusion that municipalities have significant powers to regulate land use even in the absence of state authorizing legislation.[11] In recent years, Boston has relied on this language to ban smoking in restaurants and city workplaces. Standing alone, this language would make the Massachusetts Home Rule Amendment as broad as any of the state home rule grants we examined. But the sweeping introductory language of Section 6 is qualified in two important ways. In combination, they make Boston's home rule grant among the weakest of the seven cities.

SPECIFIC EXEMPTIONS

The first limitation, detailed in Section 7, lists six areas in which cities and towns are expressly denied home rule power. The categories excepted from the home rule grant of Section 6 are the powers: (1) to regulate elections; (2) to levy, assess, and collect taxes; (3) to borrow money or pledge the credit of the city or town;

(4) to dispose of parkland; (5) to enact private or civil law governing civil relationships except as incident to an exercise of independent municipal power; and (6) to define and provide for the punishment of a felony or to impose imprisonment. For these categories, Boston is in the same position as it was before home rule. It may act only if it has been specifically authorized to do so by a state statute.

Because the exceptions for regulating city elections, taxing, borrowing, and regulating most private or civil affairs cover such a wide range of issues that are of concern to cities, Section 7 makes home rule in Massachusetts something of an illusion. Perhaps this explains why so many local officials complain they can do little without the permission of the state legislature. Or why a Boston city official told us that the Home Rule Amendment was viewed less as a source of power than as a reason for concluding that local action would require state authorizing legislation. Or why the state legislature still spends almost as much time on local legislation as it did in the years leading up to the passage of the Home Rule Amendment.

The importance of these exceptions is magnified by the way state courts have interpreted them. The Massachusetts Supreme Judicial Court has held that the list of excepted areas is not exhaustive. Local governments also lack home rule over some matters not mentioned by Section 7, such as those that have significant impact on other cities and towns in the metropolitan region. In addition, the Supreme Judicial Court has construed the private or civil affairs exception to invalidate local ordinances that arguably fall outside its scope. For example, it invoked this limitation to invalidate local rent control ordinances absent statutory authorization and to uphold local antidiscrimination ordinances only if they lack strong enforcement mechanisms. The state courts have also construed the tax exception to strike down local revenue measures that one might think are not taxes, including impact fees imposed on new development.[12]

Other cities we examined also confront obstacles when they engage in creative policymaking on their own initiative. But no other city operates under a grant of home rule that exempts taxing, borrowing, the regulation of private or civil affairs, *and* the regulation of municipal elections from its coverage. The Illinois Constitution's home rule provision is a case in point. It is a mirror image of the Massachusetts Home Rule Amendment. Rather than broadly conferring governmental authority to localities and then expressly denying them a range of important powers, it grants municipalities only those home rule powers that pertain to local matters but then expressly defines them in an expansive fashion. The list of Chicago's home rule powers includes the power to tax (albeit with some important exceptions), to borrow, and to "regulate for the protection of the public health, safety, morals, and welfare." Moreover, the Illinois Constitution provides—as the Massachusetts Constitution does not—that the "powers and functions of home rule units shall be construed liberally." Consistent with that instruction, the state supreme court has construed the grant of home rule to include the power to regulate municipal elections, including the authority to require that they be nonpartisan.[13]

Denver enjoys a similarly generous home rule grant. The Colorado Constitution specifically establishes Denver as a home rule entity with the power to issue bonds, to construct, own, and operate public utilities, and to exercise the power of eminent domain "within or without" the city's territorial limits. It grants municipalities control over local and municipal matters, as well as the power to regulate municipal elections, consolidate park and water districts, and assess, levy, and collect property taxes for municipal purposes and improvements. Colorado's constitution instructs the courts to construe the home rule grant liberally, and the courts have held that the state constitution's recognition of cities' right to control local or municipal matters includes the right to impose taxes—including the sales tax—for local purposes. As the state supreme court explained, when the people adopted home rule in the state constitution "they conferred *every power* theretofore possessed by the legislature to authorize municipalities to function in local and municipal affairs."[14]

Like Chicago and Denver, San Francisco possesses the home rule power to tax, borrow, and regulate municipal elections. These powers flow from the California Constitution, which states that municipalities that adopt their own charters (as San Francisco has done) have home rule over municipal affairs. The state's supreme court has construed this term liberally. San Francisco has used its authority to adopt a public campaign financing system and to levy taxes—such as a business license tax—that the state legislature has not expressly sanctioned. California's home rule amendment contains no prohibition against the regulation of private or civil affairs like the one that the Massachusetts Supreme Judicial Court relied on to invalidate local rent control ordinances.[15]

New York City's home rule grant is like Boston's in that taxation is expressly exempted from its scope. But it still contains a number of powers that Boston does not have. Charter amendments have considered whether the city should move to a system of nonpartisan elections and have authorized municipal financing of local elections. Each of these measures is likely to be beyond the scope of Boston's home rule authority. New York City has also barred discrimination by private clubs, cigarette vending in public places, and discrimination according to place of residence by rental car companies. And it has regulated aspects of the conversion of rental housing to co-ops and condominiums as well as residential rents. Boston's power to adopt these measures is seriously constrained by the exception for private or civil affairs set forth in Section 7.[16]

Only the home rule grants for Seattle and Atlanta are limited in ways comparable to Boston's. The Washington Constitution authorizes cities, like Seattle, that have adopted home rule charters to "make and enforce within [their] limits all such local police, sanitary and other regulations as are not in conflict with general laws." This delegation of authority has been read quite narrowly in a series of state court decisions stretching back nearly a century. The result is that Seattle, like Boston, must seek state legislative authorization to obtain the power to tax or regulate in a wide variety of areas. Georgia's grant of home rule expressly exempts the regulation of private or civil affairs, just as the Massachusetts Home Rule Amendment does. Moreover, the Georgia Supreme Court has held that "powers of cities must be strictly construed, and any doubt concerning the existence of a particular power must be resolved against the municipality."[17]

Still, even Seattle and Atlanta appear to enjoy more independence from their state legislatures than Boston. Washington's constitution does not expressly deny the broad range of home rule powers that the Massachusetts Home Rule Amendment does. There is thus more room for state judges to construe its terms in a manner favorable to home rule. In recent years, the Washington Supreme Court has relied on the home rule grant to uphold Seattle's power to run its own electrical utility and to provide domestic partnership benefits to city employees. Seattle has also adopted local campaign finance measures, as well as a private cause of action for unfair real estate practices, pursuant to its assertion of home rule powers— powers that the express exceptions to the Massachusetts Home Rule Amendment would appear to preclude Boston from exercising. As for Atlanta, its home rule statute, although narrow, neither expressly exempts the power to borrow nor wholly exempts the power to tax, as does Boston's. In fact, the city's state-drafted charter expressly confers a general power to tax, which Atlanta has exercised frequently, as well as a general power to borrow.[18]

PREEMPTION

The Massachusetts Home Rule Amendment's other important limitation concerns what lawyers refer to as preemption: the power of the state legislature to override conflicting local laws. The Amendment provides that cities and towns may exercise their home rule powers only to the extent their actions are not inconsistent with the state constitution or state legislation. There is no area of local concern that is immune from state interference. Even when the city is not taxing, borrowing, regulating elections, or regulating private or civil affairs, its laws must therefore conform to those established by the state legislature. At most, then, the home rule grant permits Boston to act when the state legislature has not said it cannot act. The state courts have gone so far as to hold that "[the state legislature's] authority includes the power to choose to provide an appointive, rather than elective, form of municipal government."[19]

Preemption works in two ways. Some state laws preempt local ordinances expressly. This was the case, according to the Supreme Judicial Court, when Boston attempted to provide health benefits to the domestic partners of city employees.[20] The Massachusetts Home Rule Amendment, however, does not say that the state legislature must have "denied" a local power in order for it to be overridden. It says only that a local law may not be "inconsistent with" the state law. Soon after the Amendment's adoption, serious consideration was given to changing this language to make it more favorable to assertions of home rule authority. Those efforts did not succeed. The Amendment thus permits state statutes to preempt local laws even in the absence of a clear conflict. It is enough if the state is found to have dealt with the general subject matter in a manner that, by implication, renders the local action inconsistent with state policy.

The problem of preemption in Massachusetts is compounded by the fact that the areas in which the state has legislated are so diverse and comprehensive that any local regulation can be understood to conflict with some state policy. The Supreme Judicial Court, for example, held that the city of Boston was prohibited from expending its own funds to inform voters about a local referendum. Because the legislature enacted "comprehensive legislation" regulating election financing after the Home Rule Amendment—legislation that did not specifically address whether a city could spend money to educate voters—the court ruled that Boston's desire to conduct the voter-education campaign was inconsistent with state law.[21] Decisions like this one have a chilling effect on municipal initiative. Local officials in and out of Boston with whom we spoke repeatedly invoked the shadow of preemption—and the litigation that a claim of preemption would trigger—as a prime constraint on independent local assertions of authority in Massachusetts.

The Home Rule Amendment does impose one important constraint on the state's power to preempt: the state cannot pass a "special law" targeted at a particular city. Section 8 of the Home Rule Amendment provides that the state can preempt only by enacting a general law—unless it obtains two-thirds majorities in each branch of the legislature following a recommendation from the governor. This is not to say that a preemptive state statute cannot impact Boston more significantly than other Massachusetts cities. The statewide referendum that banned rent control affected only three cities (Boston among them), and the initiative failed to earn a majority in those three cities. It nevertheless was upheld by the Supreme Judicial Court as not constituting special legislation.[22] Still, the ban on special legislation does protect Boston from targeted restrictions to some extent: it makes it difficult for such measures to be adopted as a matter of course.

The ban on special legislation contains an important limitation: it is not ret-roactive. It has no application to state laws enacted prior to the recognition of home rule. Given that home rule came so late to Boston, and given that Boston has been such a peculiar object of state legislative attention, there are many such special laws. A search of the state code turns up scores of statutes with phrases such as "except for the city of Boston." Many of these special acts are trivial but burdensome, such as the law (recently changed) that severely limited the fee that Boston (and Boston alone) could charge to tow a car or the one that restricts the late fees that the city school committee can impose on evening students to a level below that allowed for other municipalities. Others are not trivial. Perhaps the most tangible legacy of these laws are those found in the city charter itself—such as the one establishing the Finance Commission.

The Home Rule Amendment also contains another exception: special legis-lation is permissible if the city files a home rule petition requesting it. Reliance on this mechanism is not a substitute for the exercise of home rule power. A home rule system that relies on localities requesting state legislative permission resembles the system that was in place prior to home rule. The state legislature is under no legal obligation to approve a petition it receives. In practice, the state tends to be reluctant to grant approval when the matter in question is controver-sial (as was the case with a recent petition concerning the provision of domestic partnership benefits) or related to a matter thought to be of state concern (such as taxation). A successful petition usually requires a substantial investment of legislative effort by the city, effort that would not be required if the city were empowered to act on its own. And, of course, whenever a city must ask the state for permission, it opens up the possibility for logrolling or approval conditioned on agreement to state demands. It was concerns of just this kind that led the Massachusetts Legislature to place the Home Rule Amendment on the ballot in the first place. All of these concerns are especially heightened for Boston—the state's largest urban center and the home of the statehouse—given the interest that so many nonresidents have in its actions.

More fundamentally, state laws passed in response to home rule petitions remain state laws. They can only be changed or repealed with the consent of the state legislature. Thus, while the state allowed Boston to reconstitute the school committee in response to a home rule petition, the state legislation specified (among other things) that the new school committee have seven members, that the members have staggered terms of office, and that there be a thirteen-member nominating panel (organized in detail by the legislation) empowered to present a list of candidates from which the mayor then selects committee members. None of these provisions can be changed without returning to the legislature. The concern about state control is even more serious when the city relies on the petition process to obtain power arguably within the scope of its home rule power. The result may be that the special state law will preempt future exercises of the home rule power. The city's reliance on the petition process to adopt many of its most innovative affordable housing initiatives may have had this consequence.

Just as many states have defined the home rule power broadly to include many areas—including taxation—that Massachusetts exempts, there is also nothing natural about the way that the Massachusetts Home Rule Amendment defines the power of preemption. Although Seattle, Atlanta, and New York—like Boston—are bound to follow general state laws, several other cities enjoy protection from them. Denver's state grant of home rule provides that "the statutes of the state of Colorado, so far as applicable, shall continue to apply to such cities and towns, except insofar as superseded by the charters of such cities and towns or by ordinance passed pursuant to such charters." Thus, even though state statutes often override city ordinances, sometimes city ordinances override state law. Indeed, the Colorado state constitution specifically identifies Denver as a home rule city and invests it with powers, including borrowing powers, that the state courts have held are beyond state control. As a result of these protections, Denver has successfully challenged directly conflicting state statutes that attempted to regulate municipal employment practices and to limit the city's ability to impose sales taxes for local purposes.[23]

California's state constitution provides that a city or county may adopt a charter giving it the power to "make and enforce all ordinances and regulations in respect to municipal affairs, subject only to restrictions and limitations provided in their several charters." The state supreme court has interpreted this to confer the "constitutional authority of a home rule city or county to enact and enforce its own regulations to the exclusion of general laws if the subject is held by the courts to be a municipal affair rather than of statewide concern." California municipalities have relied on this immunity to overturn state laws regulating local bidding procedures, municipal employment rules, local elections, and even some city taxing powers.[24]

Chicago's home rule grant flatly prohibits legislative preemption in several circumstances. Under the state constitution, the legislature cannot limit a city's borrowing power below an amount equal to 3 percent of its total estimated assessed value; it cannot deny or limit its power to levy special assessments for local improvements; and it cannot deprive it of the power to impose additional taxes for the provision of "special services." For other matters, including local exercises of the home rule taxing power, the constitution requires preemptive state legislation to be passed by supermajorities. Finally, the Illinois Constitution specifically instructs courts to construe the home rule grant liberally and to recognize the power of home rule municipalities to legislate in areas of "concurrent" state and local concern. In practice, the Illinois Supreme Court has held that these interpretive instructions were designed "to eliminate or at least reduce to a bare minimum the circumstances under which local home rule powers are preempted by judicial interpretation of unexpressed legislative intention."[25]

The Ethos of Home Rule

"Home rule" means different things in different states. The Massachusetts version of home rule makes it difficult for Boston to create its own city charter; it specifically excludes from Boston's authority the power to impose taxes, engage in borrowing, or regulate private or civil affairs; and it gives Boston virtually no protection from state laws that overrule local decision making. On every one of these points, home rule in Massachusetts forbids what home rule in some other states allows. Yet even in these states, the grant of home rule power is simultaneously a limit on local power—sometimes by restricting the home rule power to "local" matters, sometimes through specific exemptions, and sometimes because of the state's ability to overrule inconsistent local laws. Given the variety of meanings of the term "home rule," determining whether a city has authority to deal with local problems without specific state authorization always require a careful legal analysis. The fact that the city is a "home rule city" doesn't answer the question of the extent of its authority. This point is worth emphasizing because so many urban scholars—and even some legal scholars—overlook it.[26]

There is more to a city's legal power, however, than the protections contained in state grants of home rule. Other aspects of state law can expand or contract city powers in ways that the terms of a home rule amendment might conceal. These other state laws are extremely important in their own right. Denver has significantly broader home rule taxing powers than Boston, but it labors under a separate state law, known as the Taxpayer Bill of Rights, that imposes very restrictive limits on its fiscal authority. Moreover, while Denver has greater power to regulate affordable housing than Boston, it is subject, like Boston, to a statewide prohibition against rent control. The next three chapters—on revenues and expenditures, land use, and education—highlight the role that these kinds of state laws play in shaping home rule.

Nevertheless, state home rule provisions are important in and of themselves. They define the fundamental legal relationship between the city and the state and set the basic parameters for the exercise of city power. They indicate whether city officials should think of taxation as something within their purview or something for the state alone. They determine whether municipal elections should be conceived of as a city issue or as an issue on which the state legislature has ultimate responsibility. And they instruct city officials to believe that there are areas of authority reserved to them or to assume that there are no such areas. In practice, home rule is a state of mind as much as it is a legal system. It only works if the officials vested with home rule power have the confidence to assert the powers arguably entrusted to them. The legal definitions set forth in provisions such as the Home Rule Amendment of the Massachusetts Constitution play an important role in creating an ethos of home rule that can either presume city power or city powerlessness.

We have not endeavored to compare, in any scientific way, the ethos of home rule that prevails among officials in the seven cities. But we have spoken with a number of present and former government officials in each city, and their impressions match with what our investigation of the legal materials indicates. Those cities that have been invested with stronger home rule measures seem to have a confidence in their lawmaking powers that other cities lack. Officials in Chicago feel comfortable with their exercise of the city's home rule power and are able to work well within its legal limits. Officials in Denver were confident that they could exercise a significant amount of authority under their home rule power. We have talked to no officials in Boston, past or present, who have voiced similar sentiments. Indeed, only officials from Seattle expressed the sense of constraint that seems so prevalent in Boston—and Seattle is the only city with a home rule grant that appears to be as weak as Boston's. We believe that the relatively weak nature of the Massachusetts Home Rule Amendment, when compared to the home rule grants that have been given to Chicago and Denver, has a lot to do with the pervasive sense of constraint we discern among Boston officials. If so, an expansion of the home rule powers contained in the Home Rule Amendment could alter the basic assumptions about city power that now predominate in Boston.

Obviously, a city's policy-making ability is not just a matter of law. It also depends on the opportunities for creative action afforded by prevailing social and economic conditions. The point here is simply that its ability to engage in innovative thinking is independently enabled and constrained by the legal powers that the state gives it.

REVENUE AND EXPENDITURES

Two of the most important powers that cities possess involve their authority to raise money and to spend it. It is commonly thought that this authority is largely within a city's control. Editorials rail against city governments for raising taxes, and there is no shortage of commentary that castigates mayors and city councils for profligate city spending. It is not uncommon for local political leaders to be attacked as well for failing to fund various projects, and even for imposing painful cuts on city services. This focus on the fiscal decisions of city governments obscures a basic fact about the capacity of cities to control their own finances: state law exerts significant control over nearly every aspect of the local budget. In fact, some of the decisions that generate the most criticism—that property taxes are too high or that city benefits for municipal workers are too generous—are often the consequence of state fiscal rules that are beyond the power of local officials to alter. Thus, although American cities are self-funded to an extent that many cities in the world are not, they do not have anything like the kind of local fiscal autonomy often attributed to them.

We begin below by describing state controls over the three main sources of city revenue: taxes, fees, and grants-in-aid. We concentrate here on the property tax, although we also demonstrate the differences among state authorizations for sales taxes, income taxes, and taxes targeted at specific activities. We examine as well differences in the state's definition of a fee and in the ways that state aid is structured. No discussion of city power, let alone of local autonomy, is adequate without a focus on these kinds of rules. Singly and in combination, they can deny a city adequate funds, leaving it unable to provide the services that residents want. They can also pressure cities to raise certain taxes time and again because they foreclose other revenue-raising options. Just as important, a state's structuring of city finances affects a city's ability to shape its own future. State-imposed limits on a city's sources of revenue influence a city's ideas about the kind of economic development that it should promote. A city is more likely to be eager to promote development that it can tax than the kind that provides no revenue. At the same time, state controls can make the city vulnerable to economic shifts and, consequently, to the influence of private investors on city policymaking. Every city we examine is affected in these ways by state law.

State controls over revenue assume added significance given the critical role that states play in determining city expenditures. Every city is subject to state-imposed rules about expenditures—and, even more important, to state mandates that require the city to spend money for specific purposes. These impositions vary from the trivial to state mandates that account for significant portions of the local budget. The way in which state expenditure rules and state limits on revenue work together also influences the exercise of local power. If the state government imposes too strict a limit on generating local revenues and, at the same time, requires a city to make too many expenditures, the city—for reasons beyond its control—can have to cut essential services simply to avoid a fiscal meltdown. Even in the absence of this scenario, the combination of state controls over revenue and state direction of expenditures generates a critical structure for city decision making: they determine, to a substantial degree, what a city government does.

Taxes

The General Legal Structure of Taxation

The first major question concerning city power is whether the city has discretion to determine how to raise money. The answer is simple but not well understood: all cities have a lot less discretion—and some cities have dramatically less discretion—than the notion of local fiscal autonomy implies.

Consider the financial powers of Boston. Boston relies on just two sources for most of its income: property taxes and state aid. Boston did not choose to rely on these two sources rather than generating revenue through additional taxes. Boston operates within state-defined constraints that restrict the types of taxes it can impose and that limit what it can raise even from the taxes that the state has authorized. Boston's entire taxing structure—what is taxed, how it is assessed, and who collects it—is determined by the state because the Massachusetts Home Rule Amendment does not empower Boston to levy taxes.

This legal structure is rejected in other states. Chicago, Denver, and San Francisco all operate within a home rule framework that makes taxation presumptively within the cities' home rule powers. In 1906, just ten years after the passage of a home rule amendment in California, the California Supreme Court adopted the language of the United States Supreme Court in explaining the importance of municipal taxing authority:

> That the power of taxation is a power appropriate for a municipality to possess is too obvious to merit discussion. As was said by Mr. Justice Field..., "A municipality without the power of taxation would be a body without life, incapable of acting, and serving no useful purpose."[1]

With this background presumption, the legal structure in California has developed in importantly different ways from the one in Massachusetts. A similar pattern exists in Colorado. There, too, taxation is considered a local power under the state constitution. Indeed, state efforts to preempt local taxation have sometimes been held unconstitutional.

The home rule framework in Illinois offers the most dramatic contrast to Boston's. A 1970 amendment to the Illinois Constitution gave Chicago broad home rule fiscal powers. As one of the drafters of this provision explained, the purpose of the measure was "to give home rule units some additional power to raise revenues as they see fit for their needs, without easy invasion or limitation by the state legislature. We agreed that home rule without money is meaningless."[2] Localities in Illinois thus have discretion to rely on a variety of sources for tax revenue, and Chicago has used this discretion by imposing a number of taxes. It has also tapped user fees and other nontax revenue sources that are not available to Boston. Even the property tax—Boston's major source of income—is subject to fewer restrictions in Chicago than in Boston.

Although Boston's taxing powers are unusually limited, its state-established revenue structure illustrates our more general point. State law controls the revenue that every city receives by barring some taxes and permitting others. Of course, even without this state control, there would be restraints on a city's taxing power. Cities have reasons to be concerned that local taxes would drive out business or fuel suburban flight. But the legal constraints by themselves play a major role in shaping city policy. This is true even for cities that enjoy substantially more fiscal freedom than does Boston.

The Property Tax

The popular idea that the property tax is the principal source of city revenue does not describe the cities we examine in this book: every one of them, other than Boston, receives most of its revenue from other sources. Still, all of them rely on the property tax to a considerable degree. The way their states define local property tax authority is therefore important everywhere. Because the tax is particularly important in Boston, we begin with that city.

THE PROPERTY TAX IN BOSTON

The property tax provided 57 percent of Boston's revenue in fiscal year 2008. (State aid constituted 22 percent, and all other sources—excise taxes, fees, parking fines, and the like—made up only 21 percent of the city's revenues.) By contrast, revenue from property taxes contributes roughly 10 percent of the city budget in Denver, 12 percent in Chicago, 15 percent in San Francisco, and 20 percent in Atlanta. Even in Seattle and New York City—the other two most property–tax-dependent cities—property taxes constitute only about a quarter of the city's total revenue.

The substantial degree to which Boston depends on the property tax makes the limits that Massachusetts imposes on its use particularly significant. The state places a ceiling on the amount of the tax, exempts certain kinds of property from the tax, and controls how the tax is allocated to residential, commercial, and industrial property. The fears of uncontrolled property taxation in Boston are not new. In 1885, a statute was passed that limited the local property tax rate elsewhere in the state to 12 percent of the assessed valuation—while placing Boston's cap at 10.5 percent. This 1885 limitation was repealed for much of the twentieth century, but Massachusetts voters approved an even more stringent statewide restriction on property taxation in 1980 by adopting Proposition 2½.

Aptly named, Proposition 2½ places two restrictions on the property tax. The total property tax for any municipality cannot exceed 2.5 percent of its total tax-able value—this is called the "levy ceiling." Annual increases in the property tax also cannot exceed a 2.5 percent increase over the previous year's levy—this is called the "levy limit." There is some wiggle room within these constraints. Most important, a municipality can, by referendum, increase its tax levy for the year over the 2.5 percent limit. This increase then becomes the baseline for the follow-ing year's calculation of the levy limit. A municipality can also exclude a specific capital project or debt from the levy ceiling. This exclusion exists only for the life of the project or debt; it is not added to the baseline for future calculations.[3]

The immediate effects of Proposition 2½, after its adoption in 1980, were swift and groundbreaking. Cities and towns laid off teachers, police officers, and other civil service personnel. Given this financial crisis, the state stepped in and pro-vided state aid to assist municipalities in maintaining basic services. State aid thus became an integral part of economic politics for every city and town in the state. Even with this state aid, however, Boston has come close to the Proposition

2½ levy ceiling on a number of occasions. Moreover, the levy ceiling makes it difficult for Boston to respond to downturns in property assessments and prevents it from reaping the benefits of economic upswings to prepare for the next stage of the cycle. Proposition 2½ also does not allow Boston to grow its property tax base to keep up with inflation rates.

One response to these kinds of problems in Massachusetts has been to obtain referendum approval for an override. Boston has not asked its voters for an override, and some state officials have demanded that Boston resort to property tax overrides before asking for other taxing authority. But it is not clear why the legal system should require Boston to put a single-issue referendum on the ballot to raise property taxes before it can obtain the additional taxing authority that other cities already have. Illinois has established a tax structure that is based on very different assumptions than those embraced in Massachusetts. Under Illinois's home rule system, cities have taxing powers unless those who oppose their exercise succeed in passing a referendum requiring the city to give it up. Massachusetts makes the referendum a prerequisite to the exercise of additional taxing authority; Illinois makes it a prerequisite to the relinquishment of taxing authority. Significantly, a large majority of municipalities in Illinois that have exercised home rule taxing powers have defeated referenda that asked voters to relinquish them.

The second major constraint on Boston's property tax is the amount of its property that is exempt from property taxation. For a city that relies so heavily on the property tax, Boston has a striking proportion of tax-exempt property. The reason is that state law excludes much of Boston's land from the tax rolls. According to a study conducted in 2002, more than half of Boston's land area is exempt from property taxes.[4] This is dramatically greater than the figures in other cities. Only 25.4 percent of Denver's land and less than 20 percent of Atlanta's is tax exempt. The largest amount of Boston's land, encompassing more than 26 percent of its total landmass, is exempt because the property is owned by the state directly or by state agencies. The city is the second largest owner of tax-exempt property, almost half of which is parkland and other open space. (Colleges and hospitals account for 2 percent, and other tax-exempt institutions 8 percent, of tax-exempt land.) To some extent, Boston is compensated for its significant amount of tax-exempt property through payment in lieu of tax contributions. But these contributions are voluntary, and they contribute only 1 percent of Boston's budget.

Another way in which the state constrains Boston's control of the property tax is by limiting the city's ability to allocate the tax burden among different types of property. In 1978, Boston and other cities in the state were empowered by a constitutional amendment to set different rates for residential, commercial, industrial, and personal property. Without this amendment, Boston would have no means of allocating the tax burden differently among different types of property owners. Even after the amendment, Boston's power to classify property remains limited by state law. State legislation, passed the same year as the constitutional amendment, enabled the city to raise the property tax levy on commercial, industrial, and personal property, with approval from the state Department of Revenue, only up to 1.75 times that of residential property owners.[5]

Even if Boston succeeded in removing all of these direct limits on its power to levy property taxes, practical limits would remain. In the world of property taxes, Boston is only one player among many well-situated communities. Any property tax increase generates concern about a flight to the suburbs and thus a decline in the city's tax base. A delicate balance has to be struck on a yearly basis. Boston needs to raise enough money to provide good services and improve its infrastructure in order to entice residents and businesses to locate or remain in town. At the same time, it must prudently keep the tax rate as low as possible to achieve the same end. Boston's recognition of this dynamic led the city to fight to secure the power to *exempt* some commercial property from local property taxes in the decades immediately following World War II. Boston voluntarily, indeed eagerly, forsook property taxes for a lesser amount of revenue in order to attract new development.[6]

PROPERTY TAX LIMITS IN OTHER CITIES

Boston's state-imposed reliance on the property tax makes the state's restrictions on it onerous. But some cities operate under legal limits on the property tax that are even more severe than those that apply to Boston. The two cities under the most significant constraints are San Francisco and Denver—constraints imposed by Proposition 13 in California and by the Taxpayer Bill of Rights in Colorado. Unlike the approach in Massachusetts, which adopted its tax limitations as a statute, both Proposition 13 and the Taxpayer Bill of Rights were enshrined in the state constitutions.

In California, Proposition 13 took property taxes out of San Francisco's hands entirely. It grants the state, rather than the city, control over the property tax base and rates. It defines assessed value as the full cash value of the property as of 1976 (two years before the amendment was passed) or at the time that the property is newly constructed or ownership changes hands. It caps the total property tax rate at 1 percent of assessed value, requires a two-thirds vote to approve any special taxes, prohibits any additional taxes related to property, and provides that any increase in tax revenue on the state level get the approval of two-thirds of the state legislature. Given the state's control over property tax receipts in California, the state can redistribute the property tax to suit its needs. With the creation of the Educational Revenue Augmentation Fund in 1992, the state did just that—shifting $3 billion of cities' and counties' share of the property tax to local school districts in order to satisfy funding requirements for education and to meet a budget shortfall. Property tax receipts in San Francisco, in short, operate functionally simply as another element of state aid.

Like San Francisco, Denver has little control over property tax revenues. Denver's property tax levy was first limited by the Gallagher Amendment, passed by the state legislature and adopted as a statewide referendum in 1982. Responding to the alarm over residential property tax increases, the Gallagher Amendment fixed residential property tax receipts at 47 percent of total receipts (the level when the amendment was passed). Then, in 1993, the Taxpayer Bill of Rights was adopted by Colorado voters. It established a formula that dramatically limited annual revenue growth and provided that any revenue raised in excess of that limit be refunded to the taxpayers. The Taxpayer Bill of Rights also required that any new taxes, tax rate increases, or changes in tax policy be submitted to the voters for approval. In 2005, Colorado voters passed a referendum that limited the impact of the Taxpayer Bill of Rights, allowing the state to retain surplus revenues to spend on education, health, and transportation and authorizing an adjustment of the tax limit formula.

Even so, the Taxpayer Bill of Rights' limitations remain much more extreme than Proposition 2½. And that's only the beginning of the story. The intersection of the Taxpayer Bill of Rights and the Gallagher Amendment has produced serious complications. Since the ratio between property taxes on commercial and residential properties is locked in, changes in valuations may require that the rate on one classification be raised to preserve the Gallagher balance. But any increase in property taxes requires voter approval under the Taxpayer Bill of Rights. If the increase is rejected, or if the municipality decides that it is not worthwhile to put it before the voters, its only option is to lower the tax rate to preserve the ratio. The intersection of the Taxpayer Bill of Rights and the Gallagher Amendment thus produces a ratchet-down effect. Indeed, since the Taxpayer Bill of Rights refund limit is calculated on the basis of the previous year's collection, any decline in revenue collection in one year has a lasting impact on a city's budget limit for all subsequent years.

The limits imposed on the property tax in San Francisco and Denver cause very serious financial problems for these two cities. Like Proposition 2½, they reflect the widespread opposition across the country to the property tax. But neither San Francisco nor Denver relies on the property tax the way Boston does. Even cities like Chicago, which do not face state-imposed caps on the property tax, have shied away from raising property taxes in recent years. Chicago is exempt from the state property tax cap that applies to other municipalities in

Illinois. Yet the city has voluntarily adopted a cap that mimics the one adopted by the state. The decision to do so reflects Chicago's conscious pursuit of a fiscal policy not to increase property taxes. City officials have concluded that tapping into other revenue streams makes more sense given the burdens on residents that the property tax imposes. Boston's limited fiscal options do not afford it the same opportunity to respond to concerns about high property taxes.

Tax Diversity

Although all states require—and thus empower—their cities to generate substantial portions of their revenue from locally imposed taxes, no city has complete discretion when it comes to raising revenue. States vary greatly as to the kinds of taxes that they permit their cities to levy, and these state-imposed limits on the extent of tax diversity have important consequences. Boston's reliance on the property tax illustrates this point. The property tax, by its very nature, encourages a city to have a territorial emphasis in its overall development policy. By relying so heavily on that tax, Boston politics is focused on a certain kind of land use development. The city has to concentrate on raising the value of its property in order to provide city services, including services (such as police, fire, sanitation, and parks) provided to visitors. Boston's focus on property development has had a major impact on every aspect of city policy, particularly on its ability to provide affordable housing. Its reliance on the property tax makes it important for the city to raise property values, even at the expense of making property unaffordable to potential residents. If property values do not increase, the city cannot raise enough money through the property tax to provide necessary services.

Such a territorial emphasis, inherent in a tax that targets land-based resources, might seem natural for a small New England town that is relatively self-contained. For a metropolitan center like Boston, this emphasis ignores the city's far more expansive role in the regional, state, and national economy. Boston serves as the economic center of the region. Commuters descend on Boston daily, and they depend on the infrastructure and services Boston provides to accomplish their goals. Boston also serves as an important tourist destination, with thousands of visitors enjoying the city's cultural, historical, and natural resources. Studies conducted in the 1990s show that, although Boston's residential population was only 574,000 according to the 1990 census, the number of people in Boston surged to approximately 1.2 million on any given workday, and to almost two million when there was a special event.[7] The reliance on the property tax not only overlooks the potential of revenue from these nonresidents but provides the city will little incentive to promote tourism and cultural development.

A lack of tax diversity can also lead cities to overlook the advantages that come from keeping property taxes low. Since state-imposed limits protect cities from the temptation to rely on property tax increases to solve a fiscal squeeze, they can serve a potentially useful role. Boston's ability to manage its budget responsibly without substantially raising property taxes has helped promote its overall economic success, while contributing to the appreciation of local property values. Moreover, although state-mandated exemptions of city land from the tax rolls deprive cities of needed revenue, they also encourage the private institutions that benefit from these exemptions to invest in the city. The future economic health of many cities, including Boston, is often thought to depend on the willingness of tax-exempt institutions—especially universities and hospitals—to maintain a strong presence in the city. Without the power to tap other revenue streams to compensate for a reduced reliance on the property tax, it is harder for Boston than for it is for cities such as Chicago to see beyond the revenue loss produced by exemptions from the property tax. The city is driven to focus more on increasing its revenues from universities and hospitals than on maximizing the advantages they offer the city.

Diversity of revenue sources can enable cities to approach their overall development strategy differently. Tax diversity enables cities to avoid being locked into a revenue source that depends on new real estate development. But there are risks in tax diversity as well. The property tax has been a stable and consistent source of revenue for Boston, while cities that have relied on the sales or income tax have seen dramatic fluctuations in receipts. Moreover, cities that rely on sales taxes become vulnerable to the attempt of surrounding cities to maximize their own income through competition for shopping malls. Cities in California are locked into a fight with their neighbors over retail dollars, and this competition has done much to scar the regional landscape. Besides, sales and income taxes can generate the same fixation with boundaries as the property tax does.

Despite these concerns about tax diversity, it seems wrong to conclude that Boston should be grateful that the state has forced it to rely on the property tax or that it has been required to forgo the revenue that a less restricted power to tax would make available. One doubts that the other cities would be willing to trade their more expansive revenue powers for Boston's limits. In Seattle, the property tax accounted for 27 percent of the city's general fund in 2006, while the retail sales tax made up 20 percent, the business and occupation tax 19 percent, and the utility tax 17 percent. Atlanta and Chicago both receive twice the revenue from a combination of other local taxes than they get from the property tax. San Francisco raises more revenue from a combination of other local taxes than from the property tax. Even Denver, which relies on the sales tax for more than half of its general fund revenues, has a more diverse tax base than Boston. Denver relies on other taxes, including the property tax, to raise another 20 percent of its revenue.

Other Local Taxes

Cities with greater tax diversity enjoy three additional sources of local income: the sales tax, the income or occupation tax, and taxes targeted at specific industries or activities. These additional sources of taxes not only relieve pressure on the property tax but give cities an incentive to generate city income by focusing on economic development policies other than raising property values. Just as no state gives cities the power to impose property taxes without significant strings, however, no state lets cities use these other taxes free of regulation.

THE SALES TAX

With a 5 percent state sales tax, Boston shoppers pay a relatively low sales tax rate compared to the other cities (which range from 7 percent in Atlanta to 8.8 percent in Seattle). More important from the perspective of the Boston city government, all proceeds from the Massachusetts sales tax are kept by the state. Every other city we examined receives a portion of its revenue from sales taxes. To be sure, the local portion of the sales tax is usually small—because state law prevents it from being larger.

In Atlanta, Chicago, and San Francisco, the local portion is 1 percent; in Seattle it is less than 1 percent. But Denver has a local sales tax of 3.5 percent—larger than the 2.9 percent state sales tax (with other sales taxes bringing the total rate to 7.2 percent). New York City has the highest local sales tax, currently 4.375 percent. Combined with the 4.25 percent state sales tax, New York's overall sales tax is 8.625 percent.

Locally-imposed sales taxes burden city residents. But they also enable cities to capture wealth from commuters and tourists who use the city's infrastructure, take advantage of its concentration of economic wealth, and enjoy its cultural, historical, and natural amenities. Boston captures some revenue from commuters and tourists indirectly through the commercial property tax and business permit and licensing fees. But tourist cities that rely on sales taxes, more extensive user fees, and similar sources are much more successful in capturing revenue from tourists and commuters than Boston is. San Francisco—like Boston, a popular tourist destination—estimates that it collects $350 million in tax revenues from tourism, over 7 percent of the city's $4.8 billion budget.

The aversion of Massachusetts to the local sales tax is not simply a product of its hostility to taxation. It is also a product of the legal structure. Because Massachusetts denies home rule taxing power to its municipalities, Boston has no power to impose a sales tax in the absence of state legislative approval. In states with a tradition of local home rule taxing power, cities have often taken the lead in initiating the sales tax. That was the case in Denver, where the state supreme court held that "the power to levy sales…taxes for the support of local home rule government is 'essential to the full exercise' of the right of self-government."[8] But even cities that have initially relied on their home rule powers to tap this revenue stream have ultimately been reined in. Many states have preempted local sales taxes and replaced them with state sales taxes to provide greater uniformity. This happened in both California and Illinois, although San Francisco and Chicago were able to maintain a claim on the sales tax after the states asserted control over it.

THE INCOME OR OCCUPATION TAX

Every city, other than Boston and Atlanta, receives a portion of its revenue from an income or an occupation tax. Seattle lacks home rule taxing power, but a state statute has enabled it to collect more than $100 million from business and occupation taxes levied on gross receipts for most business activity. The New York state constitution gives the state power over taxation decisions as well, but New York City has been empowered by statute to impose a personal income tax at a rate set by the state; its personal and corporate income taxes represent nearly one-third of its tax receipts. The Illinois state constitution expressly denies Chicago the power to levy its own income tax, but a state statute guarantees it a percentage of the state income tax. Chicago received nearly $200 million from the tax in 2003. Denver lost in its bid to assert home rule authority to impose an income tax in 1958. But it has used its otherwise expansive home rule powers to impose an occupational privilege tax, and it nets roughly $20 million annually, or about one-third of what it receives in property taxes. San Francisco imposes a payroll tax pursuant to its home rule authority that has generated nearly $300 million— more than its sales and hotel room tax combined. Although Atlanta lacks home rule taxing power, it has been authorized by statute to impose a local income tax of 1 percent if voters approve the tax by referendum. (The city so far has chosen not to pursue this option.)

It is somewhat ironic that Boston is the one city without the power to tax personal or business income. Boston is the only city other than San Francisco that is home to more jobs than residents. In fact, only one other city in the nation— Washington, D.C.—provides a similar proportion of jobs for its area. And Washington, D.C., like San Francisco, receives revenue from an income tax. Of course, there are policy reasons for not imposing a local income tax, the most notable being the concern that doing so would encourage residents and businesses to move outside the city limits. But Boston could continue to be denied the local power to tax income and instead be given—as Chicago is—a percentage of the state income tax. A statewide tax would not drive employers or residents from the city, yet it would take account of the unique role that Boston plays in regional employment.

That other cities have so much more power to tax income shows how important state law is in shaping local fiscal authority. Yet even the cities empowered to impose income or occupation taxes remain subject to extensive state regulation. Indeed, while Chicago benefits from a state decision to allocate a percentage of state income tax, the city is powerless to determine how high or low that tax should be. The state statutes authorizing local income or occupation taxes in other cities also contain caps.

TARGETED LOCAL TAXES

In addition to the property, sales, and income or occupation taxes, cities have been empowered to impose a wide array of targeted taxes. Denver has a lodger's tax, a telecommunications tax, a franchise tax, a car rental tax, a food and beverage and liquor stores tax, a facilities development admissions tax, and an aviation fuel tax, among others. San Francisco levies a business license tax, a real property transfer tax, a utility users' tax, a parking tax, and a transient occupancy tax. Chicago has more than a dozen taxes. Even the three cities without home rule taxing power impose a wide range of additional taxes. New York City lists twelve taxes in its budget plus an additional line for "other taxes." Seattle levies an admissions tax and a utility tax on seven types of services; its budget also lists a separate line for "other taxes." Atlanta imposes a hotel/motel tax, an alcohol tax, a public utility tax, a car tax, and an insurance premium tax, and it has the statutory authority to impose a host of additional taxes—not only an income tax and an occupation tax—that it has not exercised.

The state has authorized Boston to impose targeted taxes only on motor vehicles, hotels and motels, and jet fuel. Revenue from the motor vehicle tax makes up most of its income from targeted taxes, with hotels and motels coming in second, and jet fuel third. Boston thus has four types of taxes (including the property tax) while other cities have from three to seven times that number. Since Boston hosts major national and international events, the hotel/motel tax is the major way in which Boston can capture revenue from tourism. Boston officials have complained that this tax does not provide enough revenue even to cover the additional costs associated with tourism. Boston has lost money on major tourist events, ranging from Sail Boston in 1992 to the soccer World Cup championships in 1994 to the Democratic National Convention in 2004. Boston has lobbied the state legislature to allow it to impose a restaurant meals tax, a parking tax, and a 50-cent surcharge on movie and entertainment tickets, but it has not been successful. As a result, Boston's targeted taxes account for only 4 percent of its total budget. Other revenue from tourism goes directly to the state through its own targeted taxes and the state sales tax.

Although other cities have more discretion when it comes to targeted taxes, these special city taxes usually need to be expressly authorized by state statutes, and the states statutes define the parameters of the taxes that the city can levy. Because of the broad state power to preempt local laws, these state laws determine the nature of the tax. Even when a city relies solely on its home rule powers to impose a targeted tax, it may be subject to state preemption if it relies on it to an extent that might generate significant opposition in the statehouse.

TAX DIVERSITY, TAX INCREASES

Our discussion of taxes might be read as a call for tax increases. That is not our objective. A city can have a diversity of sources of income or can have only one source of income and, in either case, have the same overall tax burden. The issue for us is not how high taxes are but where they come from. Each form of taxation—not just property, sales, and income taxes but each of the targeted taxes as well—has an impact on city policy. They encourage the city to promote the income-generating objective and discourage policies that produce no revenue. The critical question regarding city power, then, is who decides how to allocate the tax burden. To the extent that the state makes this decision—as it plainly does in Massachusetts—it deprives the city of choices about its future regardless of the kinds of taxes that it allows. The argument for a city role in tax decision making is not an argument for local autonomy on tax issues. Everywhere it is recognized that the state, as well as the city, has an interest in the level of taxation imposed on its residents. Every city is therefore subject to at least some limits imposed by the state regarding its taxes. The issue here, as elsewhere, is the design of the city structure: how to allocate authority on the critical issue of revenue. This issue requires decisions not only about taxes but about fees and state aid as well.

Fees

Taxes are not the only way that cities obtain revenue. Locally imposed fees—ranging from charges for issuing licenses to requirements that commercial developers provide, or pay for, affordable housing—are another source of cash. Cities that have made extensive use of fees have generated a considerable source of income. Like taxes, the imposition of user fees influences local politics. In California, where fees have played a large role for years, an increased reliance on fees has generated a fee-for-service mentality, and it, in turn, has transformed what a city government is—what it provides, and whom it exists to serve. In the place of a general service government providing public goods to all residents, local governments increasingly function as a retailer of services purchased and consumed by individual users. Here again, the source of revenue affects the nature of the city that receives it. And here again, the dynamic is shaped—and sometimes wholly defined—by decisions made at the state level.

Fees are potentially an important form of local power for Boston. Although the Massachusetts Home Rule Amendment denies Boston the power to levy taxes without state authorization, Boston can assess and collect fees on its own. The state's authorizing legislation is quite broad, and the procedure for obtaining fees is simply passing a local ordinance (approval by the city council and mayor). Because the legal treatment of fees and taxes is so different, there often is a legal battle in Massachusetts over whether a specific assessment is a fee or a tax. If it is interpreted as a fee, the assessment is typically upheld as within the municipality's power. If it is read as a tax, it is struck down because the Home Rule Amendment requires a specific delegation of power from the state legislature. Court decisions in Massachusetts have tended to follow the second option, thereby limiting the ability that Boston would otherwise have had to generate revenue from fees.

The Massachusetts Supreme Judicial Court articulated the test for determining whether an assessment is a fee or a tax in *Emerson College v. City of Boston*. As the court explained, fees differ from taxes in three ways. A fee is

> charged in exchange for a particular governmental service which benefits the party paying the fee in a manner not shared by other members of society; paid by choice, in that the party paying the fee has the option of not utilizing the governmental service and thereby avoiding the charge; and the charges are collected not to raise revenues but to compensate the governmental entity providing the service for its expense.[9]

The *Emerson* decision addressed an "augmented fire services availability" fee assessed upon buildings in Boston that required significantly more personnel and resources for fire protection than more conventional buildings. Although the ordinance imposing the fee was established pursuant to specific state authorizing legislation, the court struck down the fee as a tax. The court noted that the benefits arising from the payment of the fee affected neighboring buildings as well as the individuals within the buildings being charged. It found that the fees were compelled, despite the fact that they could be reduced if the building owners installed fire safety equipment. Finally, it found that the proceeds of the fee were not targeted to support the augmented fire services but supported fire and police services generally, a fact that was consistent with the revenue-generating purpose of a tax rather than the compensatory purpose of a fee.

In other cities, differences in legal language and judicial interpretations have facilitated more reliance on fees. This is particularly the case in California, where, on average, fees constituted 25 percent of city budgets in the late 1970s and 41 percent in the mid-1990s. California cities turned to user fees primarily because of the legal constraints on taxation imposed by Proposition 13, and judicial decisions have facilitated the transition. The legal issue in California courts is different from the tax/fee controversy in Massachusetts. Proposition 13, in addition to imposing strict limits on property taxes, required that any "special taxes" passed by a local government receive a two-thirds majority. California courts have read this restriction narrowly. Many assessments have been categorized not as special taxes but as fees. The California Supreme Court justified its narrow reading by criticizing the initiative procedure that led to Proposition 13's restriction, calling it "inherently undemocratic" because a statewide majority of voters sought to prohibit a majority of local voters from providing services that would benefit local residents.[10]

Many charges that would fall squarely in the tax category in Massachusetts are considered fees in California. San Francisco, for example, passed a transit fee that imposed a $5 per square foot charge on new developments downtown to "provide revenue for the San Francisco Municipal Railway system to offset the anticipated increased costs to accommodate the new riders during peak commute hours generated by the construction of new office space in the downtown area." The benefit of this fee was not exclusive to the owner of the building (in fact, very little benefit can be said to be attributable to the developer). It ultimately benefited the commuters of San Francisco. But a California appellate court looked directly to the "impact" that the developer was causing to justify the fee. The court explained that the fee imposed was a good estimate of the increased costs caused by the construction. Furthermore, the court noted, "developers have been required to pay for streets, sewers, parks and lights as a condition for the privilege of developing a particular parcel" even though they ultimately benefited the public as a whole.[11] The insistence of Massachusetts on a particularized benefit to the person paying the fee is strikingly absent here. California's leniency toward impact fees appears to stem from its willingness to interpret fees as a negative imposition (like a "fine" for imposing a cost) as opposed to a purchase of special benefits.

The judicial classification of potential fees as taxes is not Boston's only problem in raising money through fees. Another problem is preemption: a fee might conflict with a state statute, either expressly or by implication. For many decades, the paradigmatic example of a state law uniquely constraining Boston was one that capped the amount of fees that Boston could charge owners of cars towed from city streets at $12, substantially less than what it cost the city to tow a car.

Although the state legislature has now enabled Boston to charge up to $75, the maximum allowable rate elsewhere within the state, the fact that this phenomenon existed for a number of years—in addition to the fact that state law still determines how much Boston can charge drivers whose cars are towed—illustrates the profound extent to which Boston cannot control its own fiscal destiny, as well as the mundane form that such restrictions often take.

Finally, as we have noted, Boston lost control over many key pieces of its infrastructure over the last seventy years, and its ability to count on fee income from infrastructure was thereby diminished. The presence of a unique fee—one often related directly to a city's ownership of a key piece of its infrastructure—enables other cities to obtain revenue from fees more easily. In San Francisco, user fees—particularly from the city-owned airport and hospital—account for almost 33 percent of the city's operating budget. In Chicago, user fees make up approximately 15 percent of the city's total budget, with almost a third of that amount—approximately half a billion dollars—coming from the O'Hare Revenue Fund, a user fee collected from the major Chicago airport. As is the case in San Francisco, these fees cover operating costs rather than providing money that the city can use as it wishes. But other unique fees can be of much more use. Chicago long received a substantial portion of its fees from tolls collected for use of the Chicago Skyway, a municipally owned highway until it was privatized in 2005. Although these fees were partially used to cover operating and maintenance costs, they helped to secure a bond issue that raised an additional $52 million for other city transportation improvement projects. Litigation to preclude the city from making use of these "extra" funds failed, in part because the state courts concluded that the imposition of the tolls was within the city's home rule powers.[12]

State Aid

Boston's dominant reliance on the property tax is accompanied by an unusual degree of reliance on state aid—it is the city's second-highest source of income, ranging from 20 to 30 percent of total revenue. Only New York is like Boston in this regard (approximately 30 percent of New York City's revenue comes in the form of state aid). Other cities receive state aid too, but it is normally for schools rather than, as in Boston, for financing other day-to-day activities as well as schools. State aid in Denver accounts for less than 3 percent of the city's general operating budget (although almost 35 percent of the school budget) and less than 10 percent of San Francisco's budget. In Atlanta and Seattle, almost no aid is transferred from the state to the municipality for general purposes.

The fact that Boston receives disproportionately more state aid than other cities might be thought to reflect its power in the statehouse. The recent history of state aid, however, suggests the opposite reading. A system that makes Boston dependent on discretionary distributions from the state does not place the city on a strong footing to plan for its future. The current structure ensures that Boston's fiscal health is entwined with state legislative budget battles. State aid can change without any input from the city, and it is always uncertain what the final figure will be. Boston cannot do anything on its own to increase or promote state aid other than lobby the state for more funds. If instead of state aid, Boston, like Denver and San Francisco, were given new taxing power to overcome the state-created limitations on its power to tax property, it would have more local control over its own finances. If a sales or income tax, rather than state aid, accounted for 30 percent of Boston's budget, Boston could promote jobs and retail sales within its boundaries and benefit from this promotion.

The other cities that receive significant funding from the state also maintain far more independence from state legislative control than Boston. Pursuant to a strict formula set forth in state legislation, Chicago (along with other Illinois municipalities) receives 10 percent of the income tax collected by the state on a per capita basis. In addition, it receives 1 percent of the state sales tax, as well as the revenue from its own sales tax, if the sale occurs in Chicago. Chicago thus receives much of its state money because of a statutory right, not as a consequence of the state legislature's annual judgment about what the city "needs" and what the legislature can afford to transfer to it. Chicago receives money from state-local revenue sharing too. These funds make up $450 million out of Chicago's operating budget of $6.1 billion. Although Boston's receipt of state aid is also sometimes based on a formula, the state legislature has adjusted the formulas both for education, the largest source of state aid for Boston, and for the revenue derived from the Massachusetts lottery. (Another form of state aid, called "additional assistance," is not based on a formula.) The fact that the formulas for state aid are readily adjustable makes Boston more vulnerable than other cities, particularly because state aid makes up such a large proportion of its overall budget.

The current system of state aid in Massachusetts creates an accountability issue. The state can cut taxes (or refuse to increase them) by reducing state aid to make up for its own budgetary shortfall. But the city cannot pass its shortfall onto another entity. The city has to increase taxes or reduce services. Thus, the state benefits from the tax reductions or a balanced budget while the city's reduction in services or increase in taxes hurts it politically. The state gets the benefit, even though it is responsible for the situation for which the city takes the blame. This lack of accountability is magnified by the state-created structure, described below, that determines the city's control over its own expenditures. A different legal structure might have an important political effect, therefore, whether or not it would increase the discretionary portion of the city budget.

Expenditures

Our survey of the sources of city revenue—taxes, fees, and state aid—describes the considerable variation in the sources of income for the seven cities, and the role that state law plays in causing it. Although state law determines what the sources of income are everywhere, sometimes the state enables cities to impose a multitude of taxes, rather than limiting the city to the property tax. Sometimes the state allows the city to substitute fees for taxes easily. Sometimes, state aid is allocated to cities as of right rather than as a discretionary year-by-year budget allocation. Within each of these categories, the specific details of the state decisions influence city policy. The city structure for expenditures is similarly diverse. Here, too, the degree of city flexibility is a product of state statutes and court decisions. And, again, the details matter a great deal.

The Basic Legal Structure for the Allocation of Resources

Most of the substantial costs that cities must incur to fund basic services do not arise because the cities choose to take responsibility for them. The state government decides whether to take on basic services itself, assign them to a state-created public authority, or delegate them to the city. The state's choice about how to allocate these obligations is the major determinant of local spending decisions. There is nothing obvious about the allocation of responsibility for different functions among different levels of government. Important variations exist. There are also similarities—public safety constitutes a very significant line item in every city's budget. Moreover, once the state has determined that paying for police and fire protection is largely a local responsibility, it becomes obvious that that is where much of the city's available revenues must go. But many cities do not fund education through general fund revenue, as Boston does. On the other hand, unlike New York City, Boston is not responsible under state law for a share of its residents' Medicaid expenses. The Massachusetts state government, unlike the New York state government, assigns to itself almost all public welfare expenditures and a large fraction of health and hospital spending.[13]

The result of these state decisions is that many cities have relatively little money left over to promote projects that implement their own vision of the city's future. Seattle spends roughly 80 percent of its budget—if the costs of utilities are included—on core services. By some estimates, San Francisco has $2 million available for discretionary spending out of a budget of more than $1 billion. Moreover, all of the cities allocate the overwhelming bulk of their spending to human resources. Denver and Chicago spend between 70 and 80 percent of their general fund revenues on personnel costs. Thus, when revenues are flat or declining, budgetary flexibility is achieved chiefly by shrinking the municipal workforce.

Boston, in this regard, is typical. The costs of education and public safety (police and fire) are Boston's two largest expenses. In fiscal year 2008, the city's spending in these areas represents approximately 67 percent of its total general fund expenditures. The city also has a number of mandatory expenses that must be financed from its general fund. Debt service and state assessments take up roughly 11 percent of the budget, while pension benefits consume another 8 percent. The six categories just named (schools, police, fire, debt service, state assessments, retirement expenses) account for approximately 86 percent of the city's expenditures. Overall, only eleven city departments are appropriated more than 1 percent of the city's budget. In addition to the six already mentioned, these are public works, snow removal, public health, transportation, and the library.

Given these spending obligations, and the limits on available revenue, providing funds for new local programs tends to be something of an afterthought in the municipal budgeting process. Rather than beginning the process by developing a list of spending priorities, and then determining the amount of revenue needed in order to achieve them, a city usually must start with the constrained structure created by its allowable revenues. A priority is then placed on ensuring that the basic city services assigned by the state will be paid for. To be sure, every city does make discretionary decisions that, in marginal ways, tilt local spending to push a particular vision of the city's future. In light of the core services they must fund, however, it is difficult to use discretionary spending as a primary means of defining a future path for the city's development.

At first glance, the legal structure in Massachusetts seems designed to produce the opposite effect. Although Boston has no power to tax without prior state legislative approval, the Home Rule Amendment presumptively entitles Boston to spend its money for whatever purposes it chooses. The problem for Boston has been that its spending decisions, like its other decisions, are subject to the general laws of the state. And the state has prohibited it from spending money for specified purposes, required it to pay for other services, and mandated its funding of state-created governmental authorities that are outside of its control. Other cities are also similarly affected by state statutes. Atlanta, like Boston, is subject to specially targeted legislation, and New York City is under the fiscal oversight of the state-created Municipal Assistance Corporation established during New York's fiscal crisis of the 1970s (although its influence has diminished in recent years). This kind of constraining special legislation, however, is not a universal feature of the legal structure of city spending power. Denver seems to be relatively free of the kind of specially targeted impositions that apply to Boston. Moreover, cities that, unlike Boston, enjoy some degree of home rule protection from state legislation generally have more local power to control their own spending because their decisions cannot be as easily preempted by state statute.

Boston's lack of power over its spending decisions is a product not only of state legislation but of judicial decision making. One noteworthy example of state control is *Connors v. City of Boston*. In that case, the Supreme Judicial Court ruled that Boston's executive order extending group health insurance benefits to domestic partners of city employees was inconsistent with state law and thus invalid. Since the ability of cities to provide health insurance benefits was governed by a state statute, the court reasoned, the state did not allow localities to provide a greater level of benefits than the state.[14] The state courts that govern Atlanta, Chicago, Denver, New York City, and Seattle have all decided the same issue in the opposite way: they have ruled that their state laws do not preempt those cities' domestic partner benefits ordinances. (San Francisco has long provided these benefits without objection from the California courts.) Indeed, in reaching the conclusion that Denver had this power, an appellate court in Colorado held that municipal employee benefits are a matter of local concern for home rule purposes.[15] This means that Colorado cities need not rely on a state statute for the authority to offer group health insurance plans to their employees; they can make the decision on their own. Since the issue is understood as being a local one, it is not surprising that the Colorado court found little state legislation regulating the provision of health insurance benefits to municipal employees. Without the thicket of state legislation that exists in Massachusetts, the court can more easily uphold city power. It is ironic that Boston is the only city without the power to spend city funds to provide health insurance benefits to domestic partners of city workers. After all, it is also the only city (other than San Francisco) that must confer marriage licenses as a matter of state constitutional law to same-sex couples.

One aspect of the Massachusetts legal structure does work to protect Boston rather than to limit its discretion: the provision that bars unfunded mandates. This provision prevents the state, from 1981 onward, from "imposing any direct service or cost obligation upon any city or town" without local approval or full funding by the state.[16] This limitation was apparently intended to offset Proposition 2½'s constraint on local taxation. But, while Proposition 2½'s limits on taxes have proved significant, the limit on state unfunded mandates has not. The principal reason for this is that the prohibition was expressly made prospective, and many significant state mandates predate 1981. Another reason is that the courts have interpreted the prohibition in ways that enable the state to continue to impose new costs without providing new money. One way of doing so is for the state to condition the receipt of other kinds of state aid on acceptance of the unfunded mandate. Other cities have sometimes freed themselves from state laws that mandate spending. Denver successfully challenged costly state-mandated training and certification requirements for local police officers on home rule grounds. But, overall, efforts to limit the state's power to compel local spending have proven no more significant elsewhere than they have in Boston. Although San Francisco benefits from a limitation on unfunded mandates, the California state courts have upheld several state laws that impose significant local costs. These laws range from one that increased local workers' compensation benefits to one that compelled local governments to extend unemployment insurance to their employees.

Local Spending Power: Specific Examples

We briefly describe below two examples of the kinds of detailed constraints that states places on local spending: bond issues and municipal employee benefits. In Boston, the state affects these two expenditures in opposite ways: it limits local spending for bond indebtedness while it mandates local spending for employee benefits. In both ways, it has a significant impact on the city budget in a manner that the city cannot alter.

STATE LIMITS ON SPENDING THROUGH BOND ISSUES

The cost of providing basic municipal services is so high—and the funds available from taxes, fees, and state aid are so limited—that cities often cannot pay for large projects and programs by spending discretionary funds. They carry out these initiatives instead by taking on debt. City borrowing can be understood as a way of raising revenue rather than spending it. We treat state limitations on city debt as restrictions on city control over its expenditures, however, because the funds raised have to be paid off either out of general revenues or from fees generated by the new service or capital improvement. To demonstrate the variety of approaches to these debt limits, we compare Boston with two other cities: Denver and Chicago.

Under Massachusetts law, Boston can authorize bonds on its own up to 5 percent—and, with the approval of a state board, 10 percent—of the valuation of the city's taxable property.[17] The state also sets the maximum maturity period for different types of bonds and details the permissible purposes for which bonds may be issued. The effect of these state regulations is that state approval is normally required for the city's long-term capital projects. Denver and Chicago operate under quite different legal regimes. Although the Home Rule Amendment that governs Boston specifically states that borrowing is not a local power, Denver is free from all state-imposed debt limitations. The only limits on Denver's ability to issue debt are set by the city itself. Denver's city charter limits its debt to 3 percent of the city's property values. Chicago's power to issue debt is even more extensive. Neither the Illinois Constitution nor the state legislature has imposed a debt limit, and Chicago thus has no borrowing limit. Not surprisingly, under these circumstances, Chicago's bonded debt is approximately 10 percent of its estimated assessed value, significantly more than Boston's.

Chicago's reliance on debt rather than state aid has made it less vulnerable to state dictates about its budget priorities than Boston is. Chicago has also been able to support an ambitious neighborhood development initiative funded by bonded debt. In a perverse way, however, its uncapped debt limit may have worked to Chicago's disadvantage. The absence of a cap has allowed the state legislature to ignore the city's fiscal problems more than it could have if the city were subject to debt limitations. One thing is clear: Chicago's indebtedness has increased enormously. Between 1998 and 2002, its long-term direct debt per capita doubled. When debt for revenue bonds is added to this total, the figure doubles again. Chicago's debt service payments consume 42 percent of its property tax revenues. Although it seems unlikely that the current trajectory can continue indefinitely, the debt rating agencies, such as Standard & Poor's, have taken no action to slow it down.

There may be long-term benefits for limiting Boston's borrowing to the relatively modest amount required by Massachusetts law. Given the costs of basic services, and the scarcity of revenue sources other than the property tax and state aid, however, Boston's comparatively restricted borrowing power constrains one possible means of undertaking the kind of investments for its future that other cities have the legal power to make.

STATE MANDATES FOR MUNICIPAL EMPLOYEE BENEFITS

Payments for municipal employees eat up a large portion of the budget for most cities. City officials are often criticized for being captured by municipal employee unions—a perception that often hampers city efforts to win new revenue-raising powers. It is important to recognize, however, that these payment decisions are not always made by the cities themselves. State law often significantly structures city choices in this area. Boston, for example, has little control over the two key elements of these employee benefit costs—the level of retirement and health care benefits—because the major elements are determined by state law. Again, our comparison cities will be Denver and Chicago, where state law creates a very different structure.

Retirement benefits for Boston's municipal employees are pervasively regulated by the state. Nearly all of Boston's city employees receive their retirement benefits through the State-Boston Retirement System. Their benefits are paid under formulas established by state law, and the state legislature has the exclusive authority to change them. The state regulates the type and amount of pre- and postretirement death benefits, sets the eligibility and funding requirements for disability retirement, mandates a number of benefit preferences and options for certain types of employees (most notably public safety officials and veterans), and establishes procedures for benefit determinations and appeal rights. The state also has control over cost of living increases. Boston, in short, is obligated to fund the cost of municipal pensions—no questions asked—but it has virtually no control over what these costs are.[18]

Denver's pension plan is controlled by the city. A city ordinance exempts city employees from the Colorado state pension plan, establishes a trust fund to manage contributions and payments, and creates a retirement board, appointed by the mayor, to administer the plan. The board defines the plan's contents, hears complaints of employees who are denied benefits, and maintains an investment manual to guide trustees' management of the fund. (Even Denver does not have complete control over its pension costs: its police and firefighters participate in the Statewide Defined Benefit Plan.) Chicago's flexibility in controlling pension costs is more like Boston's than Denver's. All benefit entitlements, including prescribed cost of living increases, are specified by state law. Because pension expenses constitute the city's fastest-growing budget item, this statutory scheme imposes significant mandated costs on the city. In 2003, however, the Illinois Legislature authorized an early retirement package that the city had drafted and pressed it to enact. Illinois law has also provided Chicago with some influence over state pension decisions by requiring that at least two city officials be ex officio members of all pension boards. Finally, the Illinois Supreme Court upheld a municipal ordinance imposing a mandatory retirement age, rejecting the argument that the ordinance was preempted by the state Pension Code.[19]

A look at the same three cities reveals equally significant differences for health benefits. In 1968, the Massachusetts Legislature authorized municipalities to provide health care coverage for their employees. Although the legislation was a local option statute, a municipality that decided to opt in could not subsequently opt out. Moreover, since the state statute established the exclusive means by which municipalities could provide health insurance coverage to their employees, it essentially required participation. Unsurprisingly, Boston chose to participate. The statute extensively details the substance of the program, including the permissible contribution levels for various employees and the types and levels of benefits. These requirements are binding once a city opts into the system, decreasing Boston's flexibility to control health care costs—costs that represent a substantial portion of its budget.

Denver and Chicago are freer to provide greater benefits to employees and also freer to reduce or limit them as a cost-saving device. Denver's home rule authority gives it power over employee benefits, which are considered matters of local concern.[20] Although Chicago does not possess the same degree of control over employee benefits as Denver, Illinois law does not mandate city or employee contribution or benefit levels. Unlike Boston, Chicago can and does negotiate the terms of its health insurance plans. With its health care costs rising about 20 percent each year, city officials stress that municipal employees will have to assume a greater proportion of the cost in the future.

State laws concerning pensions and health benefits are simply illustrative of state controls over expenditures. Boston is also required to make payments to the Massachusetts Bay Transportation Authority to support the mass transit system. It has to pay tuition costs for the more than four thousand students who attend charter schools even though most of these schools are authorized by the state without any city input. And it must allocate almost $321 million to the purposes specified in targeted federal and state grants. Like our review of the legal structure affecting the city's ability to raise revenue, these examples, together with those mentioned above, demonstrate the extent to which expenditures do not reflect the city's own decision making about what is essential in order to promote its vitality, prosperity, or competitiveness.

Every city operates under some kinds of state-imposed constraints over expenditures. But because the constraints differ significantly from city to city, the phrase "city power" means different things in different places. A freer hand on matters ranging from debt service to employee benefits and from voter education to school funding enables some cities to foster their own priorities more than others can. Similarly, as we have seen, a diversity of sources of income—not to mention the extent of the authority to determine where the income comes from—changes the options available for city development. It seems unlikely that the widely divergent revenue and expenditure rules applicable to the seven cities can all be defended as beneficial to their economies. On the contrary, existing rules about revenues and expenditures tend to push cities to favor some ideas about their future over others, regardless of the desires of their citizens or of their elected leaders.

LAND USE AND DEVELOPMENT

In this chapter, we discuss city power to control the built environment—the physical aspects of a city's growth and development. Cities do not make decisions about the built environment in a transparent way. Land use authority is embedded in a maddeningly complex array of statutes, judicial decisions, ownership structures, and public authorities. This complexity makes a city's land use policy obscure even to the most interested of observers. Yet land use powers affect the look of a city in a way that no other city powers can. Unlike the home rule power or decisions about finance and education, city power over land use is visible to everyone—not only in the gentrifying neighborhoods sporting new office buildings and high rises for high-end living but in neighborhoods where little change is evident. Although economic decisions by private developers also have much to do with the transformation of the urban landscape, local government law has an effect on their decisions too.

Urban scholars have often singled out planning and development as an area over which cities enjoy autonomy, downplaying the importance of the state legal structure on city land use decision making.[1] We see the legal structure differently. Here, as elsewhere, we envision city decision making in terms of both city empowerment and disempowerment. The structure produced by what the state allows and disallows has an overall impact on the built environment, and this impact encourages cities to pursue some land use policies rather than others. We investigate this city structure by focusing on two major ingredients of a city's land use power: decisions about the city's physical development and about the supply of affordable housing. We turn first to the basic rules governing city power over land use: the general power to zone and plan, the extent to which the state has excluded a portion of the city from city control, and the city's ability to use innovative fiscal tools to promote its land use policy. We then examine a city's ability to provide affordable housing. Both of these aspects of a city's power over land use are important no matter which vision of the future it adopts. As this chapter will demonstrate, cities do have considerable power over land use. But the way that power is exercised is significantly influenced by the details of state law.

City Power over Land Use

Zoning and Planning

The state-created institutions for zoning and planning structure the debate, and determine the decision makers, for a city's land use policy. Decisions made by a city council are likely to be different than decisions made by a zoning authority organized in terms of particular interest groups. City planning decisions are equally likely to be affected by a state's decision to combine planning and development decisions into one city agency rather than separating them into two. Notwithstanding the importance of these allocations of authority over land use decisions, they are generally not made by the cities themselves. Indeed, on both of these dimensions, Massachusetts state law treats Boston differently than other cities—not only other cities across the country but other cities in Massachusetts. These other cities are subject to state control as well: they cannot choose to adopt the allocation of authority that Massachusetts has imposed on Boston.

ZONING POWERS

The Massachusetts Home Rule Amendment gives Boston the power to zone and to plan without a specific delegation of state power. Boston has taken considerable advantage of this authority. It has promoted downtown physical development, helped major institutions fulfill their growth plans, enhanced street life, and improved the vibrancy of longstanding neighborhoods. As we have seen, however, the Home Rule Amendment also enables the state legislature to preempt Boston's exercise of its zoning power. The legislature has taken considerable advantage of its power too. Most important, it enacted a special legislative act, known as the Enabling Act, that applies only to Boston and that determines how Boston exercises its zoning authority.

The initial effect of the Enabling Act, passed in 1956 before the adoption of the Home Rule Amendment, was to give Boston land use powers that it had previously lacked.[2] Other municipalities in the state had been granted the zoning power in 1920, but Boston had been given very little zoning authority. The

Enabling Act for the first time empowered the city, rather than the state, to regulate the height and size of buildings, the amount of open space, and population density. But the Enabling Act did not end the state's traditional practice of singling out the city on land use matters. In the early 1990s, for example, the legislature passed statutes that prohibited Boston officials from granting permits for new buildings that would cast a "new shadow" on any portion of the Boston Common or Public Garden.

More important, the Enabling Act sets up a very different structure for zoning decisions in Boston than the one that exists elsewhere. It establishes two zoning authorities—the Zoning Commission and the Zoning Board of Appeal. The Zoning Commission is responsible for adopting and amending Boston's zoning code and maps; the Zoning Board of Appeal hears zoning appeals and grants variances from the zoning code's requirements. The statute that governs the zoning power of every other city and town in Massachusetts mandates a very different structure. Instead of requiring the creation of separate zoning boards, it vests zoning authority in the city council (or its equivalent).[3] The same is true for the other cities we have examined: their rules also provide for city council (or, in the case of San Francisco, the Board of Supervisors') approval for zoning decisions. Elsewhere, in other words, zoning authority is in the hands of politically accountable actors rather than appointed officials. Only Boston traces its zoning structure to a special legislative act, rather than a general zoning enabling statute, and only in Boston does the state statutory framework virtually exclude the city council from the zoning process.

There are other unusual features of the Enabling Act. In Boston, the mayor must select members for the Zoning Commission from candidates nominated by the AFL-CIO, the Greater Boston Real Estate Board, the Greater Boston Chamber of Commerce, the Contractors Association, and Boston architecture societies; three members have to represent neighborhood associations. The Board of Appeal is required to have a similar structure. No other city follows the Enabling Act's requirement that appointees to zoning boards be drawn from a list of specific state-identified groups. Other cities enable their mayor to appoint board members with complete discretion (Chicago, Denver) or permit appointments to be made without membership qualifications but with significant input from local legislative bodies (San Francisco). The closest that other cities come to the practice that the state requires Boston to follow is that some cities are required to identify certain professions from which at least a few board members must be selected. Yet the two cities that impose these professional qualification requirements—Atlanta and New York City—have not opted to follow the course set for Boston by the state legislature. Boston's board members must represent groups (ranging from the real estate industry to the construction trade) that would have an interest in overriding zoning restrictions to promote development. Atlanta's charter provides that two of the five members of the Board of Zoning Adjustment be planners, architects, or in related professions, and that the remaining members be laypeople. New York City's charter provides that, of the five members of the zoning board that hears petitions for zoning variances, one must be a registered architect, one a professional engineer, and one a planner. Perhaps Boston's zoning structure was designed to foster more development than might occur elsewhere. One way to do so would be to vest authority in a separate zoning commission with a membership organized to promote the interests of builders. If this were the original plan, Boston cannot alter it. Only the state, not the City of Boston, can decide how to change the current administrative structure for the city's zoning.[4] In other cities, state law is restrictive in a different way. By making land use decisions heavily influenced by the city council, and by requiring different voices to serve on zoning boards, state law can prevent a mayor from pursuing a prodevelopment agenda even if he favors it.

Another important difference between Boston and other cities is very technical, but it illustrates the detailed ways in which the Enabling Act affects Boston's ability to make zoning decisions. It also illustrates the ways in which all states play an important, albeit often invisible, role in shaping local land use policy. The difference we have in mind concerns what lawyers call the "vested rights" doctrine. This legal rule freezes zoning regulations so that owners who have taken steps toward development under existing legal rules do not become subject to new, more onerous rules that are adopted later. This doctrine can have very adverse consequences for urban planning. The situation in Seattle, which is constrained by a similar vested rights rule, illustrates how. Washington law provides that development rights vest on the date of the development's permit application regardless of when development actually takes place. As a result, developers in the Seattle area search for old subdivision applications, so that they can build new housing under the old standards rather than under later, more restrictive land-use and environmental laws.[5] Boston enjoys greater flexibility from vested rights claims than Seattle, but the vested rights protection in the Enabling Act is still significant. It provides that, unless the city has given the developer notice that a hearing on the new zoning rule is pending, a developer's right to freeze zoning vests when a permit has been issued to build *or* when construction has "lawfully begun." California, by contrast, provides that property owners acquire vested rights in prior zoning regulations only when permits have been issued *and* when they have made substantial financial and material investments relying on prior approval under the old regulations. California also requires that the money be spent on actual physical work on the site, not just the creation of detailed plans and blueprints. Unlike the situation in Boston, then, California cities have flexibility to change zoning rules much later in the process—not only after the permit has been issued but after money has been spent on plans. Intricately detailed rules like these have a significant impact on the development process.

PLANNING POWERS

As it did for zoning, the state of Massachusetts has established a very different administrative structure for planning in Boston than for other cities in Massachusetts. The state-established framework for Boston vests the planning power in a separate governmental entity, the Boston Redevelopment Authority, which is also charged with promoting and implementing redevelopment in the city. Other Massachusetts cities are required to establish a separate board responsible only for planning, with members appointed by the mayor and confirmed by the city council. Other cities around the country, like other Massachusetts municipalities, also have a city-controlled planning body that is not responsible for (indeed, is often not permitted to influence) the promotion of particular redevelopment projects. The development and planning structure in Denver is typical. The Denver Urban Renewal Authority, appointed by the mayor, is a redevelopment agency that undertakes neighborhood revitalization, economic development, and housing rehabilitation. The Denver Planning Board, also appointed by the mayor, is responsible for the supervision of the city's planning office and for recommending amendments to the city's comprehensive plan to promote the city's growth and development. Chicago, New York, and Seattle have separate agencies for planning and development too, each with their own members and purposes. Boston alone is required to rely on a single quasi-independent public agency to oversee both planning and economic development.

Of course, the approach adopted in other states is no less constraining: it requires cities to operate through a fragmented structure. And consolidating planning and development in Boston has benefits. Fragmenting these tasks can stifle development, while permitting a single entity to make trade-offs between adherence to a plan and compliance with requests from developers can make planned development more likely to occur. Moreover, a streamlined process for making zoning concessions provides Boston with the power to act quickly when developers express interest in building in the city. The Boston Redevelopment Authority's dramatic remaking of the central part of the city in the decade immediately following its creation in 1957 is a testament to the capacity of a single entity to make major changes in the city's physical appearance.

But there are also substantial risks in combining the roles of planner and developer. One concern is the flip side of the ability of a consolidated planning and development agency to move quickly and efficiently. The agency can move too quickly to remake the city's physical landscape without sufficient consultation with those who will be affected. The unease about the Boston Redevelopment Authority's push for urban renewal in the 1950s and 1960s reflects these concerns. Consolidating planning and development also has the potential to enable the development power to overwhelm the planning power, effectively leaving the city with no real planning. Having the power to plan is important, critics argue, and having the power to alter, amend, and vary plans in developmental negotiations can compromise the plans—even render them irrelevant.

The choice between these alternatives represents a decision about the importance of planning in a city's development policy. An independent city planning board can have a substantial influence on city land use policy. In 2002, Denver's planning board's proposed "Blueprint Denver," the first major revision of its planning process since the 1950s, which the city council then adopted. This integrated land-use and transportation plan calls for a massive overhaul of Denver's zoning code and greater intergovernmental cooperation, and it divides the city into "areas of stability" and "areas of change."[6] Other cities have master plans too. Atlanta's city charter requires the city to prepare a comprehensive development plan every fifteen years, and Washington's Growth Management Act requires Seattle to update its comprehensive development plan every ten years. Boston is not required to formulate a master plan for the city—and it has not done so.

Boston also does not have the mechanisms that other cities use to oversee zoning changes. In New York City, San Francisco, and Seattle, the planning commission must approve proposed zoning amendments before they are sent to the city council for final adoption. In San Francisco, state law requires the city to exercise land use regulation in accordance with a long-term, comprehensive general plan. Although Boston's Enabling Act requires proposed zoning amendments to be reviewed by the Boston Redevelopment Authority, it does not require that the Boston Redevelopment Authority approve them. Boston also has a different mechanism to oversee planning decisions. Boston's Zoning Commission, not the Boston City Council, has power to adopt zoning amendments to constrain planning board actions. As a result, the Boston City Council has far less power to control its planning agency than other cities, a deficit magnified by the fact that the Boston Redevelopment Authority has the authority to develop and not just plan.

Institutions matter. The presence or absence of a strong, independent planning agency—like the presence or absence of city council review of zoning decisions—has an impact on the kind of decisions the city makes. Although Boston has a considerable amount of authority to make zoning and planning decisions, specifying *who* makes these decisions for the city is a choice made by the state. Although the state made an unusual choice for Boston in this regard, it is not unusual for states to make the choice. On the basic question of who should decide contentious questions of local land use policy, the state regularly provides the answer.

State Exemptions of Property from Local Land Use Control

Whoever the decision makers are, there remains the question of what decisions they are permitted to make. Here too the influence of state law is pervasive. Boston represents a dramatic illustration. When Boston exercises its zoning and planning powers, it can affect only a portion of its territory. The state maintains its own detailed master plans for the Charles River Basin, which constitutes an important part of Boston's recreational and natural landscape, and also regulates "designated port areas" and "tidelands," which together comprise much of Boston Harbor.[7] Even more important, the state exercises land use control by holding title to key parcels in the city. The state and entities under its control own nearly twice as much land in Boston as the city itself owns. (New York City owns roughly eight times the number of parcels within the city as are owned by the state, with an assessed value twenty-six times greater than the state-owned land.) We focus attention here on two examples: the airport and major roads.

Sixteen percent of the tax exempt land in Boston—over twenty-three hundred acres—is occupied by Boston's Logan International Airport. Since 1956, the airport has been owned and operated by an independent state authority, the Massachusetts Port Authority (Massport). Boston exercises virtually no control over this part of the city. Denver, Chicago, and San Francisco are different: they all own their airports. Indeed, they own their airports even though (unlike Boston) the airports are not located within the conventional understanding of the city limits but are built on annexed land located some distance from the core city. Even in New York City, where the Port Authority of New York and New Jersey operates both LaGuardia and Kennedy airports, the city owns the land on which the airports are built and leases it to the Port Authority. This arrangement represents a guaranteed source of airport-related income and gives the city some leverage over long-term planning decisions at the two airports. Boston is entitled only to its receipts from the jet fuel tax, despite the fact that the airport, along with Massport's other Boston properties, produces substantial surpluses for Massport each year.[8]

Denver illustrates the value of the alternative ownership structure. During the early 1980s, the city realized that Stapleton Airport—built in 1929 and owned and run directly by the city—was no longer able to meet the region's needs. It therefore began planning to build a new airport. Its most significant hurdle was insufficient land within the city on which to build. The city turned to neighboring Adams County and convinced the country to allow it to annex fifty-three square miles of land for the new airport, a deal that was strongly supported by state legislators and the governor. The new airport opened in 1995 and is already a source of revenue for the city; in the long term, it seems likely that the city's ownership will be a significant source of nontax revenue. Meanwhile, the old city-owned Stapleton Airport, close to the Denver urban core, offered the city the potential for future growth. In fact, with forty-seven hundred acres, the area provided the largest urban development site in the nation. Because the city owned the airport, it was able to redevelop it according to an ambitious plan approved the Denver City Council. The property is being developed by a nonprofit organization called the Stapleton Development Corporation, an entity created by the city's redevelopment authority and controlled by mayoral appointees. Plans envision twelve thousand homes, three million square feet of commercial space, ten million square feet of office space, more than one thousand acres of parks, a medical center, and schools, all influenced by new urbanist ideas.[9]

Boston's comparative lack of control over its airport is demonstrated by its thirty-year battle with Massport over the construction of a controversial fifth runway at Logan Airport. The city vigorously opposed the project, often in the courts, but the state government, along with the Federal Aviation Administration, ultimately approved Massport's expansion plans. Although Massport was required to take a number of measures designed to mitigate the air and noise pollution concerns of East Boston residents, if the city itself were in control of the airport—as other cities are—it seems clear that the debate over Logan's expansion would have proceeded very differently.

Like for its airport, the key decision maker in Boston about toll roads, tunnels, and bridges is not the city. The Tobin Memorial Bridge, which connects Boston and Charlestown, is owned and operated by Massport. The three tunnels that connect Boston to East Boston are owned and operated by the Massachusetts Turnpike Authority. One consequence of this ownership structure is that the city gets no revenue from the tolls. (From 1958 to 2005, Chicago's Skyway, owned by the city and funded through user charges, generated city revenue.) An even more important consequence of the state agencies' ownership of Boston's transportation infrastructure relates to land use control. The Turnpike Authority owns over two hundred acres of city land and is a major player when it comes to important development proposals affecting Boston. The most dramatic example is the Turnpike Authority's ownership and management of the Central Artery/Tunnel Project (the "Big Dig")—the largest public works project in the history of the United States. The project created a third tunnel underneath Boston Harbor connecting downtown and Logan Airport, a "Turnpike Extension" connecting the tunnel to the Massachusetts Turnpike, and an underground highway culminating in a new Charles River crossing. From the beginning, the city sought

ways to exert control over this extensive development, but under state legislation enacted in 1997 the Turnpike Authority "owns and is responsible for the
construction, maintenance, repair, reconstruction, improvement, rehabilitation,
financing, use, policing, administering, control and operation" of the entire metropolitan highway system, including the Big Dig.[10]

This power affects much more than roads and tunnels. The 1997 legislation
exempted the lease of air rights over the Turnpike property from Boston's building, fire, health, and zoning laws, and it gave the Turnpike Authority control over
the development of the relevant parcels—over forty-four acres of potential real
estate estimated to be worth more than $500 million. This arrangement has gen-
erated a great deal of controversy, including over a proposal to build a massive,
forty-nine-story tower on a deck over the Turnpike and on an adjacent parcel.
The controversy has been exacerbated by the state's decision to exempt the land
and air rights (although not the buildings) from city property taxes, contrary to
the usual practice when a state agency leases land to businesses. Another source
of conflict concerns the Turnpike Authority's control of the series of parks—
called the Rose Kennedy Greenway—situated on the land that covers a portion
of the Big Dig in downtown Boston. In 2004, the city and the Turnpike Authority reached an agreement that a nonprofit organization, supported by private
donations with contributions from the Turnpike Authority, would manage
the land. Half of the ten-member nonprofit board of directors is appointed by
the Turnpike Authority, with two appointed by the state, two by the city, and one
by the Kennedy family.

The Turnpike Authority's holdings are but one example of the consequences,
both positive and negative, of the state's ownership of important parts of Boston. On the positive side, the state's landholdings ensure that there are significant capital improvements in Boston that the city does not have to pay for with
its own funds. The Massachusetts Bay Transportation Authority, a state-created
public authority whose members are appointed by the governor, owns and
operates all subway, bus, and commuter rail service in Boston. Although the
city is assessed for a financial contribution to the Transportation Authority,
the assessment is offset by its capital spending in the city. The Massachusetts
Convention Center Authority provides another example. The authority, largely
appointed by the governor and established by the state legislature in 1982, was
made responsible for the design, construction, and operation of the Boston
Convention and Exposition Center on a sixty-acre site in South Boston.

The fact that so much capital spending on physical development within Boston occurs at the behest of state-controlled entities means, however, that the
state, not the city, is often the lead planning decision maker for Boston. Other
cities work under analogous kinds of state control over city land use. In Denver,

new sports stadiums have been built under the control of state-created public authorities much like the Massachusetts Convention Center Authority. In Chicago, a state-controlled public authority runs both McCormick Place and the Navy Pier, two of the most important tourist sites in the city. In New York City, the Port Authority of New York and New Jersey is the lead actor in the redevelopment of the Ground Zero site. And New York state's Empire State Development Corporation—governed entirely by gubernatorial appointees—has assumed a critical role in such major New York City projects as the Times Square redevelopment project, the 125th Street corporation, the Apollo Theater, the Audubon ballroom, a 74.5 acre mixed-use development along the East River in Queens, the redevelopment of the main U.S. Postal Facility on 34th Street, and, most important, the coordination of the rebuilding and revitalization of lower Manhattan, south of Houston Street, in the aftermath of the September 11 attack.

These state limitations matter. But so does the scope of state control over the physical territory of cities. In these other cities, it is possible to identify transformative development projects that have taken place on city-owned land with minimal state involvement. New York City has developed an ambitious housing program with city-owned housing stock, and Denver has run the major redevelopment project related to its city-owned airport. There are no comparable projects in Boston. One reason is that other cities hold title to assets, such as airports and roads, that Boston doesn't own. Another reason is that they benefit from the fact that state-created public authorities give them greater power to influence development. To mention but one example, the Chicago Transit Authority is governed by an eight-member board with four members and the chairman appointed by the mayor of Chicago, albeit with the approval of the city council and the governor. (The governor's three appointees similarly require the approval of the mayor and the Illinois Senate.) The City of Chicago thus has substantially more say in dealing with transportation issues than Boston does.

Limits on Fiscal Tools Used in Urban Redevelopment

The most basic way that state-imposed limits on city finance affect land use policy is through the decisions they make about how cities can raise tax revenue. Another method is defining cities' powers to use innovative fiscal tools. We discuss here state definitions of city authority over two of these fiscal tools: tax-increment-financing districts and business improvement districts.

Tax increment financing is a mechanism that uses property tax revenues to pay off bonds issued to promote development. Under tax increment financing, cities issue bonds to fund land acquisition, planning, and infrastructure improvements for designated districts. The revenue generated by the increase in the property tax valuation of properties within these districts is then pledged to pay off the bonds. Tax increment financing is therefore much more than a revenue-generating device. It is a tool for promoting new physical development and, consequently, an important ingredient in land use policy. By permitting a city to lay claim to the future economic benefits of a physical development even before construction takes place, tax increment financing helps a city generate the revenue needed to fund the public planning and infrastructure that can entice a developer to build in the first place.

Pioneered in Minnesota in 1947, tax increment financing was available in about forty states before its adoption in Massachusetts in 2003. That Boston had to wait for a state statute is a direct consequence of the limited terms of the Home Rule Amendment, which expressly excludes the power to tax from the powers it gives cities. There was no possibility, as there was in Chicago, for Boston to develop its own framework for tax increment financing. Moreover, Boston has not used tax increment financing as much as other cities. The reason can be found in the details of its authorizing statute. In some respects the Massachusetts statute is quite broad. It does not require that the designated area be underdeveloped or blighted, as is the case in Atlanta, nor does it vest the power to establish districts in a separate redevelopment authority, as is the case in Denver and San Francisco. Instead, the Massachusetts statute vests the power in the city itself, with the city's elected leaders empowered to draw the districts. Under the Massachusetts scheme, unlike Chicago's, a maximum of 25 percent of the municipality's geographic area may be designated as an improvement district, and, unlike other states, Massachusetts requires that a municipality's development plan be approved by the state Economic Assistance Coordinating Council before it can take effect. Perhaps most important, it requires that the bonds issued for tax increment financing be counted against the overall municipal bond limit. This restriction does not exist in San Francisco or Denver, cities that rely on redevelopment authorities to create these taxing districts. (In cities with more generous debt ceilings—or, as is the case in Chicago, no debt ceiling—such a requirement would have little meaning.) Only Seattle has a tax increment financing system with constraints that are equivalent to Boston's. Not surprisingly, Seattle, like Boston, has not used tax increment financing in any significant way.

Business improvement districts are territorial subdivisions of cities that are designed to raise additional tax revenues from property owners to fund services beyond those provided by the city itself. Once authorized by state law, their creation requires approval by the city government. As was the case with tax increment financing, business improvement districts are best understood as a component of city land use policy. The business improvement district structure permits a city to delegate a measure of its regulatory power over land to property owners who can then work together to exercise control over the area in which they have invested. The existence of the business improvement district structure can itself play a role in making parts of the city attractive to further investment. It is important to note, however, that business improvement districts are quite controversial. The reason is that they are usually governed by a board of directors elected by property owners—that is, not by the district's residents or by the tenants who occupy the commercial premises but by the property owners even if they live outside the city. Critics' objection to business improvement districts is based on this form of organization: business improvement districts, they argue, generate serious problems of democratic accountability and promote the privatization of traditional municipal services.[11]

Despite the controversy, business improvement districts have been employed with increasing frequency throughout the United States as a means of revitalizing urban neighborhoods. They are most often created in downtown business districts, providing services such as sanitation, policing, social services, and infrastructure improvements. There are over one thousand business improvement districts in operation nationwide. New York City alone has over 130 business improvement districts, and Chicago has twenty-five (one of which includes property representing 34 percent of the city's total assessed value). In Denver, the most significant business improvement district is the 120-block Downtown Denver Business Improvement District, which funds cleaning and maintenance services, safety initiatives, consumer marketing campaigns, and economic development efforts. Seattle and Atlanta have a number of business improvement districts, and San Francisco has one major one.

Only Boston has no business improvement district. This is not for lack of effort. Property owners in Boston's downtown shopping district—Downtown Crossing—have actively, but unsuccessfully, sought state legislation authorizing a business improvement district since 1996. Given this concerted effort, it may be surprising to learn that Massachusetts already has enabling legislation, passed in 1994, allowing municipalities, including Boston, to create business improvement districts. Boston has not established a business improvement district because this enabling legislation gives every landowner the ability to opt out of the assessment fees required to operate the district. Massachusetts is the only state in the nation that enables property owners in a business improvement district to opt out in this way, and the provision has been an obstacle to the creation of these districts in the state. Business improvement districts usually require a great deal of support within the district in order to be created, but, once created, they tax all property within the district according to an established schedule. Other cities have the statutory authority to impose additional taxes on the property in business improvement districts—and, in some instances, to issue bonds—without the unanimous consent of the property owners. Given the problems created by a scheme permitting individual property owners to opt out when they of necessity share the benefits of the business improvement districts' efforts, Boston's property owners have not shown any interest in pursuing this device.

It should be clear by now what we mean by "details." Boston has authority to raise money through tax increment financing and create business improvement districts. But the exact wording of its statutory authorizations for these tools determines whether Boston can effectively use them. This is the same point that we made earlier regarding home rule. Boston is a home rule city, but that doesn't mean that it can engage in tax increment financing or establish business improvement districts without specific state authorization. These kinds of issues of detail affect every aspect of a city's land use policy, above all what it can do about its need for affordable housing.

Providing Affordable Housing

A serious and growing affordable housing problem exists throughout the Boston metropolitan region, as it does in many other metropolitan areas in the United States. One way that state law influences the central city housing markets is through its impact on the ability and desire of the suburbs to provide affordable housing. In Massachusetts, the state provides incentives to suburban communities to increase affordable housing—in particular, through the state's "Anti-Snob Zoning Act."[12] In other metropolitan areas, such as those of Atlanta, Chicago, and Denver, there are no equivalent state laws. Even in Massachusetts, however, if the incentives provided by state law are insufficient to motivate nearby municipalities to increase their supply of affordable housing, Boston will end up with a disproportionate share. Moreover, some state laws in Massachusetts create disincentives for surrounding towns and cities to provide affordable housing. State limits on taxation make the suburbs dependent on the property tax, thereby reducing their interest in opening themselves up to residents of modest means. State law prohibits municipalities from adopting rent control measures. The state's Subdivision Control Law limits local review of subdivisions that front existing roads, thereby reducing a suburb's control over important new development projects. Although there is less state pressure exerted in other states to encourage suburbs to provide affordable housing, the suburbs there may have more freedom to take on affordable housing issues on their own initiative.

We do not discuss this regional housing issue in this chapter—important as it is. (We return to the regional issue in chapter 10.) We focus instead on the ability of large, successful cities to provide affordable housing on their own. The phrase "affordable housing" does not refer to a single issue. One concern is the lack of housing for people with low and moderate incomes, usually defined as households at or below 80 percent of the region's median household income. Much of state and city housing policy across the country is directed toward this population. But there is also another affordable housing problem: the unavailability of housing affordable by the middle class, that is, for people with even substantially more than the median household income. For example, only 351 of the 5,726 single-family houses or condominiums sold in Boston in 2003—6 percent of the sales—were sold at a price a family with a median household income could afford. And only 9 percent of the rental apartments were listed at prices affordable to the average Bostonian.[13] San Francisco and New York City illustrate that this dimension of the affordability problem is by no means unique to Boston.

We will discuss these two affordable housing problems separately. We begin with housing policies for the low and moderate income population: subsidized housing, linkage programs, and inclusionary zoning. We then turn to the problems generated by the high price of housing in successful cities—both rental and owned—for all city residents, existing and potential.

Housing the Low and Moderate Income Population

All seven cities—even those, like Boston, that are characterized by high housing prices—have a considerable amount of affordable housing within their borders. Boston has 40 percent of the region's affordable housing stock. Moreover, Boston is making efforts, as are other cities, to maintain or even increase its supply of housing for its low and moderate income city residents. But every available device for doing so is limited by state law. Some of these limits, such as for subsidized housing, derive from budgetary constraints; others, such as for linkage, inclusionary zoning, and rent control programs, derive from interpretations of the cities' home rule authority or the absence, or specific provisions, of statutory authorization from the state legislature. Despite these limits, every city can— and does—address the needs of its low and moderate income residents to some extent. Boston, in this regard, has been a leader. But, as in other cities, the problem in Boston is much bigger than its available resources and its legal authority permit it to address.

SUBSIDIZING HOUSING THROUGH DIRECT
SPENDING OR USE OF CITY ASSETS

In Boston, public housing is the single largest source of housing that low-income families can afford. Owned by the Boston Housing Authority, it constitutes two-thirds of the city's subsidized housing, and demand for it has never been greater: there are twenty-two thousand people on the waiting list for the city's fourteen thousand units. A variety of other federal, state, and city programs subsidize housing units in Boston as well: overall, almost 20 percent of its housing stock (in some neighborhoods, over 40 percent) was subsidized in 2000. These figures are not unusual. The New York City Housing Authority, the largest in the nation, has more than 178,000 apartments in 343 developments throughout the city, housing more than 400,000 people. Chicago's Housing Authority houses more than 5 percent of the city's population. Subsidized housing requires money, however, and constraints on city revenues significantly limit what cities can do. Federal and state support for housing has declined substantially over the last twenty years. Even with the existing amount of subsidization, over thirty-two thousand Boston residents are spending more than half their income on rent and the number of homeless people in Boston is at an all-time high.[14]

An alternative way to increase the existing affordable housing stock is for the city to assume title to properties that were previously privately owned. Cities do this by foreclosing on properties that are delinquent in paying city taxes. Boston and Chicago have pursued this policy to some extent, but New York City has used this mechanism as a key tool in its affordable housing policy. Its program began in the late 1970s when many landlords were in default on taxes. In order to spur their payment of back taxes, the city foreclosed on properties in default. Many property owners were happy to have the city take the buildings off their hands. As a result, the city became title holder of tens of thousands of residential units. It recognized that these units were a potential means of increasing the affordable housing stock. Through a variety of programs, the city promoted the development of these properties, known as "in rem" properties. In a fifteen-year period, more than two hundred thousand new or rehabilitated units were created across the city. Some filled entire blocks, while others were in-fill units of two to eight houses. In 2002 Mayor Michael Bloomberg put forward a plan, called "The New Housing Marketplace," to invest $3 billion over five years to preserve and create sixty-five thousand units of housing for low, moderate, and middle-income New Yorkers, in part by providing city-owned land for the construction of seven thousand units of housing. A key component of this plan is the disposition of the remainder of the city's stock of "in rem" housing.[15] Boston is not in a position to follow New York City's model because it has relatively few formerly privately owned properties under its control.

LINKAGE AND INCLUSIONARY ZONING

Given the limits on Boston's ability to increase its supply of affordable housing on its own, it must, like other cities, rely heavily on efforts by the private sector. Despite the limits imposed by its grant of home rule, Boston has been a

pioneer in asserting its regulatory authority in order to increase housing for low
and moderate income families. One of its most significant efforts is its linkage
program, officially known as Development Impact Project Exactions. In 1983,
the city established the program in order "to mitigate the impact of large-scale
development on the supply of housing and jobs available to low- and moderate-
income people." It did so by requiring developers of large-scale commercial,
retail, hotel, or similar buildings to pay for affordable housing or to make an
equivalent in-kind contribution. From its inception through June 2000, almost
$60 million in linkage funds were awarded, generating almost six thousand
housing units, most of which have been allocated to those with incomes at or
below 80 percent of the region's median household income.[16]

Boston's authority to pursue this innovative strategy has depended on its ability to secure special authorizing legislation from the state legislature. In 1986, the
zoning commission's authority to enact the linkage program was challenged on
the grounds that it lacked home rule authority to adopt it. The trial court sided
with the challenger, holding that the linkage fees amounted to the imposition
of an unauthorized tax. In *Bonan v. City of Boston*, the Supreme Judicial Court
rejected the trial court's judgment.[17] But it did so on the grounds that the plaintiff did not have standing to bring the suit. The court did not discuss the merits
of the plaintiff's legal argument, although it did note that the question of the
city's statutory authority could be cured by legislation. In 1987, the legal uncertainty surrounding Boston's ability to adopt its linkage program was eliminated
when the state passed a law explicitly authorizing the program. The authorizing legislation was quite specific. It detailed, among other things, the amount of
permissible exactions and the length of repayment periods. And, while it allowed
Boston to increase the exaction amount periodically within prescribed limits, it
provided that other changes required state approval. Other cities have been able
to act more independently, and their greater power has shaped their approach to
linkage policies. San Francisco has had a linkage ordinance in place for roughly
as long as Boston has, and, due to its broad home rule grant, it has been able to
amend its ordinance several times to require higher contributions and broaden
its coverage. The process for doing so simply requires a proposed amendment to
the local zoning code by the planning commission, followed by approval by the
board of supervisors.

Another important Boston initiative is its inclusionary zoning policy.[18] In
February 2000, Mayor Thomas Menino signed an executive order requiring certain housing developers—those with projects of ten or more units that require
zoning relief and those with projects financed by the city or developed on city
land—to contribute to the city's affordable housing stock. In its current form,
the executive order requires these housing developers to set aside 15 percent of

the units within a new development for affordable housing or, at the discretion of the Boston Redevelopment Authority, to create a greater number of affordable housing units offsite either directly or by contributing money to the city's affordable housing fund. Half of the housing is to be reserved for those at or below 80 percent of the area's median income; the other half is available to those between 80 percent and 120 percent of the area's median income.

Because this policy has taken the form of an executive order, critics fear that the policy could be set aside by a new mayor or, indeed, by the current mayor in order to lure attractive developments. For this reason, they have argued that the policy ought to be written into the zoning code. Even if it did become part of the zoning code, however, it is not certain that the inclusionary zoning policy would withstand court scrutiny under the Enabling Act. The Enabling Act contains no explicit grant of authority for inclusionary zoning. It merely states that exceptions to normal zoning regulations may be granted and that the exceptions may be subject to "appropriate conditions and safeguards." Moreover, the legislation that explicitly authorized Boston's linkage program, which was adopted after the *Bonan* decision, did not specifically authorize inclusionary zoning. Thus, although Boston's authority to impose an inclusionary zoning requirement may well be defensible, it does not have the definitive kind of authorization available to other cities across the country.

This lack of clarity stands in sharp contrast to the authority exercisable by Denver.[19] In 2002, the Denver City Council adopted an inclusionary zoning ordinance with the creation of its Moderately Priced Dwelling Unit program. The ordinance applies to all new residential developments of thirty or more units and requires that 10 percent of the units be affordable. It commits the city to expedite the zoning permitting process for these developments, to provide a density bonus, and to pay developers a subsidy ranging from $5,000 to $10,000 for each unit of affordable housing constructed. Given Denver's status as a home rule city under the Colorado Constitution, Denver clearly had the authority to enact this ordinance. It is important to recognize that the structure of home rule in Colorado reverses the presumption under Massachusetts law. In Massachusetts, due to the exemption of the power to tax and the power to regulate private or civil affairs from the scope of the home rule grant, Boston's ability to enact programs such as linkage or inclusionary zoning is in doubt absent relatively clear authorizing legislation. In Colorado, neither of these limitations on the home rule grant exists, and Denver's ability to act in the first instance is thus unquestioned. In fact, shortly after Denver enacted its ordinance, a Colorado legislator introduced legislation that would have prohibited local legislation requiring developers to sell property at below fair market value. The legislation was not enacted, and it is not certain that it would have been effective. In Colorado, state legislation preempts local legislation only if a court finds that the state legislation deals with matters of state concern. Given Colorado precedent, it is not clear whether the state legislation, if passed, would meet this standard.

Other cities benefit from a broad home rule grant similar to Denver's. Cities in California can generate support for linkage ordinances by relying on their local taxing power. Indeed, the possibility that Sacramento might adopt a local real estate transfer tax induced local realtors to support a proposed linkage ordinance instead. Given the exemption of taxation from the home rule grant in Massachusetts—an exemption that does not exist in California—Boston would not have the power to adopt a transfer tax on its own. It therefore could not use the possibility of such a tax to generate political support for an alternative such as a linkage ordinance. Although the advisory group that initially helped formulate Boston's linkage policy proposed a "neighborhood impact excise tax" on new development, the tax has not been imposed.[20] And it could not be imposed without state legislation authorizing its adoption.

Seattle is like Boston—and unlike Denver and San Francisco—in needing specific state legislative authority to impose impact fees on housing developers. Like Boston, it has received the necessary authority from the state. Chicago seems to have the power to adopt an inclusionary ordinance under its expansive home rule grant, but it has not adopted one. Chicago appears to be unwilling to take measures (either regulation or taxation) that might trigger the loss of business and development to the suburbs. Chicago is also potentially constrained by the state's unusually strict standard for evaluating the lawfulness of exactions.

RENT CONTROL

Two-thirds of Boston's housing units are rental units. The price Boston residents have to pay for rent is thus an essential factor in determining whether the city's housing supply is affordable. For more than twenty years, the measure employed by Boston (along with Brookline and Cambridge) to control the cost of housing was rent control. In 1970, the Massachusetts Legislature passed a rent control enabling act, which gave municipalities of fifty thousand or more the option to enact local rent control ordinances. The enabling legislation was needed because the Supreme Judicial Court had held that Massachusetts municipalities lacked home rule authority to impose rent control. Rent control was a regulation of the landlord-tenant relationship, the court found, and therefore was a private or civil law specifically exempted from city power by the Home Rule Amendment.[21] Boston thus enforced its rent control ordinance pursuant to special authorizing legislation. The goal was to ensure the availability of affordable rental housing for low income, elderly, and handicapped people and, at the same time, provide landlords with a reasonable return.

The question whether rent control is an effective means of promoting hous-ing affordability has, of course, been a subject of intensive academic and policy debate. But another issue is more relevant to our concern: What level of govern-ment should be empowered to make the policy judgment that resolves this debate? In Massachusetts, the state's citizens as a whole have resolved the debate, denying Boston the power to do so. In 1994, a statewide referendum prohibited rent control ordinances throughout the state. Although the ballot measure narrowly succeeded in statewide voting, a majority of those voting in each of the cities where rent con-trol ordinances were then in place voted against the measure. At the time, approxi-mately twenty-two thousand units in Boston were under a form of rent control that prohibited raising rents until the unit changed hands; another sixty-three thou-sand units were subject to a less stringent form of rent control under which rents could be raised annually up to a ceiling—usually 10 percent—set by city officials. Rents within the city increased by almost 50 percent from 1995 to 1999, after the statewide referendum repealed rent control. More recently, rents have stabilized, even moderately declined, in most Boston neighborhoods. Still, the median renter income in Boston is approximately \$33,000, and 54 percent of renter income is needed just to pay the rent. This figure is among the highest in the region.[22]

It is by no means clear that Boston would choose to impose rent control again even if it could. The Boston City Council has defeated a proposed rent con-trol ordinance. One of the reasons was its fear of the impact on the city's finances, given Boston's disproportionate reliance on the property tax. On the other hand, after the 1994 referendum prohibited rent control, Boston's City Council did pass condominium conversion regulations designed to preserve a balance of rental housing in the city, particularly for the elderly, handicapped, and people with low or moderate income. The ordinance provided rent increase and eviction pro-tections to tenants occupying units that had been converted to condominiums. Boston passed this legislation pursuant to what it thought was specific autho-rization from the state legislature. Although the legislation implementing the 1994 referendum expressly repealed a number of laws relating to the operation of rent control, it did not repeal legislation authorizing ordinances designed to protect tenants in buildings undergoing condominium conversion. The Supreme Judicial Court, however, struck down the Boston ordinance. The court held that Boston's attempt to protect prospective tenants of units converted to condo-miniums (as opposed to tenants occupying the units being converted) was an impermissible end run around the legislation prohibiting rent control.[23] Over twenty-five hundred rental units within Boston were lost to condominium development during the 1990s.

The rent control experience of other cities has been mixed. San Francisco and New York City continue to have rent control laws. In San Francisco, the rent control law limits the annual allowable increase according to a schedule based upon inflation, and it covers the vast majority of rental units within the city. San Francisco's rent control laws have become stricter in recent years, due in large part to citywide ballot initiatives. In New York City, on the other hand, recent state legislation has cut back on what once were the nation's most stringent rent control laws. Most units are no longer under strict rent control but, instead, are under a form of rent regulation known as rent stabilization. In 1993, the state legislature passed a law that removed luxury units or high-earning tenants even from rent stabilization. In 1997, with the statute authorizing rent control about to expire, the legislature further scaled back the rent protections available in New York State, including New York City. In 2003, again facing expiration of rent control authorization, the legislature again weakened rent protections. The 2003 legislation specifically targeted rent control in New York City.

Seattle and Denver are like Boston: they too lack the power to impose rent control. (Chicago has never attempted to adopt rent control.) Seattle had a local rent control ordinance in place for a number of years, but in the 1980s the state legislature passed a law outlawing any local ordinance regulating rents. Denver has no power to pass a rent control ordinance because Colorado courts have interpreted its normally broad grant of home rule authority as not being able to override conflicting state anti-rent-control legislation. Because rent control measures address a "mixed" issue of local and statewide concern, the Colorado Supreme Court ruled, home rule municipalities could not enact rent control in the face of conflicting state law.[24]

Middle Class Housing

In 2000, there were roughly 250,000 housing units in Boston, of which 160,000 were rental units.[25] Only rent control (now gone) and subsidized housing (continually in jeopardy) have affected a substantial part of this housing stock. And most of Boston's efforts remain directed at low and moderate income residents, not at Boston's housing problem more generally. Yet the high cost of Boston's housing affects every existing city resident as well as potential future residents. One way to confront this problem is to build considerably more housing for the middle class within the city. Indeed, unless this happens, it is hard to see how Boston can begin to make a major dent in the significant increases in housing prices—and high rents—that have characterized the city in recent years.

Is there something that Boston could do to address the high price of housing within the city? There clearly are major constraints on its doing so. One derives from the state laws and revenue constraints already discussed: key methods of increasing the housing supply or limiting price increases, ranging from subsidized housing to rent control, are not within Boston's capacity to implement. San Francisco, like Boston, has an affordability problem.[26] But San Francisco has tools to respond to this problem that Boston lacks. Unlike Boston, the city has the power to impose rent control and to control condominium conversions. Chicago too is an expensive city, but it uses tax increment financing funds to help subsidize affordable housing construction. And Cook County, of which Chicago is a part, decreases property taxes when multifamily buildings are rehabilitated and the required number of apartments are leased to low and moderate income households. Either strategy would be difficult for Boston to adopt given its lack of power over tax administration, although its recently granted tax increment financing authority now provides some room to follow Chicago's lead.

Another problem that Boston faces derives from the contradictions that bedevil its development policy even under the current legal regime. On the one hand, gentrification—and the attendant rise of property values and, therefore, housing prices—is one of the city's goals. Its economic development ideas fuel gentrification, in large part because of its state-imposed reliance on property taxes. In addition, the city itself has the understandable desire to improve the quality of housing in its neighborhoods. To be sure, the city is also committed to preserving and even increasing its amount of affordable housing. These policies, however, conflict with each other. And the gentrification policy now has the upper hand. This is not to say that gentrification and the availability of housing affordable to the middle class, as well as to the poor, are necessarily in conflict. A class-diverse city is a possible goal. Diverse cities have existed throughout history. But these days income diversity requires an extensive legal regime—one that ensures that existing and new housing remain affordable to the overwhelming majority of Boston residents while the city is upgraded. Such a legal regime might include regulations and subsidized housing: European cities have traditionally provided rent subsidies to a large spectrum of society and offered two to three times the amount of public housing that American cities provide. It might also include a wide variety of innovative property regimes, such as the promotion of limited equity ownership. Many of these kinds of initiatives are not within the city's power to implement.

Nevertheless, Boston is making efforts to address its overall affordable housing problem. The city is using the powers that it does have to promote affordable housing for the middle class through programs to offer mortgage protection, to stimulate housing production, and to provide assistance to small developments, including the production of dormitories for its colleges and universities.[27] Other cities are exploring additional possibilities. Under the Chicago Partnership for Affordable Neighborhoods, the city provides incentives to developers who agree to include affordable units, targeted at buyers within the range of 60 to 120 percent of area median income, in their market-rate developments. The sale price of affordable units cannot exceed $155,000. Chicago offers a variety of other incentives to developers as well: permit fee waivers of up to $10,000 per affordable unit, marketing assistance, perimeter site improvements and landscaping, density bonuses, and streamlining the permitting process. Its program also provides incentives for home buyers by granting a deferred interest-free loan at a level determined by the buyer's income (buyers are required, however, to obtain a first mortgage from a private lender).[28] It is not clear whether Boston could use these tools without first obtaining state legislative authorization to do so.

Under New York City's HomeWorks Program, builders can create one to four family homes in vacant, city-owned buildings and sell them to individual homebuyers at market prices. No income limits are imposed for buyers in most cases, and there also are no income or price limits for rental apartments. Home buyers are chosen through lotteries, although a preference is given to residents of the communities where the homes are located. Another condition is that buyers have to occupy at least one unit as their primary residence. Builders usually work with lenders to offer mortgages with low down payments, and, since the lenders take into account income from the rental apartments when qualifying homebuyers for loans, many of the homes are affordable to moderate- and middle-income buyers. To help make the program workable, the city also conveys the buildings to the builders at nominal prices, and it provides a partial tax abatement or a subsidy to homebuyers, as well as imposing a resale restriction.[29] As noted above, Boston does not have the city-owned housing that would enable it to adopt New York City's program. But, working with developers, elements of the program could help stimulate new housing initiatives.

These programs are valuable. But no one would contend that they constitute an intervention in the housing market powerful enough to make the cities affordable to the middle class. Moreover, it is important not to lose sight of the point that we made at the beginning of this section: the affordable housing crisis in the Boston metropolitan area, like elsewhere in the country, is regionwide. No real solution is likely until the regional context in which central cities' housing problems are located becomes a focus of government policy. Some cities have begun to recognize this point. In Chicago, a proposal has been made to establish a linkage program akin to Boston's that would operate on a regional scale. Such a regional approach seems to offer the most potential for Boston in the long term, while highlighting the extent to which Boston does not have the power to address some of its most pressing issues on its own.

EDUCATION

Education is perhaps the most important service city government provides. Many cities spend as much on education as on all other functions combined. But the role that public schools play in city life is much more fundamental than their impact on city finance. A strong school system affects the nature of a city's population: it attracts families with children to the city, and it keeps them in the city. The reverse is also true: the strength of a city's public school system is affected by the kind of people who live in the city. A school system that disproportionately serves children from poor families faces pressures—fiscal and otherwise—that many suburban school systems can avoid. These pressures may lead fewer new families to move to the city and cause existing residents to move out. There is, then, a direct relationship between the strength of a city's public schools and a city's politics. A city without many families with children is likely to pursue different goals than one with a different population. A strong public school system can affect the city's image for others as well. As the schools improve, companies considering where to locate—and state officials determining the scope of local powers—gain confidence in the city's ability to govern itself. An inadequate school system, on the other hand, can hinder a city's ability to attract investment and obtain the powers of self-government necessary to respond to the needs of the city's school system.

Not only is education important in all seven cities but the problems facing their school systems are remarkably similar. Some of the problems stem simply from their size. The school districts in the seven cities are significantly larger than any of the other school districts within their regions. There are 135 public schools in Boston, providing education to roughly sixty thousand students. Most of the other cities are comparable to Boston in terms of their school population, but New York City educates more than one million students in fourteen hundred schools and Chicago has almost 440,000 students in more than six hundred schools.[1] All of the school districts are coterminous with the city boundaries in which they are located.

But size is only one challenge to central city school systems. The demographic makeup of the students they serve is equally important. The composition of the student body in the public schools in all seven cities is significantly different from the composition not just of the neighboring suburbs but of city residents. There are more poor students than poor city residents. Seventy-two percent of Boston's students qualify for free or reduced-cost meals, although the percentage of Boston's population below the poverty line is only 19.5 percent. The number of students in other cities qualifying for reduced-cost lunches is high too, ranging from approximately 75 percent in Atlanta to roughly 40 percent in Seattle. Boston's schools are also significantly more populated by African Americans, Hispanics, and Asians than is the city as a whole. Although the city of Boston was 49.5 percent non-Hispanic white in 2000, only 14.6 percent of Boston's public school students were non-Hispanic white.[2] The non-Hispanic white population is small in every other city as well, although the distribution among the minority groups differs.[3] Two other characteristics of the school population are also important. The schools in six of the seven cities (all but Atlanta) are significantly affected by immigration. Children learning English as a second language make up 21 percent of Boston's student population; in San Francisco, the figure exceeds 30 percent.[4] And special education students make up 20 percent of the students enrolled in Boston's public schools, an unusually high figure. The percentage of students receiving special education in other cities ranged from 14 percent to 7 percent.[5]

The size and demographics of a school system are critical ingredients in the task of offering a quality education. And they are plainly not within a city's control. This in itself is a significant constraint on local control of education. These kinds of constraints are often either taken for granted or attributed to larger demographic forces that can only be solved through reforms that can involve completely redrawing municipal boundary lines. The role of state-imposed limits on local power is thus not usually seen as a factor in cities' inability to affect the size and demographics of their school systems. Indeed, there is often a strong assumption that if there is anything for which cities are responsible, it's "their" schools. The definition of what "their" schools are is seen as uncontroversial. And the conventional understanding of local matters usually places education near the top of the list. For many in search of local autonomy, education seems to be just the place to look. In the eyes of many education reformers, this is precisely why urban school systems are in such bad shape. The state has given them too much control.

In fact, however, there is no more local autonomy over education than in other areas critical to urban success. In Boston and elsewhere, state law affects local educational policy by regulating the organizational structure of the city's school system, the amount of funding available to it, and the content of the instruction that it provides. The state also defines the variety of educational alternatives—ranging from private schools to suburban schools—that are available to families whose children might otherwise attend the city's public schools. We address these forms of state intervention in this chapter. To be sure, within these limits, there are a variety of decisions cities can make to improve the quality of public education. We conclude by examining some of these options. But we begin by explaining why there is nothing natural about the ways in which states organize control over city schools. Indeed, while in the previous chapters Boston exemplifies how much a state can do to make it difficult for city government to address some of its most pressing problems, here Boston represents a notable example of how states sometimes recognize the important benefits that can come with giving cities a meaningful amount of control over the school system.

The Governing Structure of Education

In Massachusetts, as in other states, the state constitution places responsibility for education on the state itself, notwithstanding the fact that education is widely understood to be the quintessential local power. States therefore have to—and do—play a major role in determining how public education is provided in America. One substantial way in which states affect local education is through the establishment of the basic organizational structure of a city's school system.

The Organization of Local School Systems

The critical organizational issue is whether the schools are run by an independently elected school committee or by a school committee appointed by the mayor. The vast majority of school systems in Massachusetts, pursuant to state law, are run by elected school committees. Of our seven cities, four elect their school board members as well. Only New York City, Chicago, and Boston select them through mayoral appointments. This difference in organizational structure affects every aspect of the school system. A separately elected school committee is designed to be isolated from traditional city politics—at least mayoral politics—but remains subject to a politics of its own. Conversely, without control over the school system, the mayor lacks power over an essential ingredient—perhaps *the* essential ingredient—defining the city's population and future potential.

The mayor's power over the public schools in New York, Chicago, and Boston is of relatively recent origin. Boston's schools had been run by independently elected school committees for two hundred years when, in 1989, Boston residents narrowly voted in favor of an appointed school committee in a nonbinding referendum. In 1991, the state legislature approved Boston's home rule petition authorizing the establishment of the current, seven-member, mayoral-appointed committee. The statute provides that the mayor must select the seven members from a list of nominees given him by a thirteen-member nominating panel. The composition of the nominating panel, also defined by state statute, includes parents, teachers, administrators, and the business community—all selected by a related organization. The panel is charged to "strive to nominate individuals who reflect the ethnic, racial and socioeconomic diversity of the city of Boston and its public school population."[6] The state legislation puts the day-to-day operation of Boston's public schools in the hands not of the school committee but of the superintendent of schools, whom the school committee appoints. The superintendent has exclusive authority over contracting and personnel, while the school committee makes broad policy and, along with the mayor, establishes the school budget.

Notwithstanding this state-mandated organization, the mayor of Boston now has more influence on the operations of the city's schools than at any time in history. With the exception of New York City, no city comes close to Boston's degree of consolidation. Boston's school committee is not only appointed by the mayor but is dependent on the city for budgetary appropriations. In cities with elected school boards, the school committee's policies and budget are not subject to mayoral control. The elected school committee runs the schools—with the assistance of a superintendent it appoints—and establishes local educational policy. This independence of elected school committees from city government does not mean autonomy from state government. The school board in San Francisco is elected by local citizens and operates separately from the city government, but the governor proposes the state's school budget and the state legislature approves it. The state legislature also earmarks education funding for specific programs. Seattle's school district is similarly independent of the city government but subject to control by the state. But, unlike San Francisco, its elected school board sets the local property tax rate, subject to the approval of local voters.[7]

Chicago's city government exercises more control over education than cities with elected school committees—but not as much as Boston. The Chicago public school system is run by a seven-member board appointed by the mayor without the consent or approval of the city council. Indeed, a nominating panel, similar to the one that exists in Boston, was abolished in order to give the mayor unfettered control over his appointments. Once appointed, however, state leg-islation makes the school board autonomous within its sphere of governance, especially regarding budgetary matters. The school budget is separate from the city's budget, and the board decides on the collection and allocation of its funds. Final approval for the school's budget, as in California, comes not from the city but from the state.

Only New York City plays a role in running the public schools akin to Bos-ton's. Its ability to do so is bolstered by the fact that New York City, like Boston, funds its schools through its local property tax. State law enabled the mayor to displace the independent board of education and, together with the school chan-cellor, effectively run New York City's public schools. In addition, although until the mid-1990s state law promoted decentralization to community school boards within New York City, state law shifted power from the community school dis-tricts to the city's school chancellor. These changes in the state-created legal structure have enabled Mayor Bloomberg and the new school chancellor to make a number of controversial changes in the school system.[8]

The State's Role in School Finance and Classroom Instruction

Whether the city's schools are run by the mayor or by an independently elected school board, they operate under extensive controls imposed by the state. The most important of these controls concern school finance, curriculum, and test-ing requirements. The importance of these ingredients in educational policy does not need to be belabored. How much money schools have to spend and the substance of what they teach together largely determine the quality of education that schools provide.

SCHOOL FINANCE

The traditional funding source for American public schools is the local property tax. This widespread reliance on the property tax is problematic. It has long been recognized that there is a significant mismatch between the local property tax base and the needs of local schools. As a result, a wave of school finance litigation has swept the nation in the last thirty years. This litigation has directly affected local school funding in Boston, New York City, San Francisco, and Seattle; in Atlanta and Chicago, where similar litigation has not been brought or did not succeed, state legislatures have reformed school financing partly in reaction to the success of litigation elsewhere. Only Denver operates in a state legal structure that does not seek to address the inequalities generated by the dependence on the property tax.

The first round of school finance litigation was based on state and federal constitutional guarantees of equal protection of the laws. The state, it was argued, could not fund schools in a way that created fundamentally unequal educational opportunities. This was the theory articulated by the California Supreme Court in *Serrano v. Priest*, often considered the first modern-day educational finance challenge.[9] Although this theory is still embraced in some states, its rejection in 1973 by the United States Supreme Court, in *San Antonio Independent School District v. Rodriguez*, spawned a second wave of litigation.[10] This time, the argument was that state courts should invalidate existing school finance systems because they violated specific educational mandates found in state constitutions. These mandates generally require states to provide "a sound basic education," an "adequate" education, or something similar.

This second theory of judicial decision making fits comfortably with the historic way that states have taken responsibility for education. For years, states have provided a "foundation budget"—a specified amount of aid to support local school budgets—and have set general guidelines for the amount that local school districts should spend as a minimum overall. But foundation budgets often have a very tenuous connection to educational realities. They tend to be more of a reflection of political power and the extent to which the state is willing to allocate funds to cities than a statement of what a basic education requires. In New York State, the average expenditure by school districts is approximately $11,000 per student, with the bottom 10 percent spending almost $9,000 per student. Yet the foundation amount set by the state is $4,000 per student. The emphasis on state constitutional minimum requirements and the litigation seeking to raise them has increased foundation budgets for urban school systems. But it has also resulted in remedies that have increased state control over education. The rhetoric of the new line of cases emphasizes the role of the state, and the cases have increased state supervision over education even as states have increased funding.

This is what happened in Massachusetts. In *McDuffy v. Robertson*, decided in 1993, the Supreme Judicial Court ruled that the state had a duty imposed by the state constitution to ensure that every student receives an "adequate" education. The court found that children in less affluent communities "are not receiving their constitutional entitlement of education as intended and mandated by the framers of the Constitution."[11] In response, the state legislature passed the Education Reform Act of 1993. Its scope was sweeping and comprehensive, affecting virtually every aspect of education from school hours to graduation requirements. One of its most fundamental elements was its changed formula for state aid for education. The state committed itself to a seven-year increase in educational funding, raising total state educational aid from $1.3 billion in 1993 to nearly $2.8 billion in 2000. Although the Supreme Judicial Court recently held that the state legislature was making sufficient progress, the controversy over educational funding in Massachusetts has continued.[12]

Notwithstanding the increased state support for public education, the amount cities raise through property taxes remains significant. None of the seven school districts could operate without locally raised revenues. The state rules governing local revenue sources are therefore as decisive as state aid in determining the amount of support the schools receive.

CURRICULUM FRAMEWORKS
AND TESTING REQUIREMENTS

The increased money from the state came at a price: increased state involvement in educational policy. Two of the most important state controls deal with the curriculum and testing requirements. In Massachusetts, the Education Reform Act required the state Department of Education and state Board of Education to establish curriculum frameworks in the core subjects of mathematics, science and technology, history and social sciences, English, foreign languages, health, and the arts. State agencies were also authorized to provide standards for subjects ranging from nutrition to the Federalist Papers and from computer skills to AIDS. (The legislature itself has mandated education on subjects ranging from the Bill of Rights to physical education.) In addition, state agencies were empowered to set teacher certification standards, provide for the length of the school day and school year, and declare a school district "under-performing" and, if so, intervene in its operation.

The Education Reform Act also mandated that students be tested on their knowledge of basic skills. In 1998, the state Department of Education adopted a method of assessment, a standardized test called the Massachusetts Comprehensive Assessment System (MCAS). It proposed the test not only to assess the capabilities of the students but to provide useful feedback to the state so that remedial measures could be taken to bring all schools up to par. Indeed, the department formally requested that local school districts adopt the test as an official and uniform graduation requirement. The test was to be taken in the fourth, eighth, and tenth grades, and would focus on English and math.

Other cities also must comply with state-established testing and curricular design requirements. One should not assume that this kind of state intervention is antagonistic to the interests of the local school system. States frequently describe their interventions as efforts to assist school systems to identify strengths and weaknesses in their educational programs. Indeed, the Chicago Board of Education has incorporated the state testing scheme into its performance-based-management regime on its own. Nevertheless, both the state-imposed curriculum mandates and testing requirements determine much of the structure of local education. And both remain controversial. One problem is the relationship between the two: testing regimes influence curricular choices. Another is the relationship between curriculum mandates and school finance. The state funding may not take into account the kind of quality education required to use the curriculum frameworks effectively. Yet another problem is the relationship between testing results and class difference. As a Boston Foundation report puts it about testing in Massachusetts: "To date, MCAS results have been highly correlated with family income: low-income communities tend to fare worse, high income communities tend to fare better."[13] Finally, from a city's point of view, there is an even more basic concern: What does "local control of education" mean? Choices do remain, but how much are these choices constrained by state-imposed requirements about the substance of and support for education?

The State's Role in Establishing Educational Alternatives

State control over organizational structure, finance, and instructional content are not the only constraints that affect the management of a local school system. Cities are also required to take into account—and compete with—a number of alternatives to their public school systems. It might seem odd to think of the state as playing a key role in making these alternatives available. But the state's role is significant. Sometimes the state directly creates these alternatives, such as when it authorizes the creation of charter schools without involving local school committees. At other times, the state's influence is less visible but no less important. The fact that school district lines are drawn to track municipal boundary lines—thereby ensuring an urban/suburban distinction in schooling—is, after all, itself an artifact of state law rather than local choice.

Educational alternatives available to city residents can play a positive role in inducing families with children to stay in the city. They can also generate useful competitive pressure on the city schools to improve. But the restrictions that the state places on local revenue collection produce a push/pull effect that leads school officials both to support and reject the available alternatives. State aid for education is dependent on enrollment, and this dependence makes it hard for the city to deal with significant, even if predictable, fluctuations in its public school population. Widespread withdrawal creates a hole in the budget that is difficult to patch, while sudden growth burdens facilities more than the extra money generated can accommodate.

One illustration of this push/pull effect is the impact of charter schools and parochial schools on the Boston public school system. Boston officials have been

vocal in their disapproval of charter schools not only because they have no control over how most charter schools are created but because every student who
enrolls in one takes money away from the public schools. At the same time, the
financial troubles of Boston's Catholic Archdiocese have generated fears that
the closing of parochial schools in the city would have a significant impact on
Boston's school system if it produces a large influx of students. This push/pull
dynamic undermines the city's ability to consider educational alternatives from
a broader perspective. School officials are understandably concerned that they
will lose money every time a student leaves for a charter school. A change in
enrollment does not change Boston's tax base, but it affects the educational aid
on which the operation of the school system depends. Parents are equally concerned that their children might be left in an inadequately funded public school
system. Charter schools and private schools can limit their enrollment or even
close down, but the Boston public school system can do neither.

Private Schools

One way to see the influence of educational alternatives is to consider the number of city residents who do not use the city schools. Approximately one quarter
of Boston's eighty thousand school-age children do not attend Boston's public
schools. Of these, almost 13,500 are in private schools, four thousand in charter
schools, and three thousand in suburban schools. Parochial schools, with eleven
thousand students, educate the vast majority of the private school population.
Only Seattle has a greater proportion—31 percent—of its students in private
schools. But the numbers elsewhere are also significant. New York, Denver, and
Chicago have nearly 20 percent, and the figure in San Francisco is almost one
quarter. Equally significantly, more than half of the non-Hispanic white students
who live in Boston attend private schools—a higher percentage than almost
anywhere in the country. While Boston's public schools are 14 percent non-
Hispanic white, the private school population is approximately 45 percent non-
Hispanic white, much closer to the citywide average (the city itself is 49.5 percent
non-Hispanic white).[14] The number of non-Hispanic white students in private
schools in Boston is often attributed to the federal court decision that ordered
the desegregation of its public schools. Whether because of racial bias or parental frustration over sending their children to schools outside their neighborhoods, the non-Hispanic white population of Boston's public schools dropped
from 64 percent in 1970, before the desegregation order, to the 14 percent level
in 2000. Many African American parents also began sending their children to
local private schools to avoid having them bused across the city. Others contend,
however, that it is the city's prior history of racial segregation—not its efforts to

integrate the schools—that has generated the increased enrollment in private schools. One thing is clear: private schools are very popular.

Despite their importance to the city, the city has little influence over the private schools that serve city residents. In Massachusetts, there is an attempt to maintain a separation between public and private schools. Private schools are not under the supervision of local school committees, although they must receive school committee approval to operate. This approval requirement is designed to ensure that private schools provide instruction that is at least equivalent to the public schools. But the Massachusetts courts have made it clear that no public money can be spent to support private schools. This is not the rule everywhere. Illinois offers a tax break for private education expenditures of up to $500. But this tax break does not translate into city power: it does not enable the city to provide similar or greater support. The Colorado Supreme Court, by contrast, struck down a state-wide voucher program that required Denver and other school districts to pay a portion of the private school tuition (including in religious schools) of children living in the school district. The court concluded that the measure violated a state constitutional requirement of local control over education because it directed the expenditure of local school funds for other than local school purposes.[15]

Boston has made significant efforts to induce parents to enroll their children in public rather than private schools even though private schools save the city a substantial amount of money. As one article pointed out: "with a per pupil cost of $7,428, private schools in New York City save the city $2.2 billion; in Chicago $924 million (1990 data)... and in Boston nearly $80 million."[16] Nevertheless, private schools remain controversial: they are perceived as offering a better education and offering it only to those who can afford it.

Charter Schools

Unlike private schools, charter schools are a hybrid institution. Their funds come from the state and city budgets, not private tuition paid by parents, but they have substantial independence from elected school boards and the city government. This is a large part of their appeal. Charter schools are designed to serve as a model for imitation, provide more opportunities for students and parents to select schools with different characteristics, and, through competition, make local school districts more accountable. The fact that charter schools are part of the public school system, however, does not mean cities control them. It is the state that plays a large role in defining the powers of charter schools and their relationship to city government.

The Massachusetts Education Reform Act introduced charter schools into the state's education system. Thus, ironically, at the same time that the Education

Reform Act established more standardization for Massachusetts public schools with the introduction of curriculum frameworks, it carved out, for a limited number of alternative schools, a space for nonstandardization. The original charter school format was the commonwealth charter school—a public school operated by a board of trustees independent of the local school committee. Any nonprofit business or corporate entity, combination of ten or more parents, or two or more teachers is allowed to apply to the state board of education for a charter to become a commonwealth charter school. (Private schools and parochial schools are explicitly denied the ability to apply.) An application for a commonwealth charter school does not require approval from the locality's mayor or school committee; all that is required is approval by the state. By contrast, a Horace Mann charter school, authorized by the state several years after the commonwealth charter school, is an attempt to allow public school committees and teachers to take advantage of this form of experimentation without having to break free from the school district. Horace Mann charter schools are initiated by the public school system itself; they require school committee support before an application can be filed with the state. Once created, however, their operation is explicitly placed outside of the supervision of local school committees. Of these two options, only the commonwealth charter school has truly taken off. There are sixteen commonwealth charter schools but only two Horace Mann charter schools in Boston.[17]

There are charter schools in every other city we examined except Seattle. In Atlanta, the charter school system is almost the opposite of Boston's. This is largely because state law gives local officials much more say over charter school approval. All charter schools are subject to approval by local school boards, and funding for charter schools is allocated by the locality. Like Boston, there are two types of charter schools—conversions and start-ups—but the schools converted by, and run by, local school districts were adopted first, while the start-ups were added later. Chicago's charter schools are not directly run by the school district either, but they must be sponsored by local education authorities; they are accountable to Chicago's Board of Education as well as to the state. California law has a very different, and unusual, structure: a request for charter approval must be submitted first to the school district, but if it is rejected, it can then be presented to the state Board of Education. The local school district retains supervisory power over the charter schools that it approves but not over the ones that it rejects and the state approves. For those charter schools, the state is the supervisory entity. (Of the eleven charter schools in operation in San Francisco as of 2002, nine were approved by the city.)

Some states have been reluctant to permit charter schools at all. Washington voters rejected statewide initiatives that would have authorized charter schools in 1996 and 2000, and legislative proposals also failed in 1998, 1999, 2000 and

2003. It was not until 2004 that the legislature approved the use of charter schools even on an experimental basis. The legislation required a statewide referendum to take effect, and a referendum has so far failed to pass.

Even where they have been accepted, charter schools are controversial. Some of the controversy relates to school financing. Under Massachusetts state law, students who leave a public school for a charter school take the average cost per student spent by the school district with them. The state gives these funds directly to the charter school and deducts the amount from state aid to the school district. Critics argue that this use of the average expense per student fails to take account of the variation among students. The figure includes the cost of students in expensive special education, English-acquisition, and similar programs. Yet charter schools take a disproportionate number of students who require only a regular education and can spend more per student than a public school can. Denver operates under a very different model. While Boston's charter schools receive more per pupil than Boston spends on a standard public school education, Colorado law limits the amount that charter schools can receive to 80 percent of what a public school spends per pupil. (Colorado's charter schools can seek budgetary increases directly from the voters through an initiative.) Denver has become more accepting of charter schools than Boston is. Charter schools now educate 3 percent of Denver's schoolchildren.

One point about charter schools is not controversial: they are much in demand. In Boston, the waiting list for the 2006–2007 school year (6,500 students) exceeded enrollment (5,200 students). An increase in the number of charter schools, however, requires additional state legislation and additional state approvals—a process bound to generate continued political opposition.

Suburban Schools

Private schools and charter schools provide alternatives to the city's public schools by offering something different than a public school. Suburban school systems offer an alternative version of the same idea. Parents move out of the central city to enroll their children in a public school located in another school district. And families choose not to move to the city either out of concerns about its schools or the perceived advantages of suburban public schools. Fundamental changes in the overall relationship between central cities and their metropolitan regions would be necessary to alter the impact that suburban schools now have on central city public schools. The legal definition of the borders that divide cities within the same region from each other is crucial to framing the meaning of the central city/suburb divide not only for schools but for all city services. Moreover, the factors that affect a family's decision about where to live within a metropolitan area go well beyond the quality of the public schools. These broader regional issues are explored in our final chapter. For now, it is important simply to note that state law is responsible for organizing metropolitan areas and, therefore, that state law would have to be reformed to reorganize them.

It is hard to overstate the impact of suburban public schools on the central city public school system. One way to see their importance is to examine the decline in the number of school-age children in central cities. In Boston, there has been a 35 percent drop in the school population since the 1960s, a figure that dwarfs the number of children living in Boston who attend private or charter schools. In San Francisco, public school enrollment is 60 percent of what it was in the 1960s. Atlanta had nearly ten thousand fewer students in its public schools in 2004 than it had a decade before, and fewer than half the students it had in 1969. Seattle's public school enrollment peaked at 99,326 in 1962, but plummeted to 47,400 by the end of the twentieth century. In 2002, Chicago's public school system had about 440,000 students, down from 580,292 students in 1969. These declines were significantly greater than population losses in any city; in some of the cities, overall population increased.

In two cities, public school enrollment is on the rise, if only slightly. In 2002, New York City's public schools had about 100,000 more students than they had a decade earlier. This increase brought enrollment almost to the level reached in the early 1970s, when a sharp decline began. A substantial part of this growth is due to an influx of immigrant children that has mitigated the effects of suburbanization. In Denver, public school enrollment in 2003 had increased by about ten thousand students over the previous decade. On the other hand, Denver's public schools have only 75 percent of the students they had forty years ago. Even in the New York City and Denver metropolitan areas, suburban schools remain *the* primary alternative to the central city public school systems.

One approach that Boston has pursued to bridge the suburban/urban school divide—one that stands out for its innovation—is its Metropolitan Council for Educational Opportunity program. The program enables parents in Boston to have access to suburban schools, with the participating suburbs getting the benefit of diversity in their schools. The program was not originally conceived as a permanent alternative to Boston's public school system. African American activists established it in the mid-1960s, before desegregation was fully implemented in Boston, as an "interim program" for about two hundred students. After almost forty years, the program is still operating. Now, approximately three thousand students are bused across city lines every morning to attend suburban schools. This is close to the number of students that stay in Boston and attend nonparochial private schools. Since the program was established as part of the civil rights movement, it has largely served African American students. (The program now serves a small percentage of Hispanic and Asian students as well.) The waiting list is over fifteen thousand students. Given the fact that the public school enrollment is approximately sixty thousand students, this demand is extraordinary. Some parents place their children on the waiting list just weeks after they are born. Critics argue that the program siphons off good students that would benefit the public school system if they remained in it. Efforts have even been made to abolish the program altogether. But the prospect of parents who participate in the program moving out of Boston slows abolition efforts.

Only a few other cities in the country have anything like the Metropolitan Council for Educational Opportunity program. No other city we examined does. Nor does any city have another kind of interdistrict solution: a consolidated school district that combines central city and suburban schools. On the contrary, most of the cities that have experimented with public–school-choice programs have restricted themselves to intradistrict alternatives.

This is hardly surprising. The current legal structure in most states permits cities to implement interdistrict options only with suburban consent or as a result of direct state intervention. Even in Massachusetts, despite the support for it, the Metropolitan Council for Educational Opportunity program has not expanded to new suburbs—or within existing suburban schools—since 1978. Hence, the long waiting list.

Educational Reform in the Public Schools

Even though cities are subject to the state-established constraints we have described, they can—and do—affect the quality of the education they offer their students. There are a variety of possible ways cities try to improve public education. We consider here six possible strategies: enriching the public schools; modifying the system of instruction; organizing the community to support education; creating different levels of education for different kinds of students; expanding school choice within the school district; and transforming the kind of student body that attends the public schools. These strategies overlap; many, perhaps all, can be pursued simultaneously. But city power to implement the six strategies varies considerably. A complex combination of detailed state mandates and local discretion shape the way cities undertake efforts to reform their schools.

Enriching the Public Schools

Since 1996, Boston has adopted two reform plans designed to enrich the public school system. Efforts include building new school buildings, buying computers, guaranteeing full-day kindergarten, and expanding 2–6 p.m. after-school programs. These kinds of undertakings are more dependent than other strategies on Boston's ability to generate revenue. But there are other complexities as well. We consider here only one illustration: reducing class size.

Reducing class size is expensive: it requires hiring more teachers and providing them with adequate classrooms and materials. The Massachusetts Education Reform Act provides funds that can be used for class size reduction, but the act does not require that they be used for that purpose. Other states dedicate funds to enable smaller classes. Reducing class size, however, is more complicated than simply spending more money. Consider the relationship between the teacher-student ratio and class size. One can calculate a teacher-student ratio by dividing the number of students by the number of teachers. Boston's student-teacher ratio is quite low: thirteen students to one teacher. San Francisco's is seventeen to one. Class size is a different number. Boston's average class size ranges from twenty-two (for grades K–2) to thirty-one (for grades 9–12). Even though San Francisco has a higher teacher-student ratio, its average class sizes are about the same as Boston's. Atlanta has a student-teacher ratio close to Boston's, but its average class size is significantly lower—in the low twenties, or dipping under twenty, across the board.

What explains Boston's combination of low teacher-student ratio and (comparatively) high class size? One major reason is that a substantial number of teachers in Boston are hired for special and bilingual education.[18] Seventy percent of Boston's school children are classified as requiring "regular" education, yet only about 50 percent of the teachers are responsible for these children. The rest of the teachers concentrate on special education or on assisting students with limited English proficiency. Other cities have special needs students too. But Boston classifies more of its students—approximately one quarter of the student population—as needing special education. Provision of special education is a state mandate, and state funding has fallen short of the needed expenditures. Class size, therefore, stems not just from the school system's overall resources but from the way that those resources must be allocated. Boston's ability to shift resources to regular education from special education is constrained by its limited home rule authority. So is its ability to determine how to educate students with limited English proficiency. In November 2002, Massachusetts voters adopted an initiative eliminating bilingual education for those with limited English proficiency, replacing it with English language immersion. Class size for regular education—and not just for English learners—will be affected by this statewide policy.

Modifying the System of Instruction

Since 1994, Boston has established nineteen pilot schools for grades K-12, with approximately fifty-seven hundred students (more students, one should note, than are in charter schools, nonparochial private schools, or the Metropolitan Council for Educational Opportunity program). Unlike charter schools, these pilot schools are not a product of state legislation. The city itself created them as models for innovation. They have considerable autonomy over their budget, staffing, governance, calendar, and curriculum. This freedom is from Boston school committee's rules—and the requirements of union contracts—not from state law. Still, although the pilot schools operate with the average per-student budget of the public schools, they are small (fewer than five hundred students), have smaller class sizes, require more hours of school, and devote significantly more time to collaborative planning and improved teaching. Their racial and ethnic makeup is close to that of the public schools—closer than are private schools or charter schools. They are also like the public school system as a whole in terms of special education students, although students are somewhat less poor than those in the system as a whole.[19] Studies indicate that the personalized learning environment, greater flexibility, and teacher collaboration in pilot schools have had a significant effect on the education of their students.

Boston's pilot schools are part of a national trend toward smaller and somewhat more autonomous schools within large, urban school systems. New York and Chicago have similar programs initiated at the local level. By 1997 there were more than 150 small schools in New York City, with fifty-two more planned, funded by almost $60 million in grants from the Bill and Melinda Gates Foundation. Chicago has twenty-four such schools, created after the 1995 Chicago School Reform Act increased the mayor's power over academic performance. San Francisco and Atlanta are also beginning to pursue small-school reforms. As the efforts of New York and Chicago demonstrate—and as Boston's pilot school program exemplifies—giving the city authority over its school system can enable innovative and effective school reform, even though revenue limits are always a constraint.

Organizing the Community

Another ingredient within Boston's capacity to implement—one that has limited financial implications—is the involvement of both parents and the community at large in the support and operation of the schools. It has become commonplace to recognize that a successful educational system cannot rely on the schools alone. The attitudes and efforts of the student's family and peers, even before the child is old enough to go to school, have important effects on the prospect for learning and achievement. According to some scholars, community engagement is an equally essential ingredient in improving urban education.[20] Boston's efforts in this regard appear to lag behind some of our comparison cities—even though the city appears to be empowered to adopt a least some of the innovations embraced by these other cities.

Chicago has gone the furthest in creating institutions for community organization. In 1988, state legislation provided all 560 of Chicago's elementary and high schools with a local school council. These organizations were given the responsibility of developing a "school improvement plan," a three-year plan created for the purpose of improving the quality of the school's education. Denver too has made school-based decision making and parent-community involvement district policy. The key innovation was the creation of collaborative decision-making teams for each school in the district. These teams include the school principal, four teachers, one classified employee, four parents, and a representative of the business community. They develop improvement plans for their school and are empowered, among other things, to schedule teachers' time, determine school budgets, and select new faculty. In Seattle, a new district superintendent decentralized operations in 1995, with individual schools gaining control of about half of district spending. New York City, on the other hand, has moved in the opposite direction. It has treated greater mayoral control, and enhanced power for the superintendent, as an antidote to the problems created by the decentralized governance structures that the city adopted in the late 1960s. In 1996, the decentralization movement in New York City effectively came to an end.

As the experiences of these cities demonstrate, decentralization of authority within the public school system is controversial. In Boston, the divergence between the demographics of the public school system and of the city as a whole complicates such an effort. For our purposes, it is important simply to note that Boston has the power to increase community participation in educational decision making more than it has.

Creating Different Levels of Education

The virtues and defects of separating out different kinds of students within the school system are widely debated. The creation of separate systems stands in considerable tension with efforts to improve the overall quality of the schools. Educators tend to consider overall improvement in the school district necessary to convince parents and students that public schools can compete with the available alternatives. This is the philosophy behind the reform efforts considered so far: enriching the schools, modifying methods of instruction, and organizing the community. Parents, however, have alternatives to the public school system, and they are often primarily interested in maximizing the benefits for their own children. In a world where differentiation sells and differences in abilities among students are significant, magnet schools and tracking may be one of the major ways to keep some families in central city public schools.

Like many other large metropolitan school systems, Boston has chosen to maintain a series of educational tiers tailored to provide different educational opportunities for students at different ability levels. Boston has three elite public examination schools and a series of formal and informal internal tracking systems that group schoolchildren into classifications based on projected learning ability. The examination schools educate more than five thousand students and are some of the best schools in Boston. These schools demonstrate that Boston is more than capable of managing an elite school. Lowell High School in San Francisco and three elite schools in New York City are comparable to Boston's examination schools. All of these schools have very competitive admission policies. Over twenty-eight thousand students take the test for admission to New York's three schools—even though, to give a sense of the space available, there are only 850 spots at its Stuyvesant High School.

The racial composition of examination schools varies. Moreover, it is likely to be affected by the June 2007 decision by the U.S. Supreme Court limiting race-conscious integration of the public schools. Racial issues were important even before the Supreme Court's decision. In Boston, non-Hispanic whites and Asians are disproportionately represented in two of the three examination schools while, at the third, about 50 percent of the student body is African American. These figures are, in part, the result of a 1998 decision by the United States Court of Appeals declaring Boston's effort to promote affirmative action in its examination schools unconstitutional under the Equal Protection Clause. Similarly, a settlement in San Francisco provided that race could no longer be taken into account for admission to Lowell High School. The school board altered the admissions criteria so that 70 percent of the new students are chosen by tests, with the admission of the remaining 30 percent based on measures such as artistic talent, athletics, recommendations, and family income. Chicago's elite magnet schools have taken race into account when selecting students, although a committee has explored alternatives, such as economic status and ZIP codes. New York City's Stuyvesant High School, on the other hand, has no racial preferences—and it also does not have many African-American or Hispanic students.[21]

The magnet schools are not the only method of providing different kinds of education for different groups of students. School officials have traditionally divided public school students early in their educational career into classrooms and programs that determine their educational trajectory. This kind of tracking was much more prominent and widespread in Boston before the Educational Reform Act was passed in 1993. It was previously difficult to move from one track to another, and tracking was criticized as a caste system that predetermined students' fate early in their life. The Education Reform Act called for an end to the tracking of students into lower, less rigorous tracks. Mandates by the state Board of Education, along with changing sentiments about tracking, altered the tracking practices of the Boston public school system. Boston was quick to eliminate tracking for "remedial" education, although advanced tracks have been retained in part to bolster placements in examination schools.

Meanwhile, students are tracked into special education at the other end of the spectrum. Many of the children in these programs require, and benefit from, special attention. Still, a large number of schoolchildren with acute learning problems are placed in programs that separate them from other schoolchildren for portions of the day. Children posing problems in overcrowded classrooms are sometimes placed in special education programs because regular education teachers lack the time and resources to dedicate themselves to giving them the kind of attention they need. And, as we have seen, teachers are hired to serve a small number of special education students, leaving fewer teachers to handle the rest of the school's population.

As the programs just discussed demonstrate, decisions about the creation of elite schools, tracking, and special education are in the hands of the local school system only to a limited extent. Decisions by the state regarding educational policy and, equally important, judicial decisions concerning the constitutional limits of policies that favor racial diversity, constrain city discretion. The school systems are also affected by the intense debate about the wisdom and nature of differential levels of education for public school students. Within the limits of state policy and judicial decision making, however, there is room for school committees to make decisions about differentiation within the public schools.

Expanding School Choice

Spatial segregation along socioeconomic lines often characterizes the makeup of individual schools within a single school district because school assignments are based on where students live in the city. One way to overcome this form of class and race segregation is to permit students within a school district to choose a school that is not in their immediate neighborhood. Boston, like many cities, allows some—albeit limited—opportunities for intradistrict school choice. Although all of the spots at every school in Boston were once reserved for students within the school's "walk zone," this proportion was reduced to 50 percent. The change withstood a constitutional attack based on the contention that the plan, which prevented some white students from attending schools within their walk zone, was adopted for racially discriminatory reasons. In New York City, which has had an intradistrict school choice program since 1993, priority is given to neighborhood children, and cross-community transfers are allowed only if there is space, which is rare. San Francisco adopted a five-year plan in 2001 creating a system of intradistrict school choice for its students. In deciding where to place their students, the school district considers factors such as parental preference, where a child's sibling attends school, the particular needs of individual students, enrollment near a child's home, and diversity. Seattle's local school choice program, which allowed race as a factor in admission, was declared unconstitutional in the 2007 Supreme Court decision mentioned above.[22]

Although subject to limitations, intradistrict choice programs are within local discretion to implement. But a more fundamental version of school choice—one that would allow interdistrict transfers between central city and suburban schools or even to private schools—are not within the city's discretion. State law determines whether the suburbs have the option of refusing to admit central city students to their schools.

Transforming the Student Body

There are fundamental questions posed by school districts in the seven cities that current policies do not address. Can the public school system, populated overwhelmingly by students from poor families, remain competitive for middle-class students against the appeal of private schools, charter schools, and suburban schools? Is there a way to attract the kind of students who now attend suburban schools, private schools, and charter schools into the public school system as a whole, not just to its elite schools? No matter how much enrichment or classroom innovation or community organizing is implemented, is the divergence between the nature of the student body and of the city population as a whole an impediment threatening popular support for, and the quality of, the city's public education system?

Questions of this kind are not often on the school committee's agenda. The school committee is obligated to educate the student body it is given, however it is constituted. But the city itself is in a different position. It needs to decide the extent to which its future will ensure that middle class residents, including middle-class families with school-age children, live in the city. If it adopts this objective, it must establish a housing and development policy so that this constituency can live in town. It must obtain revenues and make expenditures to achieve the same end. And, of course, it must improve the quality of education—in ways such as those canvassed above—in order to entice residents not just to live in the city but to send their children to the public schools rather than to the alternatives. Every one of these kinds of policy initiatives, we have argued, is both constrained by state law and, to some extent, permitted by it.

Part III
CITY FUTURES

The detailed constraints explored in part II serve as the background for the final four chapters: our exploration of alternative futures for cities in the twenty-first century. The specific legal structures explored in part II—home rule, revenue and expenditures, land use and development, and education—are key ingredients in whatever alternatives cities might want to pursue. We limit ourselves to the four futures we have already introduced: the global city, the tourist city, the middle class city, and the regional city. In the chapters that follow, we emphasize not only the kinds of constraints imposed by the legal rules but a number of additional limits on the cities' ability to pursue policies designed to achieve these goals. We emphasize as well the choices that cities can now make. But these choices often generate state responses—and, sometimes, more constraints. Within this structure/agency dynamic, the future of American cities and the new urban age that they will represent is being forged.[1]

The four futures are not equally available to American cities. Limits on finance and on city power have made it hard for major American central cities to support the kinds of services that middle class residents tend to want. This legal structure has led central cities to turn away from making service provision their primary function and to concentrate instead on becoming a facilitator for city economic development. Economic development has itself become defined largely in terms of a focus on outsiders—on investors who drive the global economy and on nonresidents who have an interest in visiting the city. These objectives are the essential characteristics of the global city and tourist city, respectively. Because the legal structure of local finance and city power enable major cities to pursue these options more easily than the alternatives, it affects a city's future whether or not city residents and city officials think it moves the city in the right direction. At the heart of the inquiry into the legal structure that governs city decision making, therefore, is the way it affects the place of local democracy in American life.

The existing legal structure also has a major impact on the kind of metropolitan region in which the central cities operate. The service delivery function—above all, education—has long been a selling point for suburbanization across the United States. This sales pitch works best if the region is fragmented into a multiplicity of unconnected cities, so that moving from the central city to a suburb, or from one suburb to another, changes one's life. In the middle of the twentieth century, this kind of resident-service vision fueled the desire for suburban living, leaving to the central cities the task of business development. Since the 1970s, however, this residential/business distinction between central cities and their suburbs has virtually disappeared. Business development has become essential to the future of the suburbs as well as the central cities, while central cities have sought to find new ways to lure more people to live within their borders. State law has not kept up with these regional implications of local governmental power. In chapter 10 we will explore how the legal structure generates the current organization of metropolitan regions—and present ideas about how it might be changed.

If cities had local autonomy, the state-created structures we describe in the following chapters would not matter. If cities had no room to make their own decisions, our focus on local options would not matter either. It is because cities are both bound by state law and the focal point for the aspirations of their residents and potential residents that exploring the differences between the global city, tourist city, middle class city, and regional city becomes important. It is hard to see the current legal structure as well designed either to facilitate or deter any of the possible futures for city life. Although the legal system has significant effects on a city's options, making some futures easier to pursue than others, many of the existing rules seem not to be based on a conception of the proper role of cities in American life. Instead, many of them seem to reflect state decision makers' suspicions about local decision making, whatever the topic. A belief in their own judgments and a distrust of local judgments characterize too many of the decisions made by state officials. This suspicion of local democracy is not a good basis for building America's urban future. The early proponents of home rule understood that local governments should be organized in a way that promotes substantive ideas about the proper direction for cities to pursue while affording them the flexibility they need to realize those ideas through their own efforts and creativity. Today's cities demonstrate a lack of this kind of understanding. Even the goals now seemingly promoted—the global city and the tourist city—are frustrated. That's why, we conclude, every state in the nation needs to revise its local government structure to make it relevant for the twenty-first century.

THE GLOBAL CITY

Over the last few decades, an increasing number of urban scholars have explored what John Friedmann called, in his seminal article, "The World Cities Hypothesis."[1] In advancing his hypothesis, Friedmann rejected the widely held view that key features of the globalization of the world economy—the dramatically enhanced mobility of capital, sharp reductions in travel time, unprecedented advances in communications technology, and large-scale domestic and international migration—have deprived cities of their historic economic advantage. On the contrary, he argued, cities have become even more important because the changing nature of the world economy requires the centralization of key functions in particular cities, even if other aspects of the production processes are dispersed. Business leaders move their companies to world cities to ensure proximity to other corporate headquarters or to a variety of specialized services (such as public relations firms, legal offices, and financial institutions) that have become indispensable to effective participation in the global marketplace. Immigrants—domestic and international, rich and poor—move to the same cities to provide the support services that the ever-more-concentrated business sector needs. There is, in short, a worldwide demand for specific locations, a demand that has organized the world's cities into a hierarchy ranked in terms of their relationship with the global economy.

What constitutes a world city is a matter of considerable dispute. In this chapter, we concentrate on one ingredient that everyone seems to acknowledge: the city's role in international finance. In her important book *The Global City,* Saskia Sassen concentrates on this ingredient. Global cities, she says, now function in four new ways: first, as highly concentrated command points in the organization of the world economy; second, as key locations for finance and for specialized service firms, which have replaced manufacturing as the leading economic sectors; third, as sites of production, including the production of innovations, in these leading industries; and fourth, as markets for the products and innovations produced.[2]

As this description suggests, not every city in the world can be a global city. At any given time, only a small number of major cities perform the role described above, and a major topic in the literature concerns which cities qualify.[3] True global cities—above all, London, New York, and Tokyo—function as international economic actors on a world scale. Other cities, however, can be somewhere on the hierarchical list, at least as a secondary actor. And every city can seek to raise its place on the list of competitors for a more important role.

The focus of the global cities literature has been on the economic activities of global private business, not the role of city governments. Indeed, the literature's references to London, New York, and Tokyo are generally not to the cities themselves but to a physical territory not coterminous with the boundaries of any local government. In John Friedmann's definition, the word "city" has

> an economic definition. A city in these terms is a spatially integrated economic and social system at a given location or metropolitan region. For administrative or political purposes the region may be divided into small units which underlie...the economic space of the region.[4]

Given this definition, the use of city names to refer to a territory larger than the city obscures the distinction between an economically defined region and individual cities. Moreover, not only do world city scholars pay little attention to the power of city governments but they suggest that cities, as they define them, have begun to loosen the bonds of national or subnational control. According to one scholar, globalization enables "wealthier 'world cities'...[to] operate like city-states in a networked global economy, increasingly independent of regional and national mediation." Another argues that "cities have become increasingly decoupled from local (i.e., regional or national) political geography as the salience of their position in international networks of investment and trade has grown."[5] Although these scholars do not suggest that global cities have separated from their host nations altogether, they do claim that global cities have entered into a new phase in history. Their orientation has become external rather than internal. Their associations have become global rather than domestic. And, insofar as they are global cities, they are becoming so important that they may be able to reverse the direction in which power flows: some cities may begin to dictate how nations behave rather than the other way around.

We take a different stance. Our focus is on city government policy: on what cities can and cannot do to foster their status of being a global city. It is important to recognize that neither Friedmann nor Sassen embraces the conception of being a global city as a normative goal. Quite the contrary. Friedmann sees the phenomenon as one of the contradictions of late capitalism, a development that generates social costs that nations cannot sustain. Sassen devotes considerable time to her concerns about the spatial inequalities that the pursuit of being a global city produces. Nevertheless, city governments around the world have embraced the notion of the global city as a goal to be pursued. One of the cities discussed in part II—New York City—is already on everyone's list as being at the top of the global city hierarchy, and most of the others are on at least one list. Even cities on no list often pursue a version of the idea, such as being a regional financial center. Two aspects of this pursuit of the global city ideal are of particular interest to us. One is the way in which the current organization of city power helps drive cities to embrace this version of their future. The other is the way in which the current structure frustrates their pursuit of the same goal by creating limitations on various ways to achieve it.

Enabling the Global City Objective

A city that wants to raise its position on the hierarchical list of global cities can pursue a number of options. As Robert Beauregard has convincingly demonstrated, city policies help determine what globalization is. "All activity is local," Beauregard writes. "The global only comes into being through the integration of numerous locally based actors and activities."[6] The basic objective of these locally based actors and activities is to make the city a desirable place for international financial institutions, creative entrepreneurs, and the attendant services (law firms, accounting firms, consultants) to locate. In addition to meetings with business leaders who might move to town, there are a variety of policies city officials might adopt in their effort to make the city attractive. Ensuring easy access to international transportation—a major airport with good connections to the world and to the central city and good port facilities where possible—is one task. Another is providing the proper office and living environment for those who work in finance and related activities: high-rise office buildings, back-office locations, and residential neighborhoods. An advanced communications infrastructure, a quick turn-around for licensing and building approvals, a low-tax environment—these too are often on the list. Those attracted to Richard

Florida's ideas might add cultural facilities and neighborhoods with the right kind of buzz; those more concerned with the support staff might stress the quality of public schools and the availability of affordable housing. The list can go on and on, particularly if the adjective "world-class" can be applied to as many of the ingredients as possible. As we shall see, cities are often limited in their ability to implement some of these ideas. But the legal framework also helps push cities to embrace this kind of agenda in two ways: by making the alternatives difficult and by empowering cities to pursue some ingredients on this list comparatively easily.

The Problem with Alternatives

Consider the options confronting a mayor seeking to choose between adopting a global city agenda and two alternatives, a middle class city and a regional city. Since we defer to chapter 9 a detailed examination of the middle class city, we will limit ourselves here to a report from the Drum Major Institute that offers an example of an agenda that might implement such a goal.[7] The Drum Major Institute, a think tank that concentrates on making New York City more livable for the middle class, asked one hundred local leaders to identify the kinds of policies that the city should adopt to respond to increasing economic polarization. Among the polices identified were the adoption of a more progressive local income tax; the requirement of mandatory inclusionary zoning; the provision of city-provided public full-day prekindergarten classes; the offering of expanded local public health care; the imposition of requirements that large businesses in the city provide their employees with health care; the adoption of living wage measures; and the elimination of tuition for city residents at the City University of New York.

These ideas rely on three kinds of city action: taxation, regulation, and service delivery. State law limits a city government's ability to adopt all three of these techniques. Even those states that do not, like Massachusetts, require explicit state authorization for taxes have state-imposed limits on local taxing authority. Even states that do not, like Massachusetts, require state legislative authorization before cities can regulate the private sector (by exempting "private or civil law" from the home rule power) restrict city regulation of private business. And service delivery is expensive and difficult everywhere, demanding resources and organizational flexibility that cities often lack. Even a city with power to adopt one or more of these techniques must recognize that it is in competition not only with cities across the country but with other cities in its own metropolitan region. Raising taxes to support services and regulating private business can encourage businesses interested in the region to locate in the suburbs rather than within the central city itself. From the global city literature's point of view, of course, it doesn't affect the "city's" global status—as the literature defines it—whether the ultimate location is within or outside of the city's geographic boundaries. But it certainly makes a difference to the city government. A move to New Jersey is not going to help New York City raise tax revenue to support city services. City officials, therefore, could easily think that adopting a middle-class-city agenda is not in their interest, given the current structure of intercity competition and metropolitan organization.

The global city agenda offers a more attractive option. Its goal is to appeal to business, not to impose costs on it. Implementing this agenda involves offering incentives, including tax breaks and infrastructure development, not imposing higher taxes or demanding business concessions. And no city-provided services for health care or prekindergarten are required. In fact, a city pursuing a global agenda might discourage the kinds of residents who would use these public services from living in the city. In addition to the incentive structure being more helpful, city governments are vested with relatively significant powers over economic development compared to their ability to tax, regulate, and provide services. Cities are often given the authority to make tax concessions to attract businesses even if they have no authority to raise taxes to support public services or to make them more progressive. They have more authority to provide infrastructure development than to condition city approval of zoning or licensing on acceptance of public policy conditions. It is also easier, given the state-imposed limits on city borrowing and discretionary expenditures, to stimulate private investment than to increase the city's own spending on city services. As we have seen, most cities operate under state-imposed debt limits, and they cannot borrow money to fund operating expenses. Infrastructure development, on the other hand, can be funded by creating an independent public authority with its own debt limit—an exception to the state-imposed city debt limit that has spurred the creation of development authorities nationwide. Moreover, offering tax breaks or subsidies to private business takes nothing out of the city budget directly, while funding city services does. To be sure, the ultimate cost to the city can turn out to be the same. Moreover, it will foster the privatization of the city. Nevertheless, given budget constraints and the limits on city power, it is not surprising that city governments have increasingly focused on promoting private economic development rather than improving public services.

One reason that cities have more legal authority to attract business than to regulate it is the contrasting judicial attitudes toward offering tax breaks to businesses compared to imposing costs on them. In *Maready v. City of Winston-Salem*, for example, the North Carolina Supreme Court upheld state legislation that authorized local governments to make economic development incentive grants to private corporations against a challenge that the legislation violated a state constitutional requirement that funds be spent "for public purposes only"—a phrase the court had earlier interpreted to forbid grants to private individuals or corporations. Despite concerns that the grants unfairly allowed the government to favor some private businesses over others and notwithstanding the objection that the policy did not in fact produce significant job growth or increases in the tax base, the court upheld the legislation as serving a public purpose. Noting that virtually every other state in the nation allowed such grants, the court expressed concern that North Carolina would suffer economically if the program were discontinued. "The potential impetus to economic development," it concluded, "which might otherwise be lost to other states...serves a public interest."[8]

The judicial attitude toward imposing costs on private business activity is considerably less generous. We have already noted the hurdles some cities face when considering inclusionary zoning ordinances or rent control designed to ensure affordable housing. We also have noted how efforts to impose costs on businesses are sometimes considered an unauthorized form of taxation rather than a special assessment. In chapter 9, we will discuss similar problems when cities contemplate measures such as a living wage ordinance. One additional restraint is worth mentioning here: restrictions on the use of eminent domain. Although the U.S. Supreme Court recently upheld the City of New London's constitutional authority to condemn private property as part of its economic development plan, the reaction across the country was quite negative. Many states enacted legislation restricting cities' ability to condemn property for economic development purposes unless the property was substandard or blighted. The result has been both an empowerment of cities to pursue economic development and a limit on their power: it depends on the property being condemned. This structure itself helps cities pursue a global city goal: it blesses urban renewal style condemnation of poor—that is, "substandard"—neighborhoods near downtown (thereby allowing gentrification and high-rise development) while protecting the wealthier neighborhoods elsewhere in the city. Of course, even these limits would be of no concern if outright grants, tax concessions, or infrastructure development were the development tools being employed.[9]

One aspect of the difficulty of pursuing the middle class city agenda is the central city's fear that it will lose investment opportunities to the suburbs. Another way to understand this fear is to compare the global city not with the middle class city but the regional city. Local government law makes it difficult to create a regional economic development policy. State law normally limits the kinds of interlocal agreements that are allowed and, equally important, fails to give incentives to cities and suburbs, either financial incentives or additional grants of local power, to pursue regional solutions to metropolitan problems. In fact, the structure of local government law itself makes regional cooperation unattractive. Every city in the region is required to raise its own funds to provide its own services, and this structure leads city officials to try to attract investment for themselves even at the expense of their neighbors. At the same time, the limits on local power—limits applicable to the suburbs as well as to the central cities—make local officials worry that any regional effort would further restrict their ability to provide for their constituents. A different legal structure—one that increased local power when exercised cooperatively with others—would change the way economic development competition within a metropolitan region operated. There is nothing inevitable about the current form of intercity competition that makes localized pursuit of the global city agenda attractive and the middle class city seem to undermine the city's competitive position. The state-established regional structure is itself a product of state law.

Empowering the Global City Agenda

The current legal structure does more than discourage alternatives to a global city agenda. It empowers cities to embrace it. This can be seen most easily by focusing on city power over finance and land use. The state's restriction of Boston to the property tax made the city dependent on increasing property values to generate revenue. The global city agenda is a major vehicle for pursuing this strategy. Of course, a state-defined dependence on the property tax is not the only way to enable the global city agenda. An income or occupation tax, authorized by state law in all the cities we examined other than Boston, can have the same effect. So too can specifically targeted taxes—such as the jet fuel tax in Boston, the business license tax in San Francisco, and the telecommunications tax in Denver. San Francisco's generation of fees from development works in the same way. Once state law makes cities dependent on raising their own revenue, and if (as is true for major cities) revenue from commercial and other business ventures is a major source of income, cities have to seek revenue from these sources.

It is therefore not surprising that, in the spring of 2006, Boston Mayor Thomas Menino announced a plan to redevelop a city-owned parcel of land in the heart of the city's financial district. He asked private developers to submit "world class" designs for a 1,000-foot office tower—"the city's tallest building yet." The mayor clearly hoped the project would boost the local economy, but he also wanted to make "a statement to the world about Boston's prominence" so that the city could continue to "lead the way as a global capital."[10] No one would suggest that the only ingredient that leads Boston or other cities to adopt this strategy is the local government structure. The work of Paul Peterson and Clarence Stone present additional ways of understanding the generation of the

desire to become a global city. Others emphasize the shifts in role of the government at the national level, the most important of which is the decline of the
welfare state.[11] Moreover, there are other definitions of economic development,
and these too can be relied on to generate income from the available sources.
The point here is more limited: the state-created local government financial
structure makes resource growth and the global city agenda consistent with each
other. The global city route is in vogue around the world, and it is easy for cities
in the United States to see it as an obvious way to grow their economy.

The state-granted fiscal incentives to become a global city are not always
straightforward. Consider the exemption from the property tax that state law
provides universities and hospitals. We have seen how this exemption limits cities' resources. But it also helps promote a global city future. Although
knowledge-based industries are not necessarily connected to the financial services industry or to the downtown business district, they perform two key roles
that facilitate the city's relationship to the global economy. They provide a pool
of highly trained prospective employees who are readily available for recruit-
ment. Firms often see the presence of a highly educated workforce as more
important than the state and local tax structures in making their locational
decisions. Universities and hospitals also conduct research and develop innovations that can be used by local industries. Many scholars discuss the importance
of concentrations of academic, and in particular scientific, knowledge to the
production of innovative business activity.[12] State tax-exemption decisions thus
do more than promote education and health care as desirable ends in themselves; they also stimulate a particular kind of business activity.

The city's power over land use works in the same direction. Indeed, land use
decisions and the structure of local government finance are inextricably inter-
connected. A key emphasis when cities exercise their land use power is enabling
private investment, and one reason for this is the need for city revenue. One
way cities pursue this agenda is to grant permissions for high-rise buildings;
another is to offer infrastructure improvements and tax incentives. Cities are
usually empowered to do both on their own, although the second option is
more constrained because of its fiscal impact. Boston's legal structure facilitates
the city's ability to attract international investment through the state-designed
membership of its zoning authorities and the Boston Redevelopment Authority's
combination of planning and development agency. Moreover, Boston's zoning
authority enables the city to offer incentives to private investment, while state-
imposed restrictions on additional taxes offers investors protection from tax
increases in later years.

Other cities make themselves hospitable to global city projects in other ways.
Some do so through the enactment of comprehensive zoning reform. Atlanta

recently amended its land use ordinances to remove height restrictions on buildings in the designated Midtown Commercial District. The express purpose of this change, along with other amendments to zoning ordinances, was to make the central city more attractive to high-value commercial and residential developments. In April 2006, Seattle similarly increased the height limits on skyscrapers in certain parts of downtown. If Seattle had sought instead to impose greater restrictions on building heights, it would have had to confront the state's unusually protective doctrine of vested rights, which, like the one in Massachusetts, can make downzoning difficult. Since Seattle was changing its zoning code in order to facilitate more intensive land use development, however, it encountered no equivalent state law obstacles.[13]

Other states facilitate economic investment by enabling a much broader use of tax increment financing than is available in Boston. San Francisco relied on tax increment financing to retrofit an aging industrial district in an area known as the China Basin, and these efforts, in turn, have enabled the city to attract the University of San Francisco to the site. Although critics derided the redevelopment project as a giveaway to the private developer, the city's investment led the state government to select the site as the home of California's new stem cell research institute.[14] As this example illustrates, efforts to attract economic development can be focused simultaneously on both domestic and international investors; local government law makes no distinction between the two when it empowers cities to engage in economic development efforts. Moreover, in San Francisco and elsewhere, the city's own land use power is not the only ingredient in the drive to become a global city. The state's development policies within the city point in the same direction. The role of the Empire State Development Corporation in New York, like that of the Turnpike Authority in Boston and similar authorities elsewhere, has been a major spur toward this kind of investment. State-generated projects affect the city's development not only directly but by changing the nature of the city itself. As they are built, other projects similar in nature can more easily be built as well.

The fact that the pursuit of a global city agenda increases revenue for the state as well as the city makes it unlikely that the state will inhibit the city's promotion of global investment. The home rule power in Massachusetts is unusually restricted, but the restrictions concern the organization of local government (elections), city finance (taxes, bonds), and regulation (private and civil law), not the stimulation of international investment. Cities pursue international business in the expectation that they have the authority to do so and that the state encourages the venture. Four of the seven cities we have examined—New York, Chicago, Seattle, and Atlanta—have created a specialized city office devoted specifically to international relations. One function of these offices is to connect local business with counterparts elsewhere in the world in order to promote international trade and to exchange information about best practices. The City of San Antonio has fourteen full-time people engaged with trade relations, focusing particularly on businesses in Mexico. Kansas City has gone further: it has signed an agreement with the Port of Manzanillo, in Mexico, seeking to link Manzanillo's port with Kansas City's large rail facility (the largest, by tonnage, in the nation). In this way, the city hopes that even a landlocked city like Kansas City can have the advantages of having an international port (and, for Manzanillo, even a port can have a larger transportation network).[15]

These kinds of efforts remain subject to state oversight or even prohibition. International trade activities are regularly performed on a statewide basis as well. The Massachusetts Office of International Trade and Investment is authorized by statute to operate offices in foreign countries and to provide technical assistance to foreign companies seeking to locate in the state; its focus is statewide, not on Boston. Similarly, the King County Office of Business Relations and Economic Development runs an export promotion program for the county in which the city of Seattle is located; it too is focused on a larger area. It is possible that the state might want to limit the central city's efforts in order to spur development elsewhere. But it is also possible to see the local, regional, and state efforts as consistent with each other—all, in their own way, pursuing a global city goal. A city's power to limit—rather than to increase—international trade and investment, on the other hand, is subject to considerable constraints. In *Crosby v. National Foreign Trade*,[16] the U.S. Supreme Court held that the effort of Massachusetts to bar state entities from buying goods from Burma was preempted by a federal statute. Local initiatives to ban the city's trade with specific countries (let alone that of businesses subject to its jurisdiction) would fare no better. They might even be prohibited by state law. Thus, consistent with the global city agenda, it is easier for cities to promote trading on an international level than to terminate it.

Restraining Global City Initiatives

It would be wrong to conclude, however, that states have decided to unleash their cities to use their energy and creativity to pursue the global city ideal in innovative and effective ways. Together with state encouragement, there are also a variety of state-imposed restraints on a city's ability to adopt a global city agenda.

The current form of metropolitan organization itself tends to undermine a city's pursuit of such an agenda. When city officials travel the world seeking economic development opportunities, they have no control over where within the region the business will locate even if it comes. The city might alert the investor to the advantages of the region but lose the investment to its suburbs. Even if the company's new office is located within the central city, the suburbs might gain advantages because employees moving to the area can locate in the suburbs and commute. It is therefore correct, from the economic vantage point of the global city literature, to see the global city agenda as regional in nature. But local government law now disregards this regional impact, organizing local power and finance so that other parts of the region can profit from the central city's development efforts without sharing the advantages they have gained. Although this result might encourage the central city to pursue becoming are regional city, its ability to do so is limited by state law. As a result, the city is likely to treat the spillover effects of attracting global business simply as an unavoidable cost.

Other restraints include those associated with the authority to use the state-granted powers over finance and land use. State-imposed restrictions on these powers can inhibit global city efforts through restrictions built directly into the grants of authority. A state's decision to exempt hospitals and universities from the local property tax, for example, can make even a city that is attracted to the global city vision worried about proposals for the expansion of these institutions. The more they grow, the more land comes off the tax rolls. State restraints can also take the form of potential state intervention and preemption. Rather than highlighting these now-familiar constraints, we concentrate here on three other kinds of state-imposed limits on a city's pursuit of a global city goal: those dealing with transportation, the provision of broadband services, and the impact on city life of the vast inequalities that are an integral part of the global city phenomenon.

Transportation

A transportation network that facilitates the connection to the outside world is widely thought to be an important ingredient of being a global city. Indeed, one way that a city's position in the global city hierarchy is measured is through the extent of its linkages with the global airline network.[17] But the quality of the airport is only half the battle: the international connection is only as good as the ease in traveling back and forth between the airport and the business center. This priority has not been lost on cities anxious to strengthen their position as, or to become, a global city. Major airport construction is taking place around the world (Beijing, London, Osaka), and global or potentially global cities already have (London, Paris) or are building (Johannesburg) fast train connections linking the airport with the city. The Maglev train in Shanghai—the world's fastest train—has become the symbol of advanced technology in the airport connection world. And airports are not the only focus. Train connections are also a priority in many places. Massive construction improving Eurostar connections to the Continent is under way in London, providing not only faster service but creating a new location for the London stop. Ports are another focus: Shanghai is moving its entire port to create the world's largest deep water container port, and Rotterdam, the largest European port, is undergoing major construction as well.

American cities do not have the power to implement this kind of transportation agenda. The basic reason can be summed up in one word: fragmentation. Authority over airports, subway lines, and ports is fractured in many ways: all three levels of government (federal, state, local) are involved, and so are numerous public authorities, community groups, transportation planning bodies, and private corporations. When some aspects of the responsibility are consolidated—such as responsibility both for ports and the airport—they tend to be given not to the city government but to public authorities, such as the Massachusetts Port Authority or the Port Authority of New York and New Jersey. The power of these authorities thus becomes a rival to city government power, not a mechanism for the implementation of its vision of being a global city. Even these authorities, powerful as they are, control only a portion of the agenda. The private sector—specifically the airlines—have a major say in, and provide a lot of the financing for, terminal construction and improvement at the airport. Moreover, the rail connection between John F. Kennedy Airport in New York and New York City's financial district is split between the Port Authority (its Airtrain) and the train services run by two subdivisions of another state-run authority, the Metropolitan Transportation Authority: New York City Transit and the Long Island Railroad. A comparable allocation of responsibility between different public authorities for the airport and ground transportation occurs in Boston. The city government is not in charge of either the airport or the airport connection, let alone both.

A story from Brooklyn, wonderfully portrayed in the *New York Times*, epitomizes the fragmentation in transportation policy while simultaneously illustrating the contrasting visions of the global city, the tourist city, the middle class city, and the regional city.[18] The Red Hook neighborhood in Brooklyn has long been a location for an important cargo terminal. The terminal is owned by the Port Authority of New York and New Jersey but is leased to a private company, American Stevedoring Inc. (By August 2007, the lease had expired and the Port Authority might be looking for another operator.) There is considerable support within the New York City Council for continuing cargo shipping there; it provides high-paying blue-collar jobs that the city badly needs (the middle class city). The Port Authority, however, would like to move the cargo shipping elsewhere, not just to Staten Island but to New Jersey (the regional city). Mayor Bloomberg has had his sights on another objective: turning the Red Hook port into a docking site for cruise ships, with shops and hotels nearby (the tourist city). Cruise lines, however, provide few high-paying jobs—much of the work is a one-day affair—and the neighborhood would be significantly affected by the change.

We have not yet mentioned one more key actor in the decision-making process about the future of the Red Hook port: the New York City Economic Development Corporation. Its job is to stimulate economic growth, oversee transportation and infrastructure projects, promote the city's central business districts, and provide financial support as well as "double and triple tax exempt revenue bonds" to fund development projects through its New York City Industrial Development Agency.[19] Although the Economic Development Corporation is New York City's primary economic development agency, it is not a government agency but a nonprofit corporation (a so-called "501(c)(3)" not for profit corporation) managed by a board of directors. The Economic Development Corporation's goal in Red Hook seems to be to bring the different parties together (in 2007 it hosted the first meeting in three years between the city, the Port Authority, and American Stevedoring). But there is some suggestion that it too has a position on the merits—namely, that it is favorable to retaining the cargo terminal.

Who's in charge here? Can New York City implement a version of the global city goal by strengthening its cargo terminal in Red Hook? In 2005, the *New York Times* reported, a German cargo company abandoned its effort to bring sixty thousand freight containers to Red Hook because the city could not guarantee that the cargo port would be open through 2009. Admittedly, this aspect of the global connection is only one of many; it does not fit with Saskia Sassen's focus on a financially oriented global city. Perhaps another global city goal—say, concentrating on reconstruction of the World Trade Center—would be better. (Of course, it too is owned by the Port Authority of New York and New Jersey.) Our point in raising this example is not to resolve the conflict among (and within) the city's development goals. We seek simply to highlight the importance of the limits that the state-created city structure has on a city's desire, if it has one, to be a global city. In Red Hook, the Port Authority, as owner, is a separate and important decision maker. Moreover, the allocation of power to community groups, the city council, and to public-private entities like the Economic Development Corporation (especially its bonding authority) will affect city decision making about whether and how to strengthen its role as a global city. These are all matters controlled by state law.

Redesigning this decision-making structure would be a very complex undertaking. But it is not inevitable that city governments in the United States have such a limited role in making the transportation decisions vital to the global city objective. Many cities own their own airports, and they have used this power to promote their global city ambitions. Of course, airports serve the metropolitan region, not just the city. Perhaps, then, a single city should not have control over such a regional asset. The only alternative states now provide to city ownership, however, is a state-controlled public authority. The absence of a state mechanism that empowers the region's cities, rather than a public authority, to make decisions regarding airport development can thus be a significant limit on any possible city role. Much the same can be said about ports and, in many cities (such as San Francisco and Boston), the mass transit system, because the economic future of many of the region's cities is at stake in these decisions too. From an economic perspective, as the global cities literature argues, the city is regional. But the state has made regional authorities, not city governments, the key actors, not only because of their regional scope but because it has given them (rather than a regional intercity mechanism) the independent authority to raise revenue through debt. Of course, changes in state law are not all that might be necessary to better enable cities to organize their transportation networks to advance a global city objective. In other countries, the decision-making responsibility for transportation improvements is clearer because there is greater national focus on the economic development of the country's global cities. Although the federal government in the United States has had a major impact on city development in general and on the urban transportation network in particular—most dramatically, through the Federal Highway Program, which paid 90 percent of the costs—its allocation for airports, trains, and ports is not now, and is not likely to be, at a level that exists in other parts in the world.

Broadband

A city interested in pursuing a global city agenda might well decide that the city's provision of high-speed Internet, or "broadband," services would contribute to its goals. Financial firms need more than office buildings and housing developments: they also need reliable, state-of-the-art Internet connections.[20] The United States is twentieth in the world in terms of broadband adoption rates, and its place on the list is slipping. (In Japan, broadband service is half the cost and twenty times the speed than in the United States.)[21] If a city can provide broadband services, city officials might think, it might stand out in the American context and become a global leader. Broadband services might serve other goals as well. Cities worried about some of its residents' lack of access to the Internet— the so-called digital divide—might want to provide the service for that reason. This would be consistent with a goal of being a middle class city. Cities focused on tourism might see the advantage of advertising wireless connections as one of the attractions that visitors to town might enjoy.

These goals for a city broadband service can be consistent each other, but they need not be. A global city orientation might limit service to parts of the city and therefore not serve those areas of concern to people worried about the digital divide. The new infrastructure for London, when depicted graphically, snakes around those parts of the city that have been untouched by the global economic transformation but reaches over to other parts of the city, such as the Docklands, that have been the focus of London's global city strategy.[22] A tourist city perspective, on the other hand, might favor "hot spots" that are located elsewhere than in the financial center. A citywide broadband service would solve some of these conflicts, but, as we shall see, even it needs to be designed.

At the end of 2006, seventy-nine municipalities in the United States had implemented citywide broadband networks, while eighty-five had built more limited wireless networks and 149 had begun the process of initiating one.[23] A city considering offering broadband service faces a number of choices. Broadband can be offered through cable, digital subscriber lines (DSL), wireless, satellite, or powerlines. Additional technologies are being developed as well. For our purposes, the critical choice might be the business model that the city should adopt. One possibility is to limit the city's involvement and financial risk by contracting with a private company to provide the service over the city's rights-of-way. Such a contract could be with either a profit-making or nonprofit enterprise. The first option might raise concerns about whether the private corporation would adequately implement the city's public policy objectives, while the second might raise concerns about financing. These kinds of concerns might lead the city to the opposite model: the city could run the broadband network itself. That way it could retain control and manage the financial risk. An intermediate choice—one adopted by Philadelphia, one of the major models for other cities—is for the city to provide the network infrastructure (the wholesale aspect, as it is called) and lease the network to a private company to provide services to the customer (the retail aspect). This model limits the city's financial risk, but it allows some control over the services provided, albeit less than municipal ownership. This public-private model has many possible designs. But it is the one that cities increasingly are favoring. All of the alternatives, however, have been adopted somewhere.

We come, then, to the question raised by this book: Can cities provide municipal broadband at all and, if so, can they choose which of these models best serves their purposes? The answer is not hard to guess: it all depends on state law. States have taken a number of different and conflicting positions on these issues. There is some judicial precedent for the notion that the provision of municipal broadband is within a city's home rule power, but the cases are rare and not dispositive. Given the current state of the law, many cities might be concerned that, without express authorization from the state legislature, undertaking a project of this scope would be unwise, even if an argument for its home rule authority might ultimately be persuasive. In any event, whether or not there is home rule authority, thirty states have either passed or are considering specific legislation on the topic. A few states have prohibited their cities from providing broadband, and a few others have prohibited municipal retail services but allowed wholesale services. A larger number of states have imposed procedural and financial requirements on cities before they undertake broadband services. These include the states that have forbidden cross-subsidizing broadband services from other municipal revenue sources and other states that have required nondiscriminatory access to the rights-of-way. Some states prohibit municipal broadband unless the city first seeks a private provider and is unable to find one. Still others have required a referendum before the city embarks on the project.[24]

It's no overstatement, then, to say that cities are limited by state law in their ability to include broadband provision in their global city vision. But state law is not the only city concern. The U.S. Congress has considered a variety of bills that propose requirements for municipal broadband that parallel the different approaches adopted by the states. The proposed legislation is a reaction to a decision by the U.S. Supreme Court in *Nixon v. Missouri Municipal League,* decided in 2004.[25] In *Nixon,* the Court interpreted a federal statute that prohibited the states from passing legislation that prevented any entity from providing telecommunications services. Although the statute expressly prevented the state from regulating "any entity," the Court decided that it did not protect cities from state power. Notwithstanding the federal statute, in other words, state preemption of municipally provided broadband remained permissible. Congressional reaction to this decision has varied from attempts to protect municipal broadband from state interference (reversing the court's result) to efforts to forbid a preference for a public provider to requiring an auction process to award the project. The legislation that will result from this congressional activity is unknown, but it seems unlikely that even states, let alone cities, will have the last word on the subject.

Polarization

Although major cities are increasingly drawn to the global city vision, one of its primary attributes is the generation of stark income and wealth polarization. As Saskia Sassen puts it,

> today growth is based on an industrial complex that leads not to the expansion of a middle class but to increasing dispersion in the income structure and in the bidding power of firms and households. There is social and economic polarization, particularly strong in major cities

which concentrate a large proportion of the new growth industries and create a vast direct and indirect demand for low-profit service jobs and low-wage jobs.[26]

This polarization affects the nationwide, indeed the world, economy. But its day-to-day effects are most powerfully felt in cities. Polarization can undermine the very gains that the global city objective is designed to achieve, making the city a less, not more, desirable place for financial investors to live. In Johannesburg, the city's global city vision statement, *Joburg 2030,* lists crime prevention as the critical ingredient in attracting the investment necessary to meet the city's economic development goals.[27]

One possible strategy to deal with income polarization is to condition access to the city by global business on the provision of assistance to the city's poor. Of course, a city cannot require too much of the private sector or it will undermine the growth of its financial businesses and thus its global city objective. Nevertheless, cities that have succeeded in attracting global investment can take advantage of the demand for particular cities that characterizes the global city phenomenon by exercising their regulatory power. The economy of global cities makes capital exit comparatively difficult because the institutional components, such as banks, law firms, and public relations and communications companies, are so interdependent. It is this interconnection that makes specific cities seem irresistible locations. Moreover, if the regulations can increase the desirability of the city as a place to live, they can reinforce the city's overall ability to attract the kinds of workers that the knowledge-based global economy rewards. There thus may be support even within the investor community for regulatory action.

One difficulty with implementing this strategy is state law. Many of the regulatory initiatives designed to help the poor, such as linkage and inclusionary zoning, are subject to state controls. To be sure, cities have some power to engage in these kinds of initiatives. Nevertheless, it seems clear that national and state governments are the primary vehicles for confronting the income inequalities generated by the organization of the global economy. Cities can contribute to this effort. But the major ingredients for action—from the tax system to social welfare programs to health care—are the responsibility of other levels of government. Cities could be empowered to do more about these essential ingredients of income inequality, but, until they are, they are limited to working at the margins.

Another city option is to concentrate on relieving the spatial segregation along class and income lines that a pursuit of the global economy produces. Organizing city land use to integrate city residents across income, ethnic, and racial lines can help address the impact of polarization even if radical differences in income levels persist. These days, city policies often point in the opposite direction. Cities trying to raise property values often consider segregation a helpful way of doing so. Such a belief is fed by the spatial polarization itself: people who live in a divided city are willing to pay for the protection provided by spatial distance because the city has failed to demonstrate in its own neighborhoods that class-diverse neighborhoods can be prosperous too. Development policy becomes a self-fulfilling prophecy: cities that do not provide the kinds of integrated learning experience offered by a more open city become increasingly segregated.[28] The result is visible for all to see. Although Boston is a majority-minority city, one can walk through some of the city's prime shopping areas (Newbury Street) or go to a Red Sox game and never know it. Atlanta and Chicago can be described in similar ways.

A change in city policy adequate to alter this dynamic requires resources and flexibility that most cities do not have available. Cities would have to steer development in a way that promotes class-diverse neighborhoods—a much more significant intervention into the real estate market than the current deal that offers developers taller high-rises in exchange for their providing affordable housing somewhere in the city. State legislatures are not likely to delegate this kind of power to cities, and, even if they did, it would succeed only if the state also created a different relationship with suburban jurisdictions to ensure that the income disparity didn't simply move across city lines. It would also require a revision of the current structure of city finance to ensure that integrated cities have more money to fund city services than segregated ones. In other words, virtually every aspect of city power that now fuels spatial polarization—land use, finance, interlocal relations—would have be revised to undermine it.

Another strategy might focus specifically on the impact on city life of the increasing immigration into major American cities. Immigrants not only represent a major force in the cities we examined in part II but are a significant part of the population of major metropolitan areas across the country. Although immigration is a very controversial subject in the United States and elsewhere, its effect on cities is widely seen as positive. Immigrants have helped revive neighborhoods in most of our seven cities, above all in New York City. Nevertheless, the connection drawn between cities and immigration is often one of conflict: immigrants are seen as threats to the city and the city as a threat to the immigrants. Thus, a common reaction people have when they link cities and immigration is a call for limitations on city power over the immigrant population. A federal courts' invalidation of Hazleton, Pennsylvania's unsuccessful efforts to crack down on illegal immigration is the most widely publicized illustration of this way of managing the city-immigrant relationship.[29]

Consider instead the opposite city strategy: empowering the city to incorporate the immigrants into the wider city. This agenda would promote a global city in a very different sense of the term: the city would be global not simply because of its business connections with outsiders but because so many people from so many different parts of the world live in the city. These days, immigrants tend to be disconnected not only from those managing the financial sector but from each other. Overcoming this kind of spatial segregation might lead to city policies such as providing affordable housing geared to newly arrived immigrants, offering economic incentives to encourage immigrant entrepreneurs, establishing welcoming centers for new immigrants, and creating employment centers that connect immigrants to jobs in settings better than street corners and parking lots. These efforts can be designed to be open to immigrants from anywhere in the world as part of the effort to break down the barriers between immigrants from different countries. They could also be connected to programs that link new immigrants to longtime city residents. These locally based efforts may even help promote the more familiar global city agenda: building connections between the city, its new immigrants, and their countries of origin can promote an internationally based economic development strategy. This is the vision of Miami as the "gateway to Latin America."[30]

Rather than focusing once again on the familiar kinds of legal and financial issues that this kind of agenda raises, we want to highlight a political question: Why would a city's citizens spend money, even if they could, on immigrants rather than on themselves? One way to affect the possible answer to this question is to change the current definition of who a city's citizens are. In most American cities, only American citizens can vote for local officials. This policy disenfranchises the large number of city residents who are legal immigrants but resident aliens rather than citizens. In 2000, almost three million residents of New York City were foreign born, and the numbers elsewhere are significant as well: 1.5 million in Los Angeles, more than 600,000 in Chicago, and almost 300,000 in San Francisco. Of course, many of these people are naturalized citizens: nationwide, in 2000, 40 percent of the foreign-born population had become citizens. Still, enabling lawful permanent resident aliens to vote, given their significant numbers, would significantly change local politics. This idea is not as radical as it might seem. In nineteenth-century America, many cities did not limit the vote to American citizens. In the European Union, every resident from a European Union country can vote for local officials whether or not they are a national citizen. (National elections remain limited to national citizens.) Some municipalities in the United States now allow resident aliens to vote. This legal structure integrates residents who are citizens of other countries into the political life of their adopted city. It is unlikely, however, that such a change in election law could be made in most cities in the United States without state legislation. In Boston, for example, elections are expressly excluded from the state's home rule grant.[31]

This strategy aimed at immigrants can be generalized: a city can undertake a broad-based community-building strategy to address polarization of all kinds. Cities are likely to have the authority to engage in community building. Indeed, city governments—engaged, as they are, in the daily life of city residents—are in a better position than either the state or national governments to perform such a task. Overcoming the tensions that divide the city could therefore become a focus of city policy. To be sure, a program that was not just symbolic would require considerable resources: the organization of neighborhood and interneighborhood democracy, the creation of community activities that cross racial, ethnic, and class lines, the organization of city services (and not just schools) to promote interconnection among city residents. The cities' lack of discretionary income—and their need to focus instead on the activities delegated to them by the state—now make these kinds of tasks difficult. Perhaps even more important, the lack of city self-confidence in its own ability to set an agenda for itself—one learned from long experience with complying with requirements imposed by state government—is likely to make this conception of the city's function not even come to mind.

Choices Left Open

Although cities are organized in a way that spurs their pursuit of becoming a global city, state law frustrates their ability to accomplish the same goal. The current combination of grants and limits on city power cannot be explained in terms of a state policy either to promote or to discourage the global city ideal. Nor does it direct the city toward any particular definition of the idea. Cities that embrace the global city agenda are thus likely to be frustrated by the difficulties they face in doing so. It's hard even to know what steps to take. Every term— from "economic development" to "global city"—needs definition. How does one make a city attractive to international investors? Is copying an existing model elsewhere—by building, say, a familiar kind of modernist office building—a bad strategy? (Why go here rather than elsewhere?) Or is it a necessary one? (Don't people look for familiar places wherever they go?) Are the ingredients that influence location decisions different for different businesses and even firm to firm? Is the immigrant population a selling point for the global city objective or is it irrelevant—or a problem? More generally, what are the alternative economic development models to the global city agenda? Are there ways to promote the local economy without increasing privatization that might supplement, or even replace, the pursuit of being global city? Indeed, what is the role of the city government, as distinguished from the private sector, in attracting business?

There plainly is room for city decision making in trying to formulate the answers to these questions. In this chapter, we have been able only to gesture toward the innumerable state-imposed limits that go along with this discretion. In any particular city, state law matters. But the law differs from state to state, and the answers even in a particular state are often unclear. Nailing down answers will require a city-by-city study to determine the legal structure that promotes and limits the global city agenda. In the meantime, with this research undone, cities need to decide on a strategy in a world of legal uncertainty. On any particular issue, the first question might be: Should the city try to get state authorization for the initiative? Or should it pursue its own definition of becoming a global city and try to deal with legal objections when they arise? These kinds of issues will arise again when the options of being a tourist city, middle class city, or regional city are being considered.

THE TOURIST CITY

In their influential book *The Tourist City*, Dennis Judd and Susan Fainstein describe the transition of major cities into vehicles for attracting tourists.[1] Tourist cities shift their focus from the needs of city residents to the desires of people living elsewhere. They therefore sell themselves as a place to visit to people in nearby suburbs, across the country, and around the world. In part, they do so by advertising in a manner similar to businesses marketing a consumer product, highlighting the value of their heritage, vitality, and unique attractions. But they also construct their infrastructure and provide amenities to ensure that the tourists will have something to do, and will be able to get around, when they are in the city.

It is not hard to understand why the tourist city has proved to be so appealing. It has been especially attractive in the postindustrial era because it does not require a city to convince people to move to the city to live. A city simply has to entice temporary visitors, and they can be directed to those parts of the city in which the evidence of the postwar urban crisis can largely be kept from view. From this perspective, the emergence of the tourist city is symptomatic of urban decline and a reflection of disparate political influence within the city. But the tourist city is influential in prosperous cities as well. Along with the embrace of the global city, it provides a familiar way to promote and sustain the local economy. Tourists come for a short time, and they spend significant amounts of money during their stay. They do not demand the social services that residents need, and they can spread the word about the city's appeal to others. In this way, visitors can help the city sell itself as an attractive place to live and work. The tourist city thus overlaps with the entertainment-focused approach to becoming a global city promoted by Richard Florida.

We begin our discussion of the tourist city by discussing in more detail the similarities and differences between its goals and those of being a global city. We then turn to the legal structure that affects cities when they seek to become, or strengthen their position as, a tourist city. There are a variety of definitions of a tourist city that a city might embrace. The first option is to make the city as a whole—or, more accurately, the neighborhoods within the city that outsiders identify as being the whole city—a place that tourists want to visit. We call this a "tourist-friendly city." The second is to create specific areas within the city—areas that John Hannigan calls the "fantasy city" and Dennis Judd calls the "tourist bubble"—that attract pleasure seekers: locations ranging from shopping environments to sports stadiums to gambling casinos to convention centers to theme parks.[2] The final idea is to focus on a single dramatic event that will "put the city on the map": the Olympics, the World Cup, or a World Exposition. These ideas can and do overlap, but, as we shall see, they are not the same, and each of them raises its own problems under the existing legal structure.

Global City/Tourist City

There are many common characteristics between the agendas of being a global city and a tourist city. The most important is that, unlike the alternatives of being a middle class city or a regional city, they are primarily focused on promoting the city's economic development. For this reason, a good deal of what we said in Chapter Seven applies, albeit with some modifications, to this chapter as well. For the global city and the tourist city, real estate development is a priority, and thus an important tool that city governments use is making deals with developers. The legal structure that facilitates these deals is similar in both contexts, particularly when the two goals are compared to the middle class city or the regional city. Of course, the tax structure affects the two goals in different ways. Boston's inability to impose a sales tax and its resulting need to rely on the property tax promotes the global city more than the tourist city. Nevertheless, the legislative and judicial attitudes analyzed in chapter 7 that favor the attraction of major businesses to town—embraced by the overall structure of local finance and land use law—applies to tourist businesses as well. Cities can use their zoning authority, their ability to engage in tax increment financing, and their power to develop infrastructure (however limited) to promote either objective. The critical issue, from this perspective, is determining which of the two visions makes the most sense to develop the city's economy.

There is also no reason to assume that the global city and the tourist city are inconsistent with each other. Both can be promoted simultaneously to attract their different, yet compatible, target audiences. Both kinds of cities are eager to organize their economy in a manner that will add to the city's tax base, and both seek to do so by making connections with people who live outside the city's borders. As a result, improvements to the neighborhoods in which middle class and low-income residents live rarely figure prominently in the redevelopment plans for either kind of city—unless, that is, the neighborhood is targeted for the exercise of eminent domain. On the other hand, improvements to the airport and its connections to the city are as useful to tourists as to those who travel to maintain their global business. The leisure and entertainment attractions that tourist cities use to entice pleasure seekers can also appeal to the bankers and consultants that work in the producer-services industries associated with the global economy. And the dramatic architectural statements that cities promote as tourist landmarks often signal the city's achievements as a global city as well. Sure, tourists usually have no desire to visit the financial center—although, as visits to Wall Street demonstrate, sometimes they do. But the opposite is not the case: even those who work in finance have a few hours off, and they may well want to go to restaurants and clubs that are also frequented by tourists.

There are also important differences between tourist city and global city goals. In any particular part of town, building a sports stadium or a convention center might detract from, rather than enhance, the neighborhood's value as a financial center. And vice versa: building a neighborhood of high-rise office buildings can create a dead "downtown" that no tourist would want to visit. Consider the vision, now abandoned, of building a stadium on the far west side of Manhattan:

> In [Deputy Mayor Dan] Doctoroff's vision, the far West Side would become, with the stadium as its anchor, a thriving center of culture, sports, tourism, and entertainment. There would be cafés, restaurants, shops, a 1,500-room hotel, office and residential space, and a ribbon of parks along the waterfront. Doctoroff's dream also includes a broad boulevard with a center esplanade nearly twice as wide as Park Avenue's. This boulevard would be carved out between Tenth and Eleventh avenues, and run from 33rd Street up to 42nd Street. On the east side of Eleventh Avenue, between 30th and 33rd streets, the other open section of rail yards would be covered by a six-acre park. On its southern edge, there is space for a cultural institution—perhaps a branch of the Guggenheim museum, whose director, Thomas Krens, has expressed interest.[3]

This vision embraces the tourist city, even though it includes, perhaps problematically, office and residential space. Since there is a limited amount of city money and energy available for development, even in New York City, critics charged that the pursuit of this tourist agenda threatened to undermine the pursuit of other ideas, including global city ideas, elsewhere.

A city oriented toward becoming a financial center will also attract different kinds of people and create a different ambience than one concentrating on casinos, theme parks, or conventions. One way to make this distinction is to say that global cities emphasize producer services (the term Saskia Sassen uses) while tourist cities are focused instead on consumption. Although there plainly is something to this distinction—a recent book, entitled *The City as an Entertainment Machine,* strongly emphasizes the notion of consumption—we think that it is overdrawn.[4] Sassen herself recognizes that consumption is one of the ingredients in the global city, and tourist cities must produce entertainment and attractions for people to come to enjoy them. A better way to see the difference is to focus on the kind of people who live and work in the city whose job requires them to connect with outsiders. A global city will need finance people to relate to similar people elsewhere. A tourist city will need people working in casinos or convention centers or restaurants or sports arenas. The feel of the two cities, as a result, can be quite different. No one would confuse Las Vegas with a financial center.

The reference to Las Vegas raises another point: the relationship between the central city and its region. Cities seeking to become a global city must recognize that global business might prefer locations within the metropolitan region outside the central city. Sometimes, this central city/regional competition has less importance for tourist cities. Tourists who want to visit New York City won't be satisfied by visiting the suburbs. At other times, the city/region conflict for tourist cities will be quite significant. The place that everyone calls "Las Vegas"— namely, the Las Vegas Strip—is not actually in the City of Las Vegas. It is in an unincorporated part of Clark County, adjacent to but outside the city. As the county's website proudly declares:

> Clark County is home to the world-famous Las Vegas Strip, heart of the Entertainment Capital of the World and site of 14 of the nation's 15 largest hotels. This jewel in the desert lures many of the 38.9 million tourists who come to the Las Vegas community each year to enjoy its world-class entertainment and hospitality, splendid casinos, fine restaurants and dazzling array of shopping venues.[5]

This suburban location is no accident. The location was chosen specifically because it was outside the city and, consequently, subject to different regulatory authorities, while the city, for its part, was reluctant to be overreliant on businesses associated with organized crime.[6] This kind of careful selection of a suburban location is not unique to Las Vegas. Walt Disney World is governed by local governmental institutions that the state specifically established to ensure that decision makers would not have to be responsive to local residents. No city of significant size in the United States is as overwhelmingly focused on attracting visitors as these suburban tourist destinations. But not all tourist sites in the suburbs are as elaborate: sports stadiums are located in the suburbs too. The nature of the city/region relationship, then, depends on the kind of tourism involved. Some possibilities are more amenable to suburban locations than others.

Finally, tourist cities seek a different relationship with outsiders than global cities. They are in search of transitory connections with the wider world, while global cities want the kind of development that will foster long-lasting economic integration of city residents with international counterparts. The two kinds of cities will therefore have different development priorities. Tourist cities are more likely to be interested in facilitating the construction of new hotels than in assisting in the development of luxury condos. They will favor subsidies for new festival marketplaces and sports arenas rather than biotechnology parks, office towers, or upgrades to the telecommunications infrastructure. And they will be less concerned with improving their financial districts than in making their waterfronts livelier or their shopping districts trendier. Most tourist cities do not even have a global focus. Although there are tourist cities that invite the whole world (Venice), many of the attractions tourist cities favor are directed at people who live in the nearby suburbs (shopping centers, sports events). Given these differences, a city that emphasizes the tourist trade is likely to end up looking quite different than one seeking to become a global city.

Tourist City Alternatives

As the discussion already suggests, tourist cities can be very different from each other as well as from global cities. There is an equally significant variation in the legal problems that cities face when deciding among the options. This becomes clear once one focuses specifically on possible alternatives.

The Tourist-Friendly City

One alternative is to make neighborhoods throughout the city the kinds of places that tourists might want to visit. It would be helpful to start with a city that seems attractive because of its vitality (New York), beauty (San Francisco), or natural environment (Miami). With or without this advantage, cities need to enable tourists to move easily around the city: by public transportation, by taxi, and (by providing adequate parking) using their own cars. The next step is to have attractions for tourists to visit. It would be good to have well-maintained and easily accessible parks (and beaches) close to the tourist areas. Well-supported museums, along with innovative architecture, are another priority. Cities with well-established historical sites, like Boston's Freedom Trail, should maintain readily accessible signs and maps. And, this being America, a variety of shopping opportunities ought to be available everywhere.

If implemented in the proper way, this agenda can make the city attractive to residents as well as to tourists. Pursuit of this vision can thus overlap with the goal of becoming a resident-focused middle-class city more than would creating a tourist bubble or staging a major event. Of course, not every city neighborhood will be a priority even for a tourist-friendly city. And city services, other than transportation and parks, will not be a priority either. This version of the tourist city, therefore, is not the equivalent of seeking to foster a middle class city. Nevertheless, residents can use the transportation network as much as tourists do, and they too can enjoy the parks, museums, and shopping (and, when friends come, even the tourist sites). Ironically, this advantage of being a tourist-friendly city generates its characteristic legal problem: the difficulties that the legal structure creates for being a resident-focused city apply here too. To implement either objective, the city government needs to be able to control the elements of the city that make its neighborhoods attractive. Some cities have more of this kind of authority than others.

Consider first the question of public transportation. A city focused on tourists might want to organize its public transportation system to make its routes and fare packages serve tourists' needs. Of course, there has to be a public transportation system that tourists, like residents, can depend on. Many cities do not have such a system, and they have no legal authority or financial ability to create one. Even those that do have an adequate public transportation system often do not control how it operates. Boston has no representatives on the Massachusetts Bay Transportation Authority, the entity that runs its mass transit system. Boston therefore has no direct voice in the Transportation Authority's decisions about routes, fares or maintenance. Chicago, by contrast, has a major role in the (numerous) public authorities that run its transportation system. And Chicago also controls a majority of the board of directors of the city's Metropolitan Pier and Exposition Authority, the entity that runs its major convention centers. This kind of dual involvement facilitated the Metropolitan Pier and Exposition Authority's $43 million funding of the city's much-admired 2.5-mile, two-lane busway that allows buses to bypass downtown traffic between downtown hotels and the city's convention center. With no control over either its convention center or transit system, Boston has no ability to follow Chicago's lead. It also cannot reduce the price of its subways for tourists—or even use fare increases to fund other tourist-related activities. Still, although control over transportation infrastructure is important, it is not necessarily decisive. Portland, Oregon's free public transit in its downtown area is provided not by the city but by Tri-Met, a public authority that covers its three-county region.[7]

Cities' control over parking facilities varies too. Consider a recent case concerning Philadelphia. The city once had no legal power to run municipal parking facilities because the state prevented it from competing with private parking operators and also subjected it to state-imposed debt limits that made it impossible to raise the necessary capital. In 1947, the state legislature authorized the state's localities to create city-controlled municipal parking authorities with their own debt limit. Once established, these authorities began not only to open parking garages but to assume a range of other parking-related responsibilities, including the issuance of parking tickets and the administration of on-street parking meters. The Philadelphia Parking Authority eventually contributed $13 million annually to the city's operating budget. In 2001, the state passed legislation that transferred control of the Philadelphia Parking Authority from mayoral to gubernatorial appointees. In addition, as a way of meeting a state funding commitment to the city's schools without burdening the state treasury, the legislation ordered the transfer of $45 million of the Parking Authority's retained earnings to the school district. The city argued that stripping it of its parking authority and its funds in this manner violated its constitutionally protected home rule authority. The Pennsylvania Supreme Court decided otherwise. Parking authorities, the court ruled, were created by state law and therefore could be modified by state law, with or without the city's consent. This back-and-forth history captures for one city some of the contradictory attitudes toward city control over parking that exist nationwide.[8] Moreover, a city's decisions about parking cannot be viewed in isolation. A city that has few revenue-raising options and little capital with which to build city-owned garages may have perverse incentives when it comes to presenting a hospitable face to visitors: a surprisingly large portion of Boston's nontax revenue comes from the parking fines it imposes.

How about parks? Here's the description of the New York City's Department of Parks and Recreation on its website:

> Parks & Recreation is the steward of almost 29,000 acres of land—14 percent of New York City—including more than 4,000 individual properties ranging from Yankee Stadium and Central Park to community gardens and Greenstreets. We operate more than 800 athletic fields and nearly 1,000 playgrounds; we manage four major stadia, 550 tennis courts, 52 public pools, 48 recreational facilities, 17 nature centers,

13 golf courses, and 14 miles of beaches; we care for 1,200 monuments and 22 historic house museums; we look after 500,000 street trees, and two million more in parks. We are New York City's principal provider of athletic facilities. We are home to free concerts, world-class sports events, and cultural festivals.

This kind of control over the city's parks facilitates tourism and enriches the lives of city residents simultaneously. Chicago, with one exception, similarly maintains all of the parks and recreational areas within its boundaries. Beginning in 1997, the city was therefore able to transform an area on its lakefront that was dominated by railroad tracks and parking lots into Millennium Park, a twenty-four-acre public space that has become a major tourist attraction; its Pritzker Pavilion, just one of its amenities, provides concerts free of charge. Once again, Boston lacks the kind of authority to follow Chicago's lead. Although the city operates major public parks too—including Boston Common—the Massachusetts Turnpike Authority controls the more than three hundred acres created by the Big Dig that will be devoted to open space, including the Rose Kennedy Greenway. The state's Department of Conservation and Recreation controls other important public recreational spaces both within the city and in its neighboring suburbs, while the National Park Service manages the Boston Harbor Islands.[9] The major venue for free concerts in Boston, the Hatch Shell, is controlled by the Department of Conservation and Recreation as well—even though the city places considerable importance on its annual Fourth of July concert and celebration at the Hatch Shell.[10]

Boston is not in a good position to support its museums and cultural activities either. Boston can provide support for the arts only by dedicating a portion of its property tax revenues to them.[11] The cities that have a dedicated funding mechanism for culture and the arts normally rely on a sales tax or a hotel tax. One reason for this is the sense that, as a matter of equity, investments in tourism should be funded by a source that comes in significant part from tourists themselves. Another is that a city that derives little income from tourism has less of an incentive to fund institutions that attract them. A third is a political reason: city residents are often more interested in funding local art projects and community theaters than in supporting a major exhibit at an internationally recognized museum. The resulting differences among cities in funding for the arts are quite dramatic. In 2007, Boston's Department of Arts, Tourism and Special Events had a budget of just over $400,000 for "arts promotion." It spent the money primarily on programs that benefit local residents by providing grants of up to $5,000 to cultural and educational programs; it made no grants to major tourist attractions such as the Museum of Fine Arts or the Isabella Stewart Gardner

Museum. San Francisco, on the other hand, has a program called Grants for the Arts, whose purpose is to "enhance our City's attractiveness to visitors." It uses its hotel tax revenues to support cultural attractions, ranging from an international film festival to a ballet company, and to help fund major museums, including $363,100 to the city's science museum and $427,775 to the San Francisco Museum of Modern Art. New York City's Department of Cultural Affairs is in another category altogether. It provides funding, both grants and payment of utility expenses, to thirty-four institutions that occupy city-owned land or are located in city-owned buildings. The list includes the Metropolitan Museum of Art, the Brooklyn Academy of Music, Lincoln Center, Carnegie Hall, and the American Museum of Natural History—all major tourist attractions—as well as community-based organizations. The department is the largest cultural funding agency in the country, with an annual budget of more than $130 million and a four-year capital budget of more than $800 million.[12]

Another amenity that cities market to tourists is their own history. Boston's Freedom Trail, which directs visitors to many of the city's leading historical landmarks, is a major tourist attraction. But the fragmented control over public land within the city impedes Boston's ability to maintain its appeal. According to the *Boston Globe,* a local resident noticed that ornamental posts designed to keep cars off the Freedom Trail were missing, thereby diminishing its attractiveness to residents and tourists alike. A reporter for the *Globe* tried to run through the bureaucratic maze to see how the problem could be resolved, and, in so doing, provides an account that illustrates the city's lack of control over one of its signature attractions:

> The city of Boston maintains the trail, but only the sidewalks and the brick or red painted line which marks the trail....The Department of Conservation and Recreation, which manages many of the urban parks and recreational areas in the Boston area, does not oversee the walkway....A spokesman for the National Park Service which oversees a number of local historical sites...said he believed that either the Massachusetts Port Authority or the Massachusetts Turnpike Authority may be in charge....A spokesman for Massport, which maintains and operates the Tobin Bridge, visited the walkway on Thursday morning to check out the posts and said the land belongs to the turnpike authority. While the first Pike spokesman contacted said the authority has no jurisdiction over the bridge or the land underneath it, senior spokeswoman MariEllen Burns was able to determine, 'That is ours.' New posts have been ordered and will be installed before summer's end, she said....The confusion about who maintains this walkway, said

Burns, is likely because there are two walkways in the area: one that goes under the Tobin Bridge that's maintained by Massport and this one, which sneaks under a ramp that leads to the Central Artery North Area Tunnel and the Tobin.[13]

Control over the waterfront is our final example. One reason this is important is that waterfront areas, like parks, become major attractions both for tourists and city residents. But another is specifically about tourism: as the example of Brooklyn's Red Hook, discussed in chapter 7, illustrates, waterfronts can become major entry points for tourism if they accommodate cruise lines. The cruise industry experienced an average annual rate of growth of 8 percent between 1980 and 2004; in 2004, U.S. and Canadian cruise lines had over nine million passengers. A city that owns its waterfront can make decisions about how much of the waterfront will be available to cruise ships, the rules that will govern the ships that use the port, and the services and amenities that will be provided to make the port attractive both to the operators of the cruise lines and to their passengers. San Francisco owns its waterfront, and the city is using that power to construct a state-of-the-art port that will include large berths to accommodate a near doubling of cruise ships, as well as commercial and retail space. The terminal will be part of a revitalized port district that will also include residential development and a public park. Seattle's port, like Boston's and New York's, is controlled not by the city but by a port authority, the Port of Seattle. It is governed by five commissioners elected by the voters of King County, which includes outlying suburban and rural areas as well as Seattle. Therefore, if Seattle's city government wanted to improve its port district to attract more cruise ships, it would need to win the support and cooperation of an agency outside of its control. No doubt, the Port of Seattle has its own incentives to undertake port improvements; it in fact has done so. But it, not the city, decides the content, extent, and timing of these improvements.[14]

What we have just said about transportation, parking, parks, museums, tourist sites, and ports is simply an illustration of the variations across the country in the extent of city control over amenities that are attractive to tourists. We have singled out Boston as an illustration of a city that lacks control over these attractions, but Boston is not unique. Every city lacks control over some of the ingredients of being a tourist-friendly city (New York over its subways; Seattle over the Space Needle, the symbol of its 1962 World's Fair, which is owned and operated by the privately owned Space Needle Corporation). And other cities across the country have a legal structure very much like Boston's. The City of Newark, like Boston, depends on property taxes and state aid for more than half of its revenue. The city's resulting lack of resources—along with the other legal limitations that the state imposes and, of course, the isolation of the city's African American community—has had a much more negative effect on Newark than state-imposed limits have had on Boston. The impact on Newark's tourist attractions reflects this. Peter Eisinger quotes a critic of the New Jersey Performing Art Center, which opened in Newark in 1997, as saying: "It is being built by nonresidents for nonresidents. They will come and get dumped off at the front, see the show, and then leave without having any impact on the community."[15] Notwithstanding the new Performing Arts Center, the critic is saying, Newark has isolated a portion of the city for the enjoyment of tourists rather than becoming a tourist-friendly city.

The problem facing a city's control over shopping is structured differently than the ingredients discussed so far. The issue is not governmental fragmentation or state interference or resource constraints. When a mall developer wants to provide an ideal shopping experience, it tries to organize the mall store-by-store to attract the mix of shoppers it is looking for. Cities cannot do this. Each store is private property. Cities can use their zoning powers creatively to promote a diverse mix of retail establishments. But the city cannot control the kind of stores that are available on a street-by-street basis, and, as a result, it cannot organize the city's shopping to bring in tourists the way that a mall can. To design shopping in a way that might attract tourists, the city cannot rely on its own legal powers. It could rely on private decision making, hoping that "the free market" alone will enliven the city streets. But if the city wants to do something itself, its best option is to help a developer acquire a large enough piece of city land so that, unlike the city, it can organize the area to be tourist friendly. A city interested in tourism, in other words, is better off if it turns away from the traditional design of shopping along city streets and toward a shopping development, such as a festival marketplace. To provide a shopping experience marketed to tourists, cities are thus led to develop not a tourist-friendly city but a tourist bubble.

The Fantasy City or Tourist Bubble

A fantasy city, also known as a tourist bubble, is generally organized around shopping.[16] But there are significant differences between a decision to develop a festival marketplace, a sports stadium, a convention center, or a casino. One difference, obviously enough, lies in the kinds of people who will be attracted to the developments. The legal structure of the choices differs as well. All the variants of the tourist bubble, however, have one thing in common: the basic legal device is privatization. Sometimes the privatization takes the form of an outright transfer of property to a private party; sometimes it leads to the creation of a public-private partnership; and sometimes ownership is transferred to a state-created public authority not subject to city control. Whichever form is used, the city's lack of control over the undertaking becomes a price that the city pays for the tourist business being generated.

The easiest way to grasp the effect of this privatization is to start with its strongest version, one adopted by the ultimate fantasy city: the Walt Disney World Resort. Richard Foglesong offers an indispensable account of the legal structure of Disney World, and we limit ourselves here to a brief summary of it.[17] Disney World, very importantly, is not in Orlando. On the contrary, the key state intervention was to carve out an area twice the size of Manhattan from a portion of two countries, near but by no means in Orlando, and to establish for the area its own government structure: the Reedy Creek Improvement District. The district is a property-owner government—that is, it is elected by landowners, not residents, on a one–acre—one-vote franchise. The prime landowner, of course, is Disney. The district is empowered by state law to regulate land use, provide municipal services (including a fire department and transportation), build roads and sewer lines, and issue tax-free bonds. And it is explicitly exempted from county and state land use laws, as well as from the impact fees that other developers are required to pay. (There are also two small municipalities within the district populated by Disney employees, but they have transferred planning and zoning power to the district.)

It is no overstatement to say that the resulting development has been a tourist success. In 2006, four of its sites—the Magic Kingdom, Epcot, Disney-MGM Studios, and Disney's Animal Kingdom—occupied four of the top five spots in theme park attendance in the United States (Disneyland was 2nd). Four were also in the top eight in worldwide attendance, with the Magic Kingdom alone being the number-one theme park in the world in 2006, with more than sixteen million visitors.[18] The effect on the entire regional area, including Orlando, has been overwhelming. Both the city and the metropolitan area have exploded in population, and many additional developments, including not just hotels but other tourist attractions, have been attracted to the area. This effect can be seen as the ultimate dream of the tourist city agenda: amazing economic growth. Given the legal structure, however, Disney World has generated problems and opposition as well. State funding for the infrastructure and other services provided to Disney has taken money from other parts of the region. The demands generated by the tourist influx, the lack of affordable housing, traffic congestion, and the low-wage economy that Disney World represents create problems for the area as a whole. The restriction on state power over the Reedy Creek Improvement District hampers the state's ability to address these problems or to ensure that Disney adequately shares in the costs of solutions. And Disney's plans to open a convention center and create Downtown Disney threaten to undermine Orlando's economic prosperity while it stimulates Disney's own success.

Disney World is not the kind of central city project on which this book focuses. But it represents a model that, on a vastly more limited scale, cities can modify and adapt to create tourist bubbles of their own. The modifications are important but the result is similar: to provide public support for a development controlled not by the city but by a private corporation or a public authority. This kind of privatization of city space is an ingredient not only of the tourist city but of the global city as well. Perhaps the most striking global city version is Canary Wharf in London, a development near London's main financial district, the "City of London." A project of Margaret Thatcher's time, the development was initiated by the London Docklands Development Corporation, a public authority created by the national government, which, in 1987, sold the site to a private company, Olympia and York Canary Wharf Investments. After quite dramatic ups and downs, including bankruptcy, the current owner, the Canary Wharf Group, now manages one of the major financial centers in the world. The development includes the three tallest buildings in the United Kingdom and employs more than eighty thousand people in its ninety-seven-acre territory. With government-financed light rail and Underground connections now in place, substantial expansion plans are being made. The project, in short, is an integral part of London's global city future. But it is important to recognize that the entire development—plazas and streets included—is private property, policed by security guards. As with many tourist city examples in the heart of American cities, the legal restraints on the city's regulation of private property are an essential ingredient in the way the development operates.[19]

The privatization fostered by the global city and by the tourist city can be—and increasingly are—combined in a single development. Canary Wharf is an example: it has become not just a workplace but a shopping environment, with more than half a million shoppers visiting the area each week. Similar dual-focused projects are multiplying in the United States as well. Consider two examples just from New York City. The Time Warner Building houses the offices of one of the world's leading media and entertainment companies (Time Warner) and high-end condominiums. But it also offers major tourist attractions: a hotel, a major concert venue, a shopping mall, and restaurants. Atlantic Yards, a $4 billion project in Brooklyn being created by the developer Forest City Ratner, goes one step further: it is envisioned as having seventeen buildings, including a sports stadium, 250,000 square feet of retail space, a hotel, and office space, along with parks and (a gesture toward the middle class city) affordable, as well as unaffordable, housing.

For many developments, then, a "tourist bubble" no longer seems the right term. The developments are also "global bubbles"—and, sometimes, more than that. We focus on the extent of privatization in this chapter, however, because tourist venues present the most striking example of privatization in the organization of city life. Many of the developments associated with the global city are single office buildings (Canary Wharf and Atlantic Yards are striking exceptions), and it is not particularly surprising to understand these office buildings as private property. The buildings are not designed to invite the public in; indeed, very often, members of the public are excluded by security guards. Tourist attractions are specifically created for the public. They present themselves to the world as a major city destination even though the "public space" they offer is controlled by a private entity. That's why we think that they represent the privatization of public space in its strongest form.

Tourist bubbles are organized in two different ways. One is to have the development run by a private company. The other is to have it operated by a public authority—a government institution, to be sure, but one that is insulated from local democratic control. (Disney World combines these two forms in a very striking manner.) The corporate model is epitomized by the festival marketplace, with the Rouse Company's Faneuil Hall Marketplace in Boston and Harborplace in Baltimore being classic examples. The city provides the land (either because it owns it or acquires it through condemnation), offers infrastructure support, and grants tax exemptions or subsidies. The corporation acquires the property, generally through a long-term lease, which it then manages as private property. In the planning stage, the two parties work together to get support from the neighborhood and other governments for the project. Once in operation, the corporation organizes the shops, imposes charges for services, provides security guards, and markets the enterprise. The result is that, while the government uses its power and resources to support private shopping and entertainment, much of the decision making about the site is made by a private company.[20]

This kind of corporate-organized development model exists not only for festival marketplaces but also for theme parks and casinos. Consider this report from the *Boston Globe* about Detroit:

> Over the past eight years, Detroit has brought three casinos into the heart of the city, revitalizing portions of its downtown and becoming the most populous American city with a casino inside its borders. The casinos, catering to high rollers and working folks, added nearly 7,000 jobs…Last year, they brought in $1.3 billion in revenue, of which… 11.9 percent, or $155 million, [went] to the city of Detroit. The city has built more hotels in the past five years than in the previous 25 years…diversifying the tax base and turning the Motor City into the fifth highest-grossing casino market, falling just behind Connecticut.[21]

Connecticut? Casino gambling is more pervasive than you might realize. And what's the article doing in the *Boston Globe*? No surprise: Boston's mayor wants to attract a resort-style casino—"with hotels, shops, and Vegas-style shows"—into the city's East Boston neighborhood. Boston cannot make this deal on its own. And it goes without saying that the casino would be run by a private corporation. One of Detroit's casinos is operated by MGM Mirage, one of the nation's major "hotel and gaming companies," as they call themselves.[22]

The alternative development model is the public authority. Convention centers are prime users of this model. As Dennis Judd and Dick Sampson explain, from the outset the reason to organize convention centers as public authorities was that that they could offer a public tourist attraction yet be managed like a private corporation.

> These public/private institutions were not bound by the rules that frustrated public initiatives undertaken by general-purpose governments. They could make decisions without worrying about maintaining an electoral coalition. They could operate like corporations, protecting their information and books, but at the same time, because they pursued policy objectives, they could borrow money just like governments and strike equity and revenue-generating relationships with developers. These new arrangements are the key to understanding how fiscally strapped cities impacted by deindustrialization were able to initiate a new era of city-building in the 1970s and 1980s.[23]

According to a recent study by the Brookings Institution, convention center business has declined in recent years. But, the study says, cities keep building and expanding them anyway.[24] Many major projects are under construction or planned—in New York, Chicago, Denver, and Seattle, among other places. How, the Brookings study asks, can this expansion and growth be explained given the declining business? The intense competition for business tourism in the United States generates an ever-increasing desire to be at the top of the convention business hierarchy. "Throwing good money after bad," is the study's name for this phenomenon. It is referring not simply to the building of convention centers. Chicago's Metropolitan Pier and Exposition Authority has built, and owns, an eight-hundred-room Hyatt Hotel next to its McCormack Place convention center, and Houston and Denver, among other cities, are following the lead. (Imagine the reaction if a city built and owned a Hyatt Hotel.) The intensity of the competition is being fueled in part by two prime suburban locations—"Las Vegas" and "Orlando"—that are attracting major events away from big cities. In Las Vegas, the competition is not just between the Las Vegas Convention and Visitors Authority and other similar venues; the Authority now has to compete with a privately owned convention center on the Las Vegas Strip, the Mandalay Bay Convention Center, which has one million square feet of exhibit space.

As Judd and Sampson argue, the public authority structure fuels this competitive frenzy. The authorities are usually state-created agencies, run by boards of directors, and not responsive to the city electorate and, sometimes, not even to the city government. Boston's two convention centers are owned and operated by a state agency, the Massachusetts Convention Center Authority, controlled by the governor. (It has completed a large hotel on the city's South Boston Waterfront, next to the city's newest convention center, a hotel that does not contribute money to the city's hotel tax because it is located on state-owned land.) Chicago's two convention centers, by contrast, are run by the Metropolitan Pier and Exposition Authority, an authority that, although established by the state legislature, is controlled by mayoral appointees. Even so, the authority structure, with its own leadership and having an ability to issue debt, can have a mind of its own. The reason to have authority-run convention centers in the first place is to isolate them from city politics. The authority is also supposed to have a limited focus on convention business and is organized to expand it. To be sure, notwithstanding its independence, the authority's debts have to be paid off. And city resources are often used to do so. By diverting resources in this way, convention centers thus take money from other city priorities.[25]

Sports stadiums are sometimes financed and run by authorities. There are major sports authorities across the country—in Chicago, Denver, and Atlanta, for example—and, like convention center authorities, they too issue debt to fund their facilities. But sports financing occurs in many other ways as well (singly and in combination): private financing, city support, state support, selling name rights, and money provided by the teams themselves. A detailed review of sports financing in the United States documents the importance of city involvement.[26] Cities often issue debt to support the construction of sports stadiums, and the public's share of the costs of construction is normally paid off with additional taxes on hotels, admissions, or general sales taxes. Cities without these sources of income or bonding authority—or with significant limits on them—thus have significant difficulty in putting together the necessary financing. Although the evidence suggests that stadiums do not generate significant economic benefits to cities, the competitive drive to build them remains strong. The new Yankee Stadium is supported largely by the Yankees themselves, and considerable state money is being provided as well. But the city is spending a considerable sum too, both directly (building parking, acquiring related property, demolishing the old stadium) and by forgoing the payment of rent or property taxes on the site. The project also requires New York City to issue tax-exempt bonds, which will be paid off by the Yankees.

Although there are many other kinds of tourist bubble developments, enough has been said about these kinds of projects to demonstrate why they, and not the tourist-friendly city, have become the major focus for cities embracing the tourist city agenda. The tourist city literature primarily focuses on this form of tourist development, most often to critique the fake historicism, the "sanitized razzmatazz," the commercialization of the culture, and the lack of impact—or the negative impact—on the city neighborhoods not visited by tourists.[27] Our emphasis has been on another aspect of tourist bubbles: how the legal structure both pushes cities to embrace them and limits their role in controlling them. As with the global city, the structure of state finance and land use law favors the production of tourist bubbles. Yet here, too, there is a major catch. The limits imposed on cities' state-granted legal authority and resources point them in the direction of privatization. Either through the private corporate structure or the creation of a public authority, cities that promote this alternative cede power over portions of their territory to others.

One-Time Events

A final strategy for cities interested in promoting tourism is to organize a single big tourist event, like the Olympics. This is almost certainly a once-in-a-lifetime event for the city. That's what makes it distinguishable from the more routine, once-a-year events that have become increasingly common across the country and around the world. These once-a-year attractions—the Seattle and New York Film Festivals, Art Basel Miami Beach, New Orleans Mardi Gras—have their own distinctive character. They are not a version of a tourist-friendly city (they are located in one or two neighborhoods) and do not require the construction of a tourist bubble either. Their closest analogy is to conventions: they are conventions not for businesspeople but for pleasure seekers. One advantage they offer is that no convention center is necessary (although Art Basel Miami Beach is held at the convention center). Like the tourist-friendly city and the tourist bubble, they are clearly focused on tourism: they welcome specialized visitors to town for a few days and hope that they spread their money around.

One-time events are different. It is often said that they are organized to put the city on the map. But consider the competition for the 2012 Olympics between London, New York, and Paris. What kind of map weren't these cities already on? The more plausible explanation for holding these events, it seems to us, is city transformation. Sure, the tourists who attend the events are very much part of the picture: they bring lots of people to town, if only for a short period of time. But no city would engage in the kind of dramatic reconstruction of its infrastructure now being undertaken—and no hotel chain would build hotels either—without there being a long-term development plan spurred by a sense of urgency about initiating it. One-time events are valuable because they become a vehicle for a dramatic reconstruction of city neighborhoods. This long-term project can sometimes conflict with the short-term event. Building a stadium and housing for athletes can produce structures that have no long-term purpose; they might even detract from the desired goal of city development. Designing the sites for the big event therefore has to focus on two stages simultaneously, one temporary, one permanent.

This scenario is most spectacularly being played out at the moment in Beijing, ten South African cities (including Johannesburg and Cape Town), Shanghai, and London—the sites, respectively, of the 2008 Olympics, the 2010 Soccer World Cup, the 2010 World Expo ("the Olympic Games of the economy, science and technology"), and the 2012 Olympics. The origins of this model can be found earlier—most impressively in Barcelona (Olympics 1992) but also in Athens (Olympics 2004), Atlanta (Olympics 1996), and elsewhere. Barcelona tore down warehouses and utility plants to open up a new beachfront that enlivened nearby neighborhoods, built underground highways, constructed two thousand apartments designed by thirty architects, and overhauled a large city park. Atlanta's efforts were more modest, but lasting results include Centennial Olympic Park and housing for the Georgia Institute of Technology. Beijing, Johannesburg, Shanghai, and London are taking this model significantly further. All four cities are expanding their transportation network in a dramatic fashion (trains and buses in Johannesburg, the world's largest airline terminal in Beijing, Eurostar connections in London). They are condemning entire neighborhoods and building new ones, and they are seeking investment for global city projects along with hotels and tourist attractions. The global city aspect of events such as the Olympics is epitomized by the Office of Metropolitan Architecture's new five-million-square-foot headquarters for Chinese Central Television in Beijing—a building that is at once an architectural tourist attraction and a link to global media and entertainment. Its completion is timed to correspond with the opening of the Olympic Games.[28]

No American city could undertake this kind of city transformation on its own. The cities elsewhere in the world can't do it by themselves either. Reconstruction at this scale requires extraordinary financial resources, and the organizing effort itself exceeds any city's capacity. In China, South Africa, and the United Kingdom, the national government is playing a major role in the funding, design, management, and promotion of the necessary city transformation. The resulting organizational structure is very complex. Consider one example: London. The London Organizing Committee of the Olympic Games and Paralympic Games, a corporation with its own board of directors, is responsible for preparing and staging the games. The Olympic Delivery Authority, created by Parliament, is the public body responsible for developing and building the venues and infrastructure for the games. Both have offices at Canary Wharf. The Department for Culture, Media and Sport is the major national government body focused on the delivery of the games. The Olympic Board, consisting of the mayor of London, the national Olympics minister, the head of the Organizing Committee, and the Chair of the British Olympics Association, provides oversight, strategic coordination, and monitoring of the project. The mayor of London's job is to try to ensure that Londoners benefit from the games.[29]

It is hard to imagine the kind of investment being lavished on these big events being made to promote the middle class or the regional city—or even other versions of the tourist city. Cities compete to have a once-in-a-lifetime event because it will enable them to leverage investment, both public and private, to reconfigure the city in global and tourist terms in a short period of time. The combination of sports fever and city competition enables such an undertaking in a way not possible even for sports or tourism alone. To be sure, sports fever is not necessary everywhere. The motto of Shanghai's 2010 World Expo is "Keeping in mind the next 60 years' development while preparing for the six months' Exposition."[30] One of us, however, was with a large crowd of Londoners the day that the city won the 2012 Olympics, and their cheers seemed to resemble nothing so much as the typical reaction to a teams' victory in the World Cup or World Series. "We won!"

Winning has its downside. The city will be remodeled in the image of a version of the global city and of the tourist city that may not be responsive to city residents' definition of these goals, let alone to their goals of maintaining their way of life or promoting a middle class city. No doubt, city residents and the city government will often be caught up in the fever themselves. But, as in London, the decisions about the future of the city will be in the hands of a public/private partnership so complex and unaccountable that it will never be easy to pin down exactly why this version of the city's future was selected or exactly who selected it.

The Tourist Future

There are dangers presented by tourist city development beyond privatization. One is that success can be failure. Perhaps the premier tourist city in the world, Venice, has lost 60 percent of its population in the last fifty years. Most economic life, other than tourism, has fled the city for its surrounding region, and the city faces the prospect of becoming a large museum. The future of Venice is not a goal even many tourist cities would embrace. For whose benefit is this city being created? To be sure, tourists overwhelm the Las Vegas Strip too. But Venice was an important city for a thousand years—and a major commercial center as well. Of course, success is not the only problem. Another is failure itself, pure and simple.

A city's failure to focus on changing tastes and fashions will lead tourists to go elsewhere. A city's failure to support its cultural attractions—and to generate new ones—will suffer the same fate. A city gambling on tourism bets on a risky future. The decline, like that of an industrial city, can be devastating.

Nevertheless, as Dennis Judd and Susan Fainstein end their book *Tourist City* by saying: "Tourists are everywhere, and they are here to stay."[31] Every city therefore has to decide what kind of tourism it wants to promote and what kind of tourist city it wants to be. The options we have explored are only examples, and it seems appropriate to end with another version of the idea. The option is historic preservation: not a dramatic city transformation or a tourist bubble, not even a tourist-friendly city as we have outlined it, but a city that preserves its distinctiveness by limiting changes to its built environment. This route will not be easy, but an essay on Boston by Bruce Ehrlich and Peter Dreier quotes no less of a tourist authority than Arthur Frommer: "Because of historic preservation and only because of historic preservation, the travel industry is now the single largest industry in Europe." Only the cities that initiated "draconian measures in support of preservation" became leading tourist destinations, says Frommer, while cities such as Brussels and Milan, which did not adequately protect their historic environments, turned into tourist backwaters.[32]

Ehrlich and Dreier point out that Boston has only partially embraced historic preservation. It has also embraced the opposite strategies, such as urban renewal and festival marketplaces. Ehrlich and Dreier are also careful to emphasize the importance of federal legislation (such as the creation of national historical sites and federal tax credits) and, above all, state legislation as enablers of Boston's preservation efforts. Boston's historic preservation decisions are made by the Boston Landmarks Commission, established by the state legislature in 1975 and appointed by the mayor. In the now-familiar Massachusetts style, the state legislation details categories from which the mayor's appointments must come (not just architects and planners but the chamber of commerce and the real estate board) and elaborately specifies—the Act is fifteen pages long—the standards that the commission must use in designating either a specific property or a district for preservation.[33] Thus, while Boston can do something to preserve its historical character, the decision is in the Landmark Commission's hands, and it has to follow the state-established framework. Moreover, opposition to the commission's decisions can come both from those who equate preservation with gentrification and from the owners of the properties involved. In the end, the authors suggest, it was Boston's economic downturn, more than popular opposition to urban renewal or city and state government decision making, that saved Boston's historical neighborhoods. Can the city do more? Sure. But wouldn't it be easier to create a tourist bubble?

THE MIDDLE CLASS CITY

For most city residents, the most familiar conception of their city—and of its future—is being a middle class city. This is a city focused on its residents not on outsiders, on its city services not on its marketing ability or financial sector, and on its ability to be the home not simply of the rich and poor but of those in between. The difficulties facing a middle class city are well known. Barry Bluestone and Mary Huff Stevenson describe these difficulties in terms of a "triple revolution" in American society: a demographic change caused by new immigration and the doubling of the minority population; an industrial revolution that led to the loss of traditional blue-collar jobs and the rise of an information-based economy; and the spatial revolution caused by suburbanization. A recent Brookings Institution study found that middle class neighborhoods in many major cities—including many of those we examined in part II—have shrunk significantly since 1970.[1]

Some argue that the decline of the middle class city is not a cause for concern. The new wave of gentrification in major American cities, they say, has simply triggered a natural process of spatial sorting, with middle class families moving to the suburbs as prices in the central city have risen. As one economist remarked, "The majority of middle-class people that have moved out have presumably found themselves better lives out there."[2] Others argue that central cities could not stop this middle class exodus even if they wanted to. The industries that once created middle class urban jobs no longer do, and the market forces underlying gentrification are too powerful to be countered by individual cities. At best, cities can hope that their pursuit of tourism and global finance will benefit the middle class families still living in town. If that doesn't work, it would simply prove that cities are no longer hospitable to the middle class.

Whether or not these arguments seem persuasive, no successful city could actually embrace them wholeheartedly. City leaders worry that, unless they adopt policies specifically targeted at increasing their share of the middle class, their cities will become a home for the rich and the very poor. The Brookings study of trends since 1970 demonstrates that such a concern is justified. And a city starkly divided in this way is not a desirable goal. Around the world, polarized cities generate insecurity for both the rich and the poor—insecurity that can take the form of violence, economic desperation, and the decline of public space and public life. São Paulo is one well-known illustration of this problem, and it is not a model to be embraced. Besides, there is no reason to think that local residents—that is, city voters—want their city's economic development strategy to focus primarily on attracting wealthy outsiders who can price them out of their own neighborhoods. At the same time, cities without a middle class can make it difficult for the poor to improve their lives. The Brookings Institution study describes the basis for this concern:

> If rising economic inequality has contributed to rising economic segregation, the ability of lower-income individuals to choose and access middle-income neighborhoods may have declined. This, in turn, may limit their access to associated amenities like jobs, decent health care, safe neighborhoods, and adequate political representation. A lack of middle-income neighborhoods may also limit opportunities for low and moderate-income homeowners to "move up" the property ladder, if the house-price differential between lower- and higher-income neighborhoods is too high.[3]

No city looks forward to a future in which a large segment of its population will be locked in poverty.

In order to promote a middle class city, one needs some idea of what the middle class is. The definitions of the term "class" are famously controversial.[4] Even if the test is to be defined in terms of income, the income level could be compared to the average income of other city residents (as the Brookings study does) or to a specified level of poverty (as the Census does). Other definitions refer not to income but to middle class desires for certain goods: education, public safety, and affordable housing. Of course, the rich and poor want good city services too. Nevertheless, it is thought, some services are peculiarly important to middle class residents because they lack the money to avoid relying on them or, unlike the rich, to leave the city if services are inadequate.

Focusing on the precise definition of the middle class, on the other hand, may be the wrong way to approach the issue. After all, a middle class city need not be one that excludes the rich and poor. It could be a class-diverse city—one that includes people at all income levels. Cities that seek to ensure diversity do not all start from a common position. A city might already have a large middle class and want to retain it. It might be trying to attract middle class families from elsewhere (in particular, from neighboring suburbs). Or it might be focused on increasing the opportunities for poor city residents to enter the ranks of the middle class. Whichever the focus, its options are limited. In this chapter, we leave undefined the precise definition of those who are neither rich nor poor but in between. We simply note that, in 1999, the middle 20 percent of American households made between $34,000 and $52,000, and the middle 60 percent made between $18,000 and $81,000. Those figures provide a standard definition of what the middle class is.[5]

We concentrate in this chapter on four major ingredients in the task of strengthening a city's capacity to be a middle class city: taxation, education, housing, and the local economy. Cities face significant hurdles when trying to exercise control in these areas. Given these obstacles, even cities that want to promote a middle class future have reason to doubt whether they have the power to do so. It is important to have a detailed sense of the impact that state law has on these issues before we turn to the final topic: the local economy. Ultimately, we contend, cities seeking to be a middle class city need to promote not just their middle class residents' welfare but their economic development. Without a middle-class economic-development strategy, a middle class city has little hope of competing with global city or tourist city ideals. One reason for this is that cities have more authority over economic development than over the other parts of the agenda. A different legal structure could change a city's approach to being a middle class city, enabling a greater focus on taxation, education, and housing. At the moment, however, the legal structure for the middle class city, like for the global city and the tourist city, makes economic development the easiest starting place.

Taxation

One possible way to promote a middle class city is through tax policy. On the national level, a progressive income tax is a principal mechanism used to generate the resources necessary to provide services to those who need them. Not surprisingly, the Drum Major Institute's survey suggested that increasing the progressiveness of New York City's locally imposed income tax would help the city retain residents of modest means. Since a middle class city is a service city, adequate resources are essential. And, given the squeeze on middle class incomes, these resources cannot come from increasing taxes on the very people who are being enticed to come, or stay, in town. Of course, not every city can adopt a policy of progressive taxation. Many cities are wary of driving their wealthiest residents out of town if they raise their taxes. But other cities—New York City being a prime example—might be able to keep both a wealthy population and a high tax rate. Very wealthy people are apparently willing to pay a premium to live and work in New York City—and in San Francisco and Boston as well. Absent legal restraints, these cities might be able to make their taxes progressive without driving away their richest residents. If so, greater tax equity can permit the city to generate more revenue without imposing undue costs on residents less able to pay them.

What the Drum Major Institute's report does not highlight is the fact that this option is unavailable to New York City and to American cities more generally. Let's start with the property tax. One tool that cities have used to make the property tax more progressive is the imposition of differential assessments. Under this approach, expensive houses are assessed at a higher rate than cheaper ones. State law generally prohibits this practice, in part because the differentiation has too often reflected political influence more than sound tax policy. In Massachusetts, the state courts have declared the practice of differential assessment a violation of the state constitution, and they have required Boston and other municipalities to assess all property at full value. Pursuant to state legislation, New York City continues to rely on differential assessments. It imposes lower assessment caps on one-, two-, and three-family houses than on high-rise condominiums. Although this differential treatment adds a progressive dimension to the local property tax, the differentials even in New York City are small and are strictly regulated by state law. New York's practice is also subject to the criticism lodged in Massachusetts: creating a progressive property tax by assessing property in different ways generates a significant potential for arbitrariness.

The requirement of full valuation does not mean that all property has to be taxed at the same rate. In response to the judicial decisions in Massachusetts, voters passed a statewide referendum that permitted Boston and other cities to categorize property for tax purposes, with different rates applicable to residential and to commercial and industrial property. This introduced an element of middle class protection; it was enacted to limit the burden on middle class homeowners. But it does not address the regressive effect of the property tax on homeowners of different means. The property tax remains a flat tax within the permitted categories, and all residential property is treated as a single category. The current scheme can therefore undermine the provision of middle class housing. Although property taxes require those in expensive houses to pay more taxes than those in cheaper ones, the poor and the middle class spend a greater percentage of their income on housing than do the rich. As a result, the formal equality of a flat tax has an unequal impact: a larger percentage of middle class income goes to property taxes than it does for the rich.

One residential property tax differential does exist in Massachusetts: state law gives cities the option of creating a local exemption for the elderly as a way of ensuring that rising property taxes do not displace long-term residents on fixed incomes. Other states, such as Colorado, go even further: they have established statewide property tax exemptions for elderly residents, without giving cities a say in determining whether the exemption makes sense. It is not clear, however, that an exemption for the elderly serves the purpose of promoting a middle class city. It may do the opposite. A property tax exemption for the elderly does not help a city that wants to protect middle class families from rising property taxes. It may even increase the pressure on the city to raise property taxes on these families to meet its expenses. Yet the only exemptions from the property tax permitted are those allowed by state law: Boston can deny the exemption for the elderly, but it cannot establish a different one that would be more tailored to the needs of young families.

As we have already noted, the property tax generates pressure on a city to increase property values and thus works against the promotion of a middle class city. High property values, and the accompanying high property taxes, tend to prevent middle class families from remaining in town. For this reason, state restrictions on local property taxes can be consistent with a city's goal of becoming a middle class city. But if property tax receipts are capped, other sources of revenue are needed. Although Boston is limited to relying on the property tax, other states enable their cities to enact a sales tax. Perhaps, then, a progressive sales tax would be a better way to promote a middle class city. Of course, progressive sales taxation might focus not on the needs of the middle class but of the poor. In New Jersey, the local portion of the sales tax is waived when sales are made in the state's urban enterprise zones, and a luxury tax is imposed on fur sales of more than $500.

Some states seek to help the middle class by establishing types of consumption that are exempt from the sales tax. A local tax that is imposed on hotels or rental cars targets taxpayers with more disposable income while exempting everyone else, thereby taking pressure off a more general sales tax. The same is true, to some extent, of a restaurant tax. (These taxes also have the added feature of targeting nonresident taxpayers.) Seattle recently considered a referendum, the Seattle latte tax, that would have imposed a 10-cent tax on espresso drinks; the proceeds would have been dedicated to providing subsidized child care. The referendum failed, but it reflects the recent interest in trying to make the city's tax system less burdensome on the middle class. (Measures like the one proposed in Seattle would likely be subject to legal challenge in many cities; it is not even clear that Seattle's latte tax would have survived a legal challenge in that state had it passed.)

Many other options are available. In Illinois, groceries and nonprescription drugs have a sales tax of 1 percent, while newspapers and magazines are exempt from the sales tax. Colorado does not impose a sales tax on groceries but it does tax clothing. Massachusetts has a long list of exemptions, including "food products" (but excluding prepared meals); residential water, gas, and electric services; returnable containers; clothing and footwear up to $175; prescription medicines, prostheses and medical appliances or services; and the American flag. In 2006, New York State enabled its cities to eliminate the sales tax on clothing and shoes with prices up to $110 per item; New York City has done so. Some of these items can be understood as efforts to make the sales tax more progressive, but not all. Whatever their impact, with some exceptions (like the New York City example just mentioned), the decisions are made by state law. Most cities cannot revise the list of exemptions—or add their own.

Finally, we turn to local income taxes. Many local governments—including many major cities, not just Boston—do not have the authority to adopt such a tax. But some states give cities the discretion to impose an income tax, although they set the rates and rules that govern it. And one state—Maryland—requires its cities to impose an income tax. Even when the tax is allowed, state law usually requires that it be levied at a flat rate. A local progressive income tax is unusual in the United States. The few states that permit a progressive local income tax require that it mirror the rates of the progressive state income tax. New York City alone has a rate schedule for its income tax that does not track the state's. Still, the progressive nature of New York City's tax is limited: the range is from 2.5 percent to 3.2 percent. And even New York City cannot make its income tax rates more progressive without obtaining state legislative approval. New York City's income tax also does not apply to commuters. Although the city was once allowed to shift some of the burden of its income tax onto nonresident commuters—and thus to shield moderate income residents from increased local tax burdens—the state has now prohibited a commuter tax. The Drum Major Institute's suggestion that New York City make its income tax more progressive is thus a good example of something that cities cannot do.

There remains the question whether, even if cities were allowed to make their tax systems more progressive, it would be wise to do so. Opponents of raising the top rates of the New York City income tax have argued that even if 5 percent of "average" millionaires left the city because their taxes were raised, the city would lose $211 million dollars in revenue.[6] Without a regional approach to revenue generation, any proposal to raise taxes on a portion of the population may be self-defeating. Besides, property taxes are due regardless of the income of the person paying the tax; raising property taxes may therefore not tap only the income of the rich. Important as it is on the national level, in sum, progressive taxation on the local level is hardly a sufficient means of promoting a middle class city. Its unavailability is indicative of the state-imposed obstacles cities face in pursuing a middle class future, although there plainly are also other reasons that proposals for progressive taxation on the local level fail or never get off the ground.

Education

We have already noted that many people consider education the critical ingredient in creating a middle class city. What can cities do to improve their schools? Although one might think that the answer is that a city can implement whatever creative ideas it can think of, the reality is far more complicated. In chapter 6, we detailed important elements of state control over education—above all, over school finance, the curriculum, and testing requirements. At the same time, we listed a variety of options that cities might undertake to improve the quality of education. With this background in place, two ideas are currently much discussed as ways to make progress in improving a city's schools. One involves increasing the city's control over the schools and the other involves decreasing it. The first option proposes mayoral control over the public school system; the second focuses on charter schools.

As we noted in chapter 6, state law usually requires school systems to be run by an independently elected school board. But change is in the air. Major cities have switched to mayoral control: Boston (1992), Chicago (1995), Cleveland (1998), Detroit (1999), Philadelphia (2001), and New York (2002). The momentum, however, is not unstoppable. Although Antonio Villaraigosa, the mayor of Los Angeles, successfully obtained state approval for such a change, the authorizing state legislation was declared unconstitutional by a state court.[7] Although the Los Angeles story is complex, it is worth summarizing because it demonstrates that sometimes not even the state legislature has the power to establish mayoral control of a school system.

The Los Angeles Unified School District is the largest school district in California and, importantly, it runs the schools in a number of adjacent cities, not just Los Angeles. The state legislation sought to give a council made up of the relevant city mayors—with voting power allocated according to population. That gave the City of Los Angeles ultimate control—the power to approve the superintendent of schools. It also enabled the mayor of Los Angeles and the superintendent to take control of the district's lowest-performing schools. This somewhat convoluted way of giving the mayor of Los Angeles more power over the city's schools was made necessary because the California Constitution provides that the voters of Los Angeles County (an area much larger than the city) have the power to decide whether the county school board is elected or appointed. Thus the mayor (or council of mayors) couldn't just take over the school board, as was done in Boston and New York. That would violate the rights of citizens of Los Angeles County who have decided to have an elected school board. The state legislation sought a way around this problem by keeping the elected school board but intervening in a way that allowed the mayor to control the superintendent and low-performing schools. This end run around the state constitution, the court ruled, didn't work: the state couldn't transfer power away from the elected school board that the voters of Los Angeles County had created.

One might be tempted to read this opinion as a victory for local control of the schools. It seems to prevent the state from invading the province of the elected county school board. This would be a misreading of the court's decision. The court conceded that the state is not obligated to give the elected county school board any authority over the schools whatsoever, that (as happened in the City of Richmond) the state could itself take over the governance of a troubled school district, and that the state's creation of charter schools was not a derogation of the county school board's constitutional authority, even though they are not subject to the board's control. It was simply mayoral control—even the complex form of it that the state legislature adopted—that was the problem. The voters had chosen an elected school board, and mayoral control was therefore not an option. In the end, then, neither the state legislature of California nor the City of Los Angeles has the power to change the organization of the Los Angeles Unified School District to give the mayor the ability to run the schools or to intervene in the city's most troubled schools.

Elsewhere mayoral control remains possible if the state legislature authorizes it. Proponents of mayoral control argue that the mayor has a unique potential to be a catalyst for change. Mayoral control, they say, increases political accountability and thereby empowers parents and other concerned citizens to press for improvement. School committees, they contend, have their own political agenda and are typically resistant to change. Opponents respond that mayoral control risks politicizing the local school system without improving educational quality and that it tends to foster a particular model of educational reform, one that emphasizes testing and other centralized approaches. We do not attempt to resolve this argument here. Even where it is implemented, the contribution of mayoral control to the improvement of the city's school system is likely to be modest. Even with mayoral control, state law varies in the extent of the discretion that the mayor has to choose members of the school committee or the superintendent of schools.

There are also variations in the amount of the city's control over the school budget. More fundamentally, there are limits on the ability of any local government body—whether the mayor or an elected school board—to affect the city's school system. We refer here not only to the state's control over finance, curriculum, and testing, but to the fundamental issue raised in chapter 6: the demographics of school systems, when compared to the population of the cities themselves, and the current lack of a regional mechanism that can confront the inequalities in the metropolitan area's schools. In many cities, a substantial majority of students are at or below the poverty line, schools are crowded, and classes are not racially diverse. Many parents simply assume that their children will be better educated in suburban schools.[8]

From our perspective, the value of mayoral control lies in its potential to influence the way that a city's political leaders think about the city's future. Whether or not mayoral control is necessary for school reform to succeed, it encourages the mayor to plan the city's future with the school system in mind. In many cities, the mayor now has strong incentives to walk away from the schools if they are failing and if improving them seems difficult. Since he has much more control over land use planning and economic development, he is likely to organize the city's future around the kinds of policies that he can influence. Increased political accountability for the schools' performance can lead the mayor instead to push for more school spending out of a fear of being deemed a failure if improvement in the schools does not occur. Sure, the opposite scenario is also a possibility. A mayor who lacks control of the schools might still have a difficult time cutting school funding. And, once in control, a mayor might still seek to reduce the local tax burden by cutting school funding in order to generate support for the global city or the tourist city. One does not have to embrace a deterministic model of mayoral decision making, however, to see the influence of the city structure on his or her priorities. Given this influence, it is important to recognize that no state in the country permits cities to decide for themselves how much mayoral control is appropriate. Some states require independent school committees, thereby prohibiting mayoral control, and others require mayoral control. At best, as in Los Angeles County, they permit local residents to make a one-time judgment on the issue through a referendum. Nowhere are cities permitted to make the relationship between the mayor and the schools a regular subject of local political contestation.

A very different method that many people favor to improve the city's schools is to expand school choice. Joel Kotkin identifies charter schools as a key way for cities to get "back to basics" and serve upwardly mobile families.[9] School choice, however, is not a choice cities can make for themselves. Just as states control school governance, they also control the authorization of charter schools.

Indeed, in many states (such as Massachusetts), it is the state, not the city, that grants their charter. For those who are supportive of increased school choice, this state control is not usually treated as a cause for concern. Local officials, they argue, are likely to block charter schools because they will be seen as a competitive threat to the existing local public schools. If so, it is better to have the state in charge of authorizing them.

This standard narrative overlooks the state's role in impeding charter schools. At the moment, ten states have failed to give their cities any legal authority to approve charter schools (in chapter 6, we noted Seattle as an example). In states that do permit charter schools, state law sometimes seems based on the fear that localities will want too many, not too few. States routinely impose caps on the number of charter schools allowed. In Illinois, no more than sixty charter schools are authorized statewide, and no more than thirty are permitted in Chicago. Massachusetts limits the number to 120, and the state also sets the maximum number of students who can be in commonwealth charter schools (4 percent of the statewide population) and restricts the amount of spending on charter schools (no more than 9 percent of the schools district's total outlays).[10] Moreover, states that allow local approval of charter schools usually vest that power in the school district, not the mayor. Yet school boards and mayors are often on opposite sides of the charter school issue. The mayor of Indianapolis is the only mayor in the country that has power to approve charter school applications.[11] A final issue is funding: state law usually requires school districts to fund new charter schools, and the details of the funding structure create disincentives for cities to support for charter schools (chapter 6 describes Boston as an example). State law, in short, requires cities to pay for charter schools even in cases when they oppose them, and it forbids cities from approving charter schools even if they want them.

As with the issue of mayoral control, the key point we are raising is not whether charter schools are a solution to the problem of the public school system. We are simply stressing that cities are not empowered to decide whether to adopt either of the currently popular approaches to school reform. Only the state can decide between mayoral control and charter schools—or (as in Boston and New York) pursue both options simultaneously.

Affordable Housing

A middle class city by definition has to have desirable housing that families of modest means can afford. The city's power over the provision of housing is structured differently, however, than its power over taxation and education.

A city's taxing power is designed to generate money from the private sector (whether they want to pay or not), and the city's provision of education is a public service (even charter schools are public schools). By contrast, cities primarily rely on the private sector to create housing, and they need to entice it to do so. To be sure, as we have seen, New York City has used its ownership of abandoned properties to provide a considerable amount of affordable housing. And public housing remains important in many cities across the country. Still, New York City's program is unusual, and American cities, unlike European cities, have never provided housing subsides and public housing that enables a large percentage of their urban population to live at affordable prices.[12] When American cities do provide public housing, it is generally allocated to the city's poor population, not to its middle class. Middle class housing is supposed to be built by the private sector.

The city's stock of middle class housing is thus largely in the hands of others. It can be increased either by large-scale developments or on a small-scale, house-by-house basis. Cities' efforts to provide affordable housing are primarily focused on developers. This aspect of a city's housing policy is built on a single concept: making a deal with a developer that involves trading concessions (usually, allowing them to build larger projects) for a certain amount of affordable housing. It is by no means clear that these deals slow the momentum of gentrification. Most of the housing built, after all, will not be affordable to the middle class. Indeed, the overall deal is likely to be consistent with the goal of being a global city more than that of being a middle class city. Large-scale developments will foster changes in the neighborhood that will attract a global city clientele. In this way, the deal can generate momentum away being from a middle class city. Yet cities have few alternatives. Because housing provision, unlike education, is understood to be a private function, cities do not have the power (with the significant, but limited, exception of public housing) to build it themselves. Nor can they simply require developers to build housing primarily for the middle class. That's why the cities seek to use techniques when dealing with housing developers—tax breaks, infrastructure improvement, zoning variances, and the like—comparable to the ones they use to promote the global city and the tourist city. They are the best tools cities have for this purpose, given the limits on their finances and their legal power.

The principal device cities employ is inclusionary zoning. Pioneered in small cities and suburbs, the idea was to take advantage of developers' interest in building new housing by requiring them to build affordable units. As urban housing markets heated up, large cities began to experiment with inclusionary zoning too. By most accounts, mandatory inclusionary zoning programs are more effective than voluntary ones, although they are also more controversial. Voluntary programs generate less opposition because they simply *permit* a process by which a city can make a deal with a developer by exchanging regulatory and financial concessions in return for promises to build affordable units. But the line between a voluntary and a mandatory program can be thin: many mandatory programs also include provisions that allow the city to grant zoning relief and other benefits to developers. Even when cities can require the provision of affordable housing before granting zoning approval, the impact on the city's housing stock is limited. This is particularly true for the middle class. Inclusionary zoning requirements typically have an income limit on those who can qualify for affordable housing, and many middle class families are above the limit. In addition, the percentage of affordable housing that can be demanded is low when compared to the large amount of middle class housing that needs to be developed.

There is another strategy that cities use to promote middle class housing: protecting the housing stock that the city already has. Cities do not have the power to define property rights in a way that would require existing housing to remain affordable.[13] But they do seek other ways to ensure that those now living in middle class housing can continue to do so. In recent years, some cities have focused on the regulation of the expansion of the subprime mortgage industry, which provides adjustable-rate loans to borrowers without the traditional indicia of creditworthiness. Although enhanced access to credit has increased home-ownership rates, borrowers become unable to meet payments when interest rates rise and are thus vulnerable to foreclosure. Proponents of local ordinances aimed at the regulation of subprime lending practices see them as ingredients in protecting these city residents and, thereby, as part of an overall urban strategy of creating stable middle class neighborhoods.

Here, too, there are significant legal obstacles. Because foreclosure is a court-ordered process, it is generally treated as a matter for the state courts to control. Some cities have tried to get around this limitation through ordinances that restrict subprime lending. But courts in California, Ohio, and Maryland have invalidated these ordinances either because cities lack the power to enact them (that is, on home rule grounds) or because state law has disabled cities from dealing with the issue (the doctrine of preemption). Since there rarely is an express indication that cities lack the power to regulate subprime lending, the courts have in effect adopted a presumption that the local interest in these measures is outweighed by the state interest in uniformity. Yet a city may have a strong local interest in adopting a stricter measure than the state, even if increased local regulation leads to a reduction in available financing in struggling neighborhoods. Cities hard hit by predatory lending practices can conclude that the benefits of increased access to credit are outweighed by the neighborhood effects of a wave of foreclosures. The dissenting opinion in the California Supreme Court case invalidating Oakland's pioneering subprime mortgage ordinance describes the local interest in adopting these regulations:

> Oakland's particular interest in regulating subprime loans goes beyond merely protecting its particularly vulnerable citizens....Predatory home mortgage lending has enormous impacts on targeted neighborhoods. Predatory lending...can result in abandoned houses and blighted neighborhoods and contribute to the physical and economic deterioration of lower-income, minority, and inner city communities. "Foreclosures, especially in low- and moderate-income neighborhoods turn what might be typically viewed as a consumer protection problem...into a community development problem, in which increased foreclosures lead to property abandonment and blight."[14]

If one puts together the widespread practice of giving incentives to developers and the limitation on local regulation of subprime lending, the constraints on city efforts to pursue a housing strategy to promote a middle class city become apparent. When negotiating with private developers, the city is limited to what it can demand; when regulating private lenders, it is limited on what it can require. These constraints stem from the private nature of the housing market and state restrictions on cities' attempts to exercise control over it.

Jobs and Wages

Given the limits on city power over taxation, the provision of services, and regulation, a city's best chance of becoming a middle class city may lie in promoting economic development. We have seen the power of cities to engage in economic development activities in the contexts of the global city and the tourist city. Many of the tools that cities use in those contexts—tax incentives, infrastructure development, and the like—can be directed instead toward the creation and maintenance of middle class jobs. The projects are likely to be different. The city might focus on industrial jobs rather than on finance or service jobs, on small-business development in working class neighborhoods rather than on convention centers, or on immigrant neighborhoods rather than on downtown. Before turning to these ideas, we begin with two other ways that cities now seek to promote middle class jobs. The first is a regulatory intervention: the passing of a living wage ordinance. The second is municipal employment—a traditional way to provide jobs for the middle class.

Living Wage Ordinances

The living wage movement began at the local level as a reaction to cities' economic polarization and the consequent rise of low-paying service-sector jobs. Important too was the failure of the national government to raise the federal minimum wage. The movement gained momentum as it became clear that many cities had room to impose regulatory burdens on business because of their increased attractiveness to global investors. The consequences of living wage ordinances on poverty reduction are fiercely contested. It seems fair to say that there is no definitive evidence either that these ordinances backfire by undermining city's efforts to create better-paying jobs or that there are substantial positive effects on local labor markets. One reason for their limited impact is that state law often prohibits local enactment of the strongest forms of living wage regulations: city minimum wage laws.

So far, more than one hundred cities—ranging from large cities like Philadelphia to smaller ones like Albany—have adopted the most common form of living wage ordinances. These ordinances require employers to pay higher wages only if the employer has a direct relationship with the city government through a city contract, the use of city-owned land, or a special tax benefit. These measures are generally thought to fall within cities' home rule powers, although they remain subject to state preemption. Although these kinds of ordinances have gained ground, only a handful of cities have adopted a living wage ordinance that applies to private employers that operate within the city. The reason derives in part from local government law. As we have seen, home rule powers often do not include the authority to regulate private or civil affairs. This exception has raised concerns about whether regulation of the private contract between employers and employees would exceed the home rule grant. There are also concerns about whether a living wage ordinance applicable to private employers would be a local or municipal affair (as the home rule grant usually requires), given its potentially significant effects on the labor market more generally. The threat of state preemption is significant too, because there usually is a well-developed regime of state wage and labor regulations. All of these concerns were voiced in recent cases that invalidated a minimum wage ordinance enacted in 2001 by New Orleans. The most detailed legal survey of the issue concludes that citywide living wage laws are possible in half the states, likely to be invalided in a quarter of the states, and uncertain in the remaining quarter.[15]

Living wage ordinances thus remain a possibility in some states. The New Mexico Supreme Court upheld a citywide minimum wage law, and, in so doing, demonstrated that even seemingly restrictive home rule grants can be construed to authorize cities to adopt such a measure on their own initiative.[16] Campaigns to preempt local living wage laws through state legislation have also been defeated. Nevertheless, there remains considerable uncertainty about the future course of either state legislation or the judicial decisions that will continue to define the scope of city power to enact these kinds of ordinances.

Municipal Employment

Another way in which cities can attempt to increase middle class jobs is by hiring workers on the city payroll. City governments—along with the state and national governments—have long been a major employer of middle class wage earners. Cities clearly have power to hire workers, but it is not automatic that the city jobs will go to city residents. To address this problem, cities across the country have enacted residency requirements that condition city employment on living within city limits. Although the U.S. Supreme Court has upheld the constitutionality of city residency requirements, legal problems remain. The California Supreme Court also upheld local residency requirements, but cities' power to impose them was later overturned by a constitutional amendment adopted by a statewide initiative. Still, residency requirements have been enacted by a number of cities, including Chicago and New York. But they remain controversial. Read literally, Boston's Residency Requirement Ordinance, passed in 1976, seems to require city employees to live in Boston. But there are hardship exceptions built into the law, and municipal employee unions have negotiated additional exceptions. As a result, only about a quarter of the City of Boston's employees are required to live in the city.[17]

There is another limit to the usefulness of municipal employment as a vehicle for creating a middle class city: the city budget. Since spending on municipal employment represents a substantial portion of every city's budget, state restrictions on city expenditures powerfully affects the number of employees cities can hire. The state affects the cities' ability to rely on municipal employment in another important way as well: by increasing the cost of hiring employees. Many cities are not in charge of determining the amount they pay for benefits. Boston's retirement and health benefits are controlled by the state, and even Denver, which has substantially more power over benefits, is subject to specific state controls. Thus, although cities are often criticized for granting overly generous pensions and health care to their employees, sometimes they become supporters of municipal employees' benefits because the state requires them to be.

Finally, the impact of municipal employees' salaries and benefits on the creation of a middle class city is uncertain. Municipal employment and state-mandated benefits can clearly be understood as part of a strategy designed to promote the middle class city. City employment provides middle class job. On

the other hand, a large municipal workforce with generous benefits can undermine efforts to retain and attract other middle class residents because local taxes
will have to rise to pay the costs of municipal employment. Since the state does
little to offset the costs of mandated benefits, cities usually must either shift the
costs to middle class homeowners through the property tax or cut services that
middle class residents rely on.

Small Business Development

Whatever their value, there plainly is a need for ideas other than living wage ordinances and municipal employment to promote a middle class city. In our chapters on the global city and the tourist city, we emphasized a very different kind
of initiative: the role that cities play in attracting businesses that promote their
economy. In our earlier chapters, the focus was on attracting global businesses
and tourism. Even now, however, cities also compete for manufacturing jobs, and
they recognize the importance of small-business development as a means of supporting its middle class. We turn to a discussion of this kind of economic development strategy, one that can supplement—and, perhaps, partially replace—the
strategies directed at the global city and the tourist city.

One way to promote small businesses is to protect them from large chains.
Big-box stores, critics charge, drive competing small retailers out of business
and, as a result, generate neighborhood decline. For this reason, some cities have
begun to use their zoning powers to exclude big-box retailers that they fear will
threaten the small businesses that generate better middle class jobs. California
cities have been especially active in addressing this issue. A number of California cities—including Los Angeles—have passed an ordinance limiting the size
of retail stores. The San Diego City Council adopted such an ordinance too,
although, when the mayor vetoed it, the council was unable to override the veto.
In 2007, the California Supreme Court, in a sweeping opinion, upheld cities'
authority to regulate in this way. This is not to say that every state will follow
California's lead. And, as the San Diego reversal demonstrates, the issue generates
considerable political conflict. Nevertheless, ordinances limiting big-box retail
might be an aspect of a strategy to protect small businesses that cities have power
to adopt.[18]

Of course, controlling the spread of big-box retail is not an economic development strategy in its own right. The goal is to encourage the growth of small
businesses, not just to limit the impact of other kinds of commercial life. Cities
have a significant amount of discretion in promoting small business development. They can modify local permitting requirements (at least to the extent
that state law allows), which many critics see as a barrier to establishing a new

business. This criticism applies especially to new small businesses. They can use their zoning powers so that parts of town might be particularly attractive to manufacturing or small retailers. And they can encourage these businesses to locate in the city through incentives such as tax breaks or infrastructure development just as they do for global and tourist businesses.

In developing such a strategy, cities have several options. One is to promote industrial jobs. It's wrong to think of this option as a return to the dark, satanic mill. These days, small industrial enterprises fit into areas of the city in ways that often cannot even be noticed, and they engage in small-scale manufacturing, in a small amount of space, that supports the rest of the economy. Some of the controversy over global and tourist development focuses on the elimination of just these kinds of small-scale industries in favor of high-rise residential development and office buildings. One objection to the Queens West Development project—a seventy-four-acre project on the waterfront facing midtown Manhattan, controlled by a subdivision of New York state's Empire State Development Corporation—is that it will eliminate a number of small industrial workplaces that provide middle class employment. As we saw in the example of Red Hook, industrial jobs also are often at stake when the city plans to redo a neighborhood for tourist purposes.[19]

Although New York City is promoting developments that threaten industrial jobs, it has also recognized the need to protect and promote industrial development within the city's boundaries. The city lost hundreds of thousands of industrial jobs after 1950, but more than five hundred thousand of these jobs remain. Most of the industrial enterprises still in the city have fewer than twenty employees, and the city is seeking to develop this sector of its economy in a number of ways. It is creating industrial business zones within the city, providing incentives to businesses to locate within them, guaranteeing not to rezone these areas to allow residential housing, seeking to restrict illegal conversions of other industrial sites to residential uses, setting aside city-owned land for industrial use, and taking steps to reduce the bureaucratic obstacles for new industrial businesses. Most of these initiatives are within the city's power to adopt on its own, although not all (for example, it needs legislative approval to extend the real estate tax reduction provided to commercial businesses to these small-scale industrial businesses). The question remains, however, whether all of these efforts—and more like them—will even begin to counterbalance the city's simultaneous efforts to promote the global and tourist alternatives.[20]

Boston's Back Streets Initiative is similar to New York's strategy, although it is focused on protecting the city's small- and medium-sized commercial as well as industrial businesses.[21] When the program was launched in 2001, the mayor noted that roughly 20 percent of the city's jobs came from these businesses, and he set a goal of ensuring no net decline in these kinds of jobs. A primary focus of the Back Streets Initiative is land use development for industrial purposes. Boston's legal powers—in particular, the combined development and planning powers of the Boston Redevelopment Authority, which administers the Back Streets Initiative—enable the city to preserve existing industrial areas. The Redevelopment Authority also can assure industrial users that the areas will not be rezoned for new luxury residential development and can help assemble parcels for businesses in need of more space. But other aspects of the state's legal structure raise problems for this effort. Because many of Boston's industrial sites are located on the city's harbor, they occupy city land that is subject to state land use controls. Boston Marine Industrial Park, one major site, has been deemed a "designated port area" by the state office dealing with coastal zone management. As a result, the state has imposed limits on the kinds of uses permitted in the area.

Perhaps even more important than these industry-focused initiatives is an attempt to promote small-scale enterprises more generally. More than 97 percent of the twenty-six million firms in the United States have fewer than twenty employees, and over the last decade these firms generated 60–80 percent of new jobs nationwide. The organization of employment is similar in major cities in the United States. In New York City, there are more than two hundred thousand small businesses (96 percent with fewer than fifty employees), and they provide two-thirds of the city's private sector jobs. An economic development strategy that focused on these kinds of enterprises might stimulate economic development for the middle class, and, at the same time, enable these small businesses to generate more attractive, thriving neighborhoods. This kind of development characterizes a multitude of city neighborhoods not on the tourist or global circuit. Paul Grogan and Tony Proscio describe one example of this kind of neighborhood revival in the South Bronx in New York City. Of course, there are problems too: advancement opportunities in these small businesses are often less developed than in large firms. Nevertheless, the space needs are small, the job locations are spread throughout the city, and the effort to match local residents with local jobs can have a positive impact on other city problems, such as the transportation system.[22]

One way to organize this effort is to focus specifically on employment opportunities in immigrant neighborhoods. A 2007 report issued by the Center for an Urban Future does just that. Unlike our reference to immigration in chapter 7, which focused on the immigrants' role in the global economy, the report concentrates on encouraging local employment opportunities for city residents in small businesses in their own neighborhoods. It begins with the observation that small-scale enterprises in immigrant neighborhoods are growing rapidly in New York City and other major cities, even as other kinds of jobs in the city are stabilizing or declining. And the jobs varied enormously: food manufacturing (fortune cookies, pita bread, empanadas, jerk chicken), child care, transportation (91 percent of New York City's cab drivers are immigrants), publishing, service businesses (insurance, medical, immigration, accounting), travel agencies, restaurants. According to the report, "Despite the increasing significance of immigrant-run businesses, city economic development officials have hardly begun to incorporate them into the overall economic development strategy." The report concludes by making a number of recommendations—ranging from regulatory reform to offering loans to changing parking rules—that would redirect the city's economic development strategy toward these kinds of businesses.[23]

Another focus for such an economic development effort can be on the city's poorest neighborhoods. Michael Porter has become a well-known advocate of this emphasis, and, in 1994, he founded a not-for-profit organization, the Initiative for a Competitive Inner City, to promote it. The focus is on high-poverty neighborhoods—areas that include census tracts with 20 percent or greater poverty rate or 50 percent unemployment or half the city's median income. The goal, in other words, is to help the poor gain access to middle class jobs. A study published by the Initiative found that there were 814,000 private businesses in these neighborhoods in the one hundred largest cities in the nation. Newly created jobs were predominately in the service sector and, given their location, proximity to the high-end global business neighborhood can be a major asset. Many of the initiatives suggested above for the immigrant city could be helpful in these neighborhoods too.[24]

There are other ideas as well. San Francisco has a Department of Economic and Workforce Development within the Mayor's Office, and its recent program, CityBuild, organized in conjunction with community organizations and the transportation department, is designed to create a one-stop location for finding construction jobs and providing training for these jobs. Denver offers loans to businesses operating within designated parts of the city to supplement private financing of new businesses. New York City has issued tax-exempt bonds to help rebuild lower Manhattan after 9/11, and the beneficiaries include small businesses.[25] And there's no reason to limit oneself to ideas already under way. In Chapter 8, we mentioned that New York City had issued bonds for the new Yankee Stadium, bonds that the Yankees themselves will pay off. If this can be done for the Yankees, could bonds be issued to provide loans to small businesses in immigrant neighborhoods and the inner city? If not, we'd need to investigate what the legal restraints are that would permit the Yankee loan but not these kinds of loans.

Many of the efforts just described are within the city's legal power as defined by state law. Even so, the existing legal structure limits the possible impact of all of them. First, the constraints described earlier concerning other ingredients of developing a middle class city—education, housing, transportation, and the like—prevent the city from organizing a comprehensive approach to attracting the middle class. Without such an integrated effort, a focus on economic development might well not succeed. It may be hard to attract the residents needed to expand the city's small-business sector if middle class housing options are few and the public schools are failing. Equally significant, much of the city's development strategy is not in the city's hands. Independent public authorities and public-private partnerships have become the major way development decisions are made. Given who the decision makers are and the kinds of investment calculations they are likely to make, these kinds of institutions can easily overlook or devalue efforts to promote middle class businesses. Their isolation from local democratic control may explain their tendency to focus on the global city and tourist city. As a result, the city's overall economic strategy can threaten, rather than enable, the ability of the middle class to live in the city.

There also is the problem of financing small-business development. Economic development for the global city and the tourist city is currently financed principally through tax increment financing. This mechanism is not well designed to promote interstitial efforts to create small businesses throughout the city. The economic development strategy for middle class business requires the city's financial support and its willingness to provide tax exemptions. To be sure, this kind of assistance is provided for global and tourist business to an even greater extent. But, in those cases, the city government (or the public authority) makes a financial calculation that the increased property values will generate tax revenue to reimburse the city's costs. This kind of calculation is less plausible when a small business strategy is the focus, if only because of its incremental nature.

There is another major problem as well—a problem that applies not only to the middle class city but to the global city and tourist city. All of these strategies have to be understood in a regional context, because the suburbs, in their own way, are organized to attract global business, tourism, and the middle class. Nowhere have the suburbs been more successful than in attracting the middle class. Given the power of the suburbs to do so, it may be that no central city economic development strategy focused on middle class jobs can succeed. No American city can pursue a vision of its future as if it were isolated from the region in which it is located. Its plans for the future—above all, its plans to nurture a middle class city—require it to confront the legally created difficulties of being a regional city.

THE REGIONAL CITY

"Most Americans today," Peter Calthorpe and William Fulton declare in their book *The Regional City*, "do not live in towns—or even cities—in the traditional sense of these terms. Instead, most of us are citizens of a region—a large and multifaceted metropolitan area encompassing hundreds of places that we would traditionally think of as distinct and separate 'communities.'" Most people, they hasten to add, do not think of themselves in these terms. They think of themselves as living in a specific city or town, even a specific neighborhood:

> But the patterns of our daily existence belie a different reality. Most of us commute from one metropolitan town to another for work, for shopping, and for many other daily activities. The businesses for which we work are typically bound up in a series of economic relationships with vendors and customers on a regional or metropolitan scale. And, even if we do live and work in one small town…, the ecological fallout of our day-to-day patterns will be felt upstream or downstream throughout the region.[1]

Every city we examined in part II is a regional city in Calthorpe and Fulton's sense of the term. For all of them, their relationship to their neighbors is one of both connection and disconnection. On the one hand, the central city's economic and cultural vitality is essential to the prosperity of the region as a whole. The central city is the economic engine of the region, it attracts a substantial commuter workforce, and it provides cultural and sports facilities that serve metropolitan residents wherever they live. At the same time, central cities are in competition with their neighbors for residents and commercial development. Indeed, although the population in the suburbs has exploded for many years, central city populations have remained relatively stable or declined. As a result, the future of the central cities depends on whether nearby suburban growth contributes to, or detracts from, their prosperity. This codependence between central cities and their neighbors is not just a matter of sustaining their economic growth. Many issues critical to their future, from environmental quality to security against threats of terrorism, are powerfully affected by the decisions made by the other localities in their region. Central cities' ability to engage with their neighbors is therefore of critical importance—not only to their own future but to that of their neighbors as well.

Local Government Law's Impact on Regionalism

Despite its importance, there is little incentive for the region's localities to work collectively on the issues of economic growth, environmental quality, or social services. On the contrary, each locality has an incentive to act in a narrowly self-interested manner. Local government law plays an important role in generating this structure, and it does so in two different ways. One is the manner in which legal power is now delegated to individual localities. The second is the state's failure to provide an alternative to the current fragmented structure, an alternative that would promote regionalism rather than parochial self-interest.

State-Generated Fragmentation

State law organizes localities to be competitors for real estate development rather than participants in a collective endeavor to further the regional economy. This competitive frame is fostered by the state-created structures we describe in this book. First, because local power derives from state law, the state-city relationship, not the intercity relationship, is the key focus for local officials. To gain the kind of legal authority that local governments need but lack, they must negotiate with the state. There is no comparable necessity to negotiate with their neighbors. As a result, many municipalities attempt to address problems with their neighbors by seeking state intervention into their neighbors' affairs, or threatening to assert their own power in harmful ways, instead of finding common ground for collective action.

The state-organized finance system has a similar fragmenting impact. Although state aid reduces the inequalities that affect service delivery to some extent, the quality of city services largely depends, under state law, on individual localities' ability to raise their own tax revenue. It is not surprising, then, that economic development policy is driven by parochial, rather than regional, interests. A locality can favor itself over its neighbors by attracting a shopping mall to locate within its boundaries. Under state law, the property tax revenues generated by the mall (and, if there is a local sales tax, the revenues derived from it) go only to the locality where the mall is located. Even though the shoppers come from neighboring jurisdictions as well, the regional nature of the shopping mall is not recognized. The same structure applies to other forms of economic development as well.

The most familiar state-created ingredient fragmenting metropolitan America is the organization of the school system. "We've moved here for the schools" is a phrase everyone has heard. This incentive to move derives from the divisive way in which school system boundaries are drawn. State law, one should recognize, draws these boundaries. In most of the country, the way of doing so allows potential residents to locate good schools and bad schools easily. If the state were to draw them so that they attracted a more regional student body rather than favoring those who can afford to buy a house nearby, the population that would profit from the better schools might change considerably.

The widespread pursuit of a narrow, parochial conception of local self-interest is thus not ingrained in the nature of decentralized power. It is a result of the way local governments are now empowered. Many people agree with this general statement, but they usually then argue that regional cooperation is inhibited by home rule—by which they mean the considerable power now exercised by local governments. There is no regional cooperation, they say, because the localities will never agree to it. As we have stressed, local governments do not have the kind of home rule that this account imagines. Indeed, in our view, it is the condition of having limited power—rather than of being autonomous—that encourages the insular and defensive mind-set that now so often makes regionalism unattractive. We call this attitude defensive localism.

Defensive Localism

Defensive localism, according to our definition, is an effort to defend local power in order to preserve the status quo. This defensive stance is spurred by a feeling of not being in control. The best way to explain this attitude toward local power is to listen to local officials and to consider their comments in light of the legal structure within which they operate. The Boston metropolitan area is a good place to study these officials' simultaneous recognition of the constraints on local power and their opposition to regionalism. As we have already demonstrated, despite the state's reputation as the cradle of New England democracy, local power in Massachusetts is more limited than in many other states. Yet opposition to regionalism is no less intense. Massachusetts thus illustrates how parochialism can be generated not from the arrogance of power but from the defensiveness generated by the lack of it. We base our understanding of defensive localism in Massachusetts on the results of a series of interviews that we, assisted by our students, conducted with representatives of a majority of the 101 cities and towns that make up the Boston metropolitan area. We summarize here the findings from these interviews; a more detailed report of our findings has been published elsewhere.[2]

Our interviews made clear that local officials in the greater Boston area feel burdened by substantial constraints on their authority. Yet this limiting legal structure does not end local attachment to home rule. Nor does it make local officials sympathetic to regionalism. In fact, officials who spent the first half of the interviews cataloguing the various ways in which the state had stripped them of home rule often spent the second half objecting to regionalism for taking away their local control. This divided response raised a puzzling question: What did local officials who spoke in these seemingly contradictory ways mean? For some, we felt, the attachment to home rule—understood as local sovereignty—seemed to exist as an ideological commitment. But for others this insular mind-set did not seem rooted in an unshakeable commitment to local independence. Many explained that the problems that their communities faced were of a greater-than-local scope, and they conceded that their own choices were powerfully influenced by decisions made by their neighbors. They also expressed concern about the viability of a go-it-alone approach. Nonetheless, they often expressed skepticism about regionalism.

Their hesitation stemmed in significant part from the limited form of local power that Massachusetts now recognizes. The state's legal structure fosters skepticism about regionalism because it gives cities and towns so little. It encourages local actors to defend the limited powers they possess vigorously and leads them to believe that a less defensive strategy is not viable. Parochialism seems a necessary stance, rather than a preferred one. The state's encouragement of this defensiveness is probably unintentional. Nevertheless, local officials repeatedly expressed hesitancy about entering into interlocal agreements because they believed that they were "risky." Although this aversion to risk reflects a cautiousness common to individuals and governments no matter what the scope of their power, the feeling seemed heightened by the limited powers that local governments have. The defense of home rule has become a defense of specific state-granted entitlements that are all the more important because there are so few other available ways to exercise control over municipal problems.

This dynamic—in which the limited nature of local power induces an enhanced commitment to its preservation—was particularly evident with respect to local cooperation in fiscal matters. The fact that municipalities are starved for revenue makes them open to forging interlocal agreements to establish economies of scale or joint purchasing groups. Yet officials with whom we spoke often expressed concern that collective action might worsen their already precarious competitive position. Administrators tended to guard their revenues against the possibility of expropriation or reallocation, knowing that they lack the power to raise revenue to make up for budget shortfalls. They seemed equally reluctant to consider cooperative arrangements involving expenditures because of the lingering risk that they may not come out ahead or that they will be seen by voters to have been snookered by a competitor. So deep is the fear of improving the financial position of a neighbor, and thus undermining their own competitive standing, that some officials expressed concern that municipal judgments about benefits were determined by comparing a municipality's own benefits with those of the other participating municipalities rather than considering whether the locality was better off when measured against its previous, noncooperating, position. In other words, municipalities were not inclined to engage in cooperative efforts if they perceived that the other municipality was getting more out of the arrangement, even if they stood to benefit too.

Officials described a similar cautiousness when it came to cooperation on land use matters, in part because of the important role of land use policy in protecting a local community's fiscal position. Officials were well aware that land use controls by neighbors affected their communities. Even so, they were reluctant to support collective efforts that might provide protection from these impacts. They seemed to regard home rule as the right to impose costs on neighbors, even if that meant that they were subjected to their neighbors imposing costs on them. This kind of self-serving action was viewed as a necessary means of augmenting the local tax base. The current fiscal structure made them reluctant to defect from a land-use strategy that provided at least some means of balancing revenues and expenditures.

State Limits on Interlocal Cooperation

States do more than simply create incentives for localities to hunker down and look on joint ventures as threatening propositions. They also place limits on the ability of local governments to enter into interlocal agreements. Moreover, except for provisions authorizing small-scale cooperation, states have not used their interventions into municipal affairs to create an atmosphere that promotes interlocal agreements. Quite the contrary: state supervision of municipal governments tends to encourage vertical interactions with the state at the expense of horizontal relationships among municipalities.

The limitations on interlocal agreements and the failure to provide an alternative to the fragmenting structure are well illustrated by the situation in Massachusetts. Massachusetts municipalities are allowed to establish (among other institutions) regional water and sewer authorities, regional school districts, regional police and fire districts, regional transit authorities, and regional charter commissions for establishing regional councils of government. And, in fact, a number of municipalities have taken advantage of these opportunities. Among the most successful cooperative arrangements have been those aimed at saving money. Joint purchasing arrangements range from office supplies to health insurance; these kinds of agreements provide benefits without compromising local authority on other matters. On occasion, interlocal contracting authority has also been used to address seemingly intractable conflicts, such as the recurrent disputes over land use development by neighboring communities.

But there are important limits on the kinds of agreements that localities can make under their current state-granted authority. Interlocal agreements often require the approval of a state agency, and state-imposed restrictions also limit the extent of municipal power that these voluntarily formed subregional organizations can exercise. Moreover, the state imposes a variety of special requirements for establishing regional bodies. For example, state law requires that a single community be the "lead" municipality for some interlocal agreements. This means that one partner must bear the brunt of the administrative costs of cooperation, a requirement that in the current competitive structure deters regionalism. Another aspect of state law requires local *legislative* approval of some joint agreements. This limitation does not apply to ordinary municipal contracts with the private sector, and it can dramatically slow down cooperative efforts.[3]

The state's failure to create institutional mechanisms that would encourage a broader way of thinking about the region is equally significant. Although local interactions with the state were frequent, they chiefly focused on individual issues that confronted particular towns. This form of state-local interaction reinforces the very isolation between localities that is often assumed to be a natural consequence of their empowerment. Yet local officials understand that they lack many of the legal powers they need, recognize that there are substantial costs to pursuing a go-it-alone approach, and realize that their own ability to meet the needs of their residents is powerfully affected by actions that occur beyond their borders. Even so, they rarely favor addressing these interlocal pressures at the regional level. Rather than viewing this picture as a hopeless jumble of contradictions, we are inclined to see it as the basis for trying new strategies for promoting regionalism. The fact that the state places so many limits on local power—and that these limits are experienced as significant by so many of the officials with whom we spoke—suggests to us that innovative approaches might be possible that would call into question the supposed conflict between local empowerment and regionalism.

Promoting Regionalism by Revising Local Government Law

Any regional approach—no matter how innovative—depends on the state's willingness to assume an affirmative role to bring it about. Some of the local officials we interviewed asserted that regionalism would happen only if the state would "get out of the way." But it is not clear to us what it would mean for the state to get out of the way. Local parochialism and interlocal competitiveness are realities. The state, as the source of local power, has created the legal structure that fosters this parochialism and competitiveness. The question, then, cannot be what localities can do without the state. The question must be: How should the state go about promoting greater intraregional coordination?

One way to do so would be to provide state aid to encourage local governments to act on a more regional basis. Such a solution seems to us problematic. It would require substantial outlays of new state money that is not now available and is unlikely to be available any time soon. Moreover, existing state grants-in-aid already have a distorting effect on municipal governments, leading them to devise programs to obtain needed revenue from the state when alternative policies might be better. And, of course, if the regionalism string were attached to existing dollars, few municipalities would experience the state as offering them a meaningful choice. The distinction between a grant-with-strings, and an outright mandate, is not one that impressed many of the officials we interviewed.

A better alternative, we suggest, is to promote regionalism by responding seriously to the widespread sentiment that the state has unduly limited home rule. The idea would be for the state to enhance local power—and relax existing limitations on that power—as a carrot to induce greater regionalism. In this way, the state would help overcome the sense of opposition between home rule and regionalism that so many municipal officials we interviewed took as a given. To make this proposal more concrete, we offer some examples from the three substantive areas detailed in part II: revenues, land use, and education. What we offer here is not a menu for legislative reform. Our goal is much more limited: our proposals are designed to demonstrate that increasing local power and regionalism can go hand in hand.

Virtually every municipal official we interviewed in the Boston region emphasized their locality's lack of power with respect to fiscal matters. These constraints are made even more onerous by the state's substantial role in mandating local spending. The result is a disconnect between revenues and expenditures that prevents local budgeting from being an exercise in expressing municipal will. Municipal officials also recognized that the state's limits on taxation, and its mandates to spend, are not the only constraints on local fiscal control. They were quick to point out that their town's fiscal health was in large part determined by its success in battling neighbors for commercial and residential development. The wealth of the residents that a municipality attracts or loses—and the costs that accompany either move—plays a large role in determining municipal fiscal capacity.

To address these two limitations on local fiscal authority, the state must do more than simply loosen restrictions on local revenue-raising power. It needs to expand local control in a way that will not simply exacerbate the interlocal battle for taxable property. One way to do this would be to grant greater local tax authority to the localities that engage in regional cooperation. For example, the state could grant a group of localities a limited power to impose a sales tax as long as they agreed to share the new revenue. The state could offer to reimburse localities (in whole or in part) for the lost revenue generated by state-owned, tax-exempt property as long as the municipalities collectively submitted to the state a plan detailing where new state properties should be located. This structure would give the region's cities an incentive to formulate joint plans about the location of new state buildings rather than to try to exclude or court the new development based on a self-interested assessment of whether it would attract more net revenue. It would also make it more practicable for the central city to impose a sales tax. So long as the city must act in isolation, it risks driving retailers to the suburbs. If the state helped to create a structure in which a central city and its suburbs could act in concert in ways now prohibited, the idea of a regional city might begin to take root. Yet another example does not involve either raising locally imposed taxes or increasing state payments. The state could enhance municipal authority to offer tax abatements to attract development as long as the locality agreed to share a portion of the generated revenue with neighboring localities. Any of these ideas—and many more like them—would increase the incentives for coordination within the region without increasing state control over local power. Regionalism would become a by-product of state efforts to enhance local power rather than to limit it.

Municipalities often have more control over land use than over their finances. Indeed, the officials we interviewed repeatedly pointed to zoning as an area in which the state had ceded significant discretion. Yet, as these respondents noted, the state also imposes a broad range of limitations on the land use powers that localities may assert. One example is the generous granting of vested rights that state law now affords property owners. The vested right provisions of state law can make changes in local land use planning difficult and, sometimes, even counterproductive. To respond to this problem, the state could relax this requirement in the name of enhancing local home rule. But this solution would not fully respond to the concerns localities have about their land use authority because they are also limited in what they can do by the relative position of their neighbors. Land use choices may be driven by a felt need to win out in the competition for new developments or affected by development policies pursued across the border. In order to think about home rule and regionalism as complements, the state could address both types of local limitation on local land use powers without exacerbating interlocal battles. It could relax the early vesting rules only for the local governments that enter into regional land-use-planning agreements. In this way, municipal power to manage growth would increase as localities agreed to work together to devise a greater-than-local land use strategy. Cooperation would thus make planning strategies possible that now are effectively foreclosed. Suburbs that are burdened by vested rights rules would have new incentives to work with the central city in formulating a land use plan for the region as a whole.

Another possible land use strategy could deal with current affordable housing regulation. Everyone realizes that the future development of central cities will not be promoted simply by those who live within its borders. Many of those who work in the central city will continue to live in the suburbs, and many of its residents will continue to work in the suburbs. The regional nature of the affordable housing problem is equally well known. But the general grant of home rule power now leaves local governments without an adequate set of tools for making affordable housing available to their residents. Expanding home rule power to adopt inclusionary zoning ordinances or other means of stimulating the building of affordable housing can promote the regional goal of more equitable distribution of affordable housing. These measures can be strengthened even more, however, if the grants of greater authority were offered to neighboring cities that worked together to develop an affordable housing strategy. Some states— including Massachusetts—now have a policy designed to override local zoning in jurisdictions without adequate affordable housing.[4] These kinds of strategies help promote a regional policy of a fair-share allocation of low- and moderate-income housing. But they are often resented by localities on the ground that they limit local power. A better alternative, then, might be to modify these fair-share requirements in ways that would treat the localities as contributors to the solution rather than the source of the problem. One way to do so would be to empower them, under state guidelines, to implement jointly new strategies that generate affordable housing, thereby enabling them to promote policies that none of them, individually, now has the power to adopt.

All of the ideas just presented could be structured so that greater authority would be transferred to municipalities as the number of localities willing to enter into the regional undertaking increased. Even if implemented, none of the proposals just sketched would fully address any, let alone all, of the problems facing American metropolitan regions. But, as we have already emphasized, we have not made these suggestions in the expectation that they would become a concrete agenda for reform. We have sought instead to propose a number of ideas that might enable readers to revise the standard notion that regionalism of necessity erodes home rule. All of the proposals—and many more like them—would restructure home rule in a way that empowered localities rather than weakened them. At the same time, they would create incentives for the region's municipalities to see the benefits of thinking regionally beyond the easy, nonpolitical matters that now bring them together. Over time, this new conception of regionalism—in whatever concrete form it is adopted—could begin to instill a regional sensibility that at present does not exist. Our proposals, it should be clear, do not seek to resurrect home rule in the sense of "local autonomy." This is what makes them attractive to us. The "local autonomy" version of home rule now stifles the discussion of regionalism more than it promotes it.

New Regional Institutions

Simply by itself, a revision of the local government law structure might suffice to promote the concept of a regional city. Creating a regional institution, in other words, is not a necessity. Nevertheless, states might find it useful to do more: they might think it desirable to create an institution designed to promote regional thinking and cooperation by neighboring cities. This need not mean that they should establish a regional government. As Anthony Downs has observed, "Almost no one favors metropolitan area government except a few political scientists and intellectuals." As a result, he said, "Proposals to replace suburban governments completely are...doomed."[5]

This opposition to creating yet another level of government with authority over localities is understandable. Centralization transfers local governmental power from entities in which popular participation in government decision making is possible to one that is more like a state (indeed, more like the federal government in 1790) than a city. It is therefore not surprising that the African Americans who now exercise governmental power in some of the nation's central cities are as opposed to regional government as are white residents of prosperous suburbs. Too often, however, the only alternative considered possible for American metropolitan areas, once regional government is taken off the table, is the status quo. Yet the inadequacy of the current system is so apparent that even the staunchest defenders of local power agree that at least *some* urban problems require regional solutions. The most commonly accepted proposal for regionalism is the two-tier model of regional government: the notion that public functions should be divided into those that could best be performed on a regional level and those that should remain at a local level. The two-tier model creates a fundamental dilemma: every traditional local function—police, education, housing, transportation, parks, sanitation—is simultaneously a matter of local concern and of regional concern. Decisions on these issues regularly affect not only the people who live within local boundaries but those who live outside of them. As a result, the very items that are most important to local citizens can be understood as proper subjects for regional governmental action.

An even more serious problem with the two-tier model stems from its conception of how local separateness and regional togetherness should be combined. Two-tier advocates have sought to preserve local autonomy while empowering a regional government to deal with matters affecting the region as a whole. This picture imagines local governments as able to make their own decisions on matters that affect local residents unless the regional government is given authority over that activity. Thus, by definition, regional and local power are seen as being in conflict with one another: increasing the power of one level of government necessarily reduces the power of the other. Given this picture, defining the authority of the two levels of government becomes the critical issue. Only if this is done correctly can the exercise of local power be protected. In fact, the only relationship considered important in this version of regionalism is the vertical one between higher levels of government and decentralized decision makers. The model imposes no requirement that local governments form connections with each other. To be sure, they *can* if they want to. But, like all contracting parties, they do not have to do so if it is not in their self-interest.

To better connect metropolitan localities with each other, we propose another alternative. It is important, we think, to put the authorizations of local power together with the constraints on local decision-making authority. By focusing on both the attachment to local power and the limits placed on it, we can begin to rethink the notion that every regional advance is a setback for local power. Regionalism can redefine the existing mix of local power and local powerlessness rather than simply reduce the first in order to increase the second. For many local governments, such a revised mix can improve their ability to promote their self-interest and the regional interest simultaneously. This is especially true for successful central cities. The lack of coordination with neighboring suburbs impedes the efforts of successful central cities to implement a bold plan for the future.

Admittedly, promoting both regional and local objectives simultaneously is not easy. Achieving a confluence of local and regional interests will take effort. There is no solution to regional problems that will make everyone better off and no one worse off. Localities need to negotiate with each other to work out the kinds of changes in local authority—both increases and decreases—that will better protect collective interests while furthering, as much as possible, local self-determination. What is needed, then, is an institution that will permit the region's local governments to work together to advance regional interests. The fundamental issue presented by this alternative version of regionalism is not how to divide power between local and regional decision makers but how to turn regional decision making into a form of interlocal decision making. Clearly, important questions need to be resolved about what such a regional entity would do. But the possible answers to these questions will vary depending on the level of citizens' confidence that the regional institution will advance local interests rather than simply override them. And this level of confidence will be affected by the structure of the regional institution. A structure that required the unanimous consent of all participating parties would inhibit the formation of any regional agenda. Nothing in America commands unanimous consent. Yet a structure that allowed local power to be overridden too easily would jeopardize the values provided by local decision-making authority. The task of creating the right structure is therefore critical.

A Regional Legislature

To spur thinking along these lines, we sketch out one idea of what an institution that could advance this alternative version of regionalism might look like—a regional legislature. Legislatures, after all, are the classic vehicles for enabling locally elected officials to hammer out a common agenda. A regional legislature can, in fact, borrow from two existing models—state legislatures and regional planning agencies. Like a state legislature, a regional legislature could be relatively large, with members popularly elected from cities across the region. Unlike a state legislature, however, it would be organized to perform a single task: to serve as a vehicle for interlocal negotiations designed to forge a regional perspective on specific issues. State legislatures are not themselves an appropriate mechanism for undertaking this task. State legislators are elected from districts that disregard city lines. It is not plausible to expect people elected in this fashion (many from rural areas) to redesign their own institution to give a voice to cities. They could, however, create a regional legislature to do just that.

To be effective, a regional legislature would have to have the power to ensure that its decisions, once made, will be followed by the region's local governments. It would thus have the power to control local policy, including the power to redefine what it means for local government institutions to pursue local interests. To be able to exercise this amount of power, the regional legislature should derive its authority from a delegation of power from the state legislature, not simply from a voluntary agreement between the region's cities. This source of power need not transform the regional legislature into a centralized regional government. The regional legislature should—and this is crucial—consist of democratically elected representatives of the municipalities themselves. If it were so organized, it would be a mechanism for giving a voice to local governments. Local representatives would be in control of the agenda. Not only could they increase as well as decrease local power but, once a regionally oriented definition of local self-interest became internalized into local decision making, they could leave the formulation and implementation of policies in the hands of local governments. Indeed, the more discussions within a regional legislature helped local officials understand the impact of their decisions on each other, the less the regional legislature would have to do. Still, a critical question remains. How can a regional legislature with this much power be organized without undermining the advantages gained by decentralizing power to local governments?

One source of ideas to address this question is the European Union.[6] The twenty-seven nations that form the European Union have not abandoned their devotion to national sovereignty. They nevertheless have created a much more connected relationship with each other than have the cities that constitute America's metropolitan areas. Those of us interested in American regionalism can learn a good deal from this European experience, notwithstanding the stark differences between the two contexts. Some of these differences need to be emphasized. The European Union was formed as a response to two devastating world wars—a level of interjurisdictional conflict that has no parallel in metropolitan America. From the outset, the European focus has been on economic integration, an issue that is a matter for national policymaking in the United States. Trade barriers and a common currency—like many of the other issues that concern the European Union, such as defense and foreign policy—are not metropolitan issues in the United States. Moreover, unlike the member countries of the European Union, American cities are not sovereign nations. On the contrary, they are subject to the very kind of power exercisable by a higher sovereignty—state governments—that the members of the European Union are unwilling to cede to centralized control. American states have the power to merge cities with each other, even to eliminate them; a European Union with this kind of authority is not within anyone's contemplation. The fact that cities are not sovereign nations is also more than a reference to their lack of sovereign power. European countries have long been understood by many of their citizens in terms of their cultural, and not just their political, unity: a common language, a common history, even a common ancestry have often been thought to distinguish one nation from another. No one thinks of municipal boundaries as dividing one prepolitical "people" from another. Finally, the European Union has established a wide variety of institutions that have no relevance in the American metropolitan context. Indeed, its complex institutional structure is not only unnecessary but cannot constitutionally be reproduced at the regional level in the United States.

Despite these differences, the European Union provides ways of thinking about separateness and togetherness that offer promise for the American metropolitan context. After all, many of the ways in which the European Union differs from American metropolitan areas might have made the formation of connections within Europe harder, not easier, to accomplish than regional cooperation in the United States. If European countries could overcome nationalist loyalties—not to mention the differences that led to two world wars—people who live in the same metropolitan area within the United States should be able to relate to each other at least as well. Although American metropolitan areas are fragmented in very divisive ways—often along lines of race, ethnicity, and class—the European Union has also faced stark differences in wealth and ethnicity across the geographic area where interjurisdictional cooperation has been built. And Europe did not have a powerful government—like state governments—that could organize the necessary institutional structure to overcome these sources of conflict. The European Union's institutional structure had to be created by interlocal agreement—that is, by treaties.

Still, it would be wrong to try to reproduce the structure of the European Union in American metropolitan areas. We intend instead simply to rip from their European context specific institutional ideas that might help us reconceptualize the relationship between local separateness and regional togetherness in the United States. We will focus solely on two specific aspects of the European Union that, once appropriately revised, suggest organizational possibilities for a regional legislature in the United States: its creation of a governing structure that cannot easily be categorized either as a voluntary agreement or as a centralized state and its establishment of a European citizenship.

An Interlocal Structure of Regional Organization

What interests us about the institutional structure of the European Union lies in its attempt to build localism into the very fabric of European institutions, rather than simply to divide authority between a "centralized government" and "local control." Some elements of this model are familiar to American readers. Two of the governing institutions of the European Union are the European Parliament (elected roughly according to population) and the Council of the European Union (a body consisting of representatives of the member governments). The European Parliament's allocation of membership according to the population of the member nations, while assuring each country a minimum representation regardless of population, parallels the organization of the U.S. House of Representatives. The Council's allocation of equal membership to representatives of the constituent governments regardless of population parallels the organization of the U.S. Senate prior to the adoption of the Seventeenth Amendment (which retained equal membership but added democratic election of representatives). A problem with this aspect of the European (and federal) method of building local control into a larger union is that it offers an unconstitutional model for elected regional institutions in the United States. The U.S. Supreme Court has rejected "the federal analogy" for state and local governments because "political subdivisions of States—counties, cities, or whatever—never were and never have been considered as sovereign entities." Thus, the familiar bicameral structure that allocates power in one of two governing bodies to political subdivisions as such is not an available option for metropolitan governance in the United States. Any regional institution has to be organized according to the one-person, one-vote principle.[7]

The one-person, one-vote principle will usually make the suburbs the dominant force in a democratically elected metropolitan-wide organization. A majority (in Boston, more than 80 percent) of the residents of metropolitan areas live in the suburbs. The suburbs, however, are not a monolithic voting bloc. The split between prosperous and declining suburbs renders uncertain the kind of alliance among political subdivisions that would control a regional legislature in most American metropolitan areas. This uncertainty presents its own problem: the requirement of one person, one vote would threaten every political subdivision within the regional legislature. Any local decision could be overruled by a coalition of other localities. Organizational ideas to deal with fear of loss of local control are therefore indispensable, given the emotional attachment to local decision making. Ideas about how to ensure that the desire for local control does not overwhelm the possibility of forging a regional agenda are also indispensable. The structure of the European Union offers two useful suggestions about how to achieve these conflicting objectives: qualified majority voting and regionwide political parties.

QUALIFIED VOTING

The Council of the European Union (consisting of representatives of each of the twenty-seven member countries) first deals with its members' fear of loss of control by seeking to establish policy through consensus. But the formal decision-making rules of the Council address the same fear. Different rules apply depending on the issue being decided: sometimes unanimity, sometimes a simple majority, and sometimes a qualified majority is required. The notion of a qualified majority is the most unfamiliar of these decision-making methods to American readers. The European Union defines a qualified majority for Council decision making by allocating votes to individual members very roughly according to their population and, in addition, establishing a minimum number of votes (and sometimes a minimum number of members casting these votes) before a policy can be adopted. The results of a vote thus depend on the specifics of how this formula is constructed—the extent of variation from a one-person, one-vote standard allowed in allocating votes to the different members; the minimum number of votes required for adoption; and the minimum number of members (if one is set) required to cast these votes. These ingredients have long been the subject of considerable controversy within the European Union. The specifics of the ways in which these various ingredients have been set and reset for the Council are not of significance here. What is significant is the idea of organizing the Council in terms of qualified majority voting. A simple majority requirement demands too little regional consensus for policymaking to be widely acceptable, while a unanimity rule would make decision making impossible given the dozens of cities represented in a region (as opposed to the twenty-seven nations represented in the European Union). The ingredients of a qualified majority voting system, however, can protect individual jurisdictions by establishing the minimum level of agreement required for action, while at the same time giving greater weight to the views of the most populous cities in the region.[8]

Creating a regional institution with a qualified majority voting mechanism in the American metropolitan setting would involve a major change from the European structure. The qualified majority rule would be adopted in a regional legislature organized not in terms of equal membership (like the Council) but according to population (like the European Parliament). By allocating votes for qualified majority voting within the Council very roughly according to population, the European mechanism itself incorporates aspects of this model. But the number of votes allocated to each jurisdiction in a regional institution in the United States would be considerably less flexible because the allocation would have to track population levels more closely. Still, much of the value of the idea remains. A qualified majority voting mechanism would enable every locality in a region to be represented in a regional legislature and would simultaneously take into account population differences among the localities represented.

Creating this kind of interlocal institution would be a major innovation in America: there is no institution in the country that allows a region's local governments to meet together and forge a common policy that is binding on all of them. The idea of giving a voice to every political subdivision would also be an innovation in the organization of population-based legislative bodies in the United States. Districts for state legislators and members of the House of Representatives routinely divide some cities while combining others; the effort to draw district lines for state and federal purposes concentrates on creating equally sized districts (and on tracking party membership and protecting incumbents) rather than on giving a voice to political subdivisions. This is one of the many ways in which the "local autonomy" that is so valued in the regionalism debate is completely disregarded in other contexts. On issues decided by the state and federal governments, cities are not decision makers at all. They are relegated, along with private corporations and interest groups, to being lobbyists. A regional legislature organized according to qualified majority voting, by contrast, would enable representatives of the cities themselves, acting collectively, to become the regional decision maker.

A principal reason why political subdivisions are not now represented in legislatures in the United States is the difficulty of squaring such a notion of representation with the constitutional requirement of one person, one vote. A qualified majority voting mechanism offers the best way to do so. It allows a legislature to be organized according to political subdivisions and to the size of local government populations simultaneously: every political subdivision would be represented in the legislature, but the number of representatives for each subdivision would vary with its population. At the same time, a qualified majority voting mechanism would prevent the domination of the legislature by a small number of the largest jurisdictions by establishing a specified minimum number of votes before a measure can be adopted.

This is not to suggest that organizing a regional legislature with a qualified majority voting system would be easy. The minimum number of votes, the minimum number of jurisdictions supporting the measure, and the minimum regional population represented by the vote would have to be worked out (or eliminated from the formula). The process of enacting state legislation establishing these figures would engender a complex negotiation, with the results varying from region to region given the different populations—and number—of cities in each metropolitan area. Of course, once a regional legislature was established, the numbers could be revised over time as experience revealed the levels that were high enough to assuage the fear of loss of local control yet low enough to enable the pursuit of a regional agenda. There certainly is no reason to assume that the figures adopted by the European Union—three-quarters of the votes, two-thirds of the members (on certain issues), or (as the Treaty of Nice proposed) 62 percent of the population—would be the right ones in any American metropolitan area, although they illustrate the kind of options available.

Yet virtually any agreed-upon figures are likely to be an improvement over the status quo. Currently, there is effectively a unanimity rule on some regional issues—those delegated to local decision making. Any jurisdiction can undermine a regional plan by refusing to cooperate with other cities. On other regional issues—those entrusted to the state or to neighboring localities—local jurisdictions need not even be consulted in the decision-making process. Every metropolitan area in the country should be able to craft a qualified voting mechanism better than this oscillation between a local veto power and local irrelevance for regional decision making.

After working out the voting rules, a decision would also have to be made about how large a legislature to create. A regional legislature with a qualified majority voting system could be organized to give the least populous local government in the region one vote. The amount of representation given every other locality could then be built on this base, enabling each legislator to represent approximately equal numbers of people. Consider, for example, the Boston region. According to the most extensive definition of the region adopted by the 2000 census, there are 129 cities and towns in the region, ranging in population from 844 (South Hampton, New Hampshire) to 589,141 (Boston). The total regional population is 3,406,829. If each local government had a representative for every 844 people—thereby giving South Hampton one representative—it would mean roughly 4,000 representatives, with Boston having 698, Newton (a city of 83,829) having 99, and Newbury (a town of 6,717) having 8. Those who think this legislature too large (most people, we assume) need not abandon the idea of creating a regional legislature with a qualified majority voting mechanism. They can simply reduce the number of representatives by giving each of them weighted votes. To ensure that every local government has a voice in the legislature, the minimum number of representatives would have to equal the number of cities. In the Boston area, the minimum number would be 129. With that number as a starting point, votes could then be allocated according to the local population. If each locality had only one representative, the Boston representative would get 698 votes and the South Hampton representative would get one. This kind of system already exists in some areas of the United States, and it too has been upheld as constitutional under the one-person, one-vote requirement. But there is no need for the number of representatives to be one per locality. Larger localities could have multiple representatives, and most smaller localities could have more than one, as long as the system allocated voting strength according to population.

In deciding how many representatives to have, it is important to recognize that the presence of people in the room—and not just their voting power—has an effect on the outcome. A one-representative-per-locality regional legislature would have many people in the room who, collectively, would have very few votes. Adding more people from the more populous towns would change the dynamic of the discussion. Besides, a one-vote-per-locality rule falsely suggests that local residents are not themselves divided on issues, while electing multiple representatives would allow local governments to have legislators who disagree with each other. It is also useful to remember that the European Parliament has 626 representatives (99 from Germany alone), the British House of Commons 659 members, and the German Bundestag 669 members—and that regular attendance in the assembly in classical Athens is thought to have been over 5,000. Whatever the number of legislators, the representatives from small towns would be in the room with representatives from the largest city. And all of them collectively would be empowered to negotiate and vote on regional matters.

REGIONAL POLITICAL ORGANIZATION

Reliance on a qualified majority voting rule emphasizes jurisdictional boundaries as the building blocks for regional decision making. Legislators are encouraged to understand themselves as representatives of their own political subdivisions and, therefore, to cast their votes with an eye toward their constituents' parochial interests. This jurisdictional emphasis may well be a good basis for the initial organization of a regional legislature. It is hard to imagine that the European Union could have been organized without recognizing the importance of jurisdictional lines. In our view, however, this amount of emphasis on jurisdictional boundaries is excessive. An additional mechanism is needed to reinforce legislators' commitment to building regional connections across local boundaries rather than simply cementing their ties to their own locality. Moreover, particularly if there are a large number of legislators, it seems necessary, to get business done, to organize the disparate members of the legislature into fewer categories than is possible under a jurisdiction-by-jurisdiction legislative structure. Both of these objectives can be advanced by adapting another ingredient of the structure of the European Union, this time taken from the organization of the European Parliament rather than from the Council.

The members of the European Parliament are elected nation by nation, but the representatives from each nation are chosen in contests among national political parties and are organized through a system of proportional representation. As a result, every delegation in the European Parliament is divided by political party. Moreover, the representatives from each national party link with like-minded people from other nations—indeed, sit with them on the floor of the Parliament—to form cross-jurisdictional political parties. Political parties therefore create a cleavage within the European Parliament that is not based on jurisdictional lines. This cleavage divides people from the same jurisdiction while it unites those from different jurisdictions who agree with each other on issues. It therefore creates a different dynamic for regional argumentation and decision making than would a system based purely on geographical representation. Jurisdictional unity can be maintained in the European Parliament only if the national representatives from different parties view their common jurisdictional tie, rather than their political divisions, as central to the issue being debated. Experience has demonstrated that left-right debates, rather than centralization-decentralization debates, dominate deliberations in the European Parliament.

Elections to the European Parliament are based on already existing political parties. Organizing the election system of a regional legislature as a competition between political parties would, by contrast, create a new type of political structure in American metropolitan areas. That, we suggest, is one of its advantages. For far too long, supporters of regionalism have perpetuated the pretense that regional issues can be decided by experts without political conflict—a position that has fostered the creation of countless regional authorities. We should embrace the opposite position. Political conflict is more likely to generate negotiations over, and support for, a regional agenda than are appeals to neutrality or expertise. After all, conflict over how to improve the public schools, reduce the crime rate, provide affordable housing, stimulate the economy, and raise local tax revenue already exists. Debate on these issues should inform regional decision making. New parties might well emerge once this is done: given the environmental focus of many regional issues, for example, regional elections might become a method for organizing the Green Party in the United States.

Combining qualified majority voting with party-based elections is a significant departure from what now exists in the European Union. Qualified majority voting in the European Union exists only in the Council; democratic elections based on proportional representation exist only for the European Parliament. The combination of these two features in a one-chamber regional legislature would thus raise complexities not faced in the European Union. But the combination of party representation and qualified majority voting seems well worth the costs in complexity. It would create a mechanism that balances jurisdictional ties and cross-jurisdictional alliances in a promising, albeit unpredictable, way. The proposal for a regional legislature, then, bears little relationship to the institutional structure of the European Union itself. No body in the American metropolitan setting would represent the constituent political jurisdictions equally. There would be no multimember Commission functioning as a quasi executive. There would be no Court of Justice. There would be no need, as there is in Europe, to work out the complex division of powers among these bodies and the European Parliament. As we have said, the point is not to suggest that the organization of the European Union can be reproduced in American metropolitan areas. The point instead is to demonstrate that there are ways to combine separateness and togetherness that cannot simply be categorized as examples either of an interjurisdictional agreement or of a centralized government.

A Regional Citizenship

The European Union offers ideas not only about institutional organization but also about citizenship. Since 1992, the citizens of the European Union's member countries have simultaneously been citizens of the European Union itself. Citizens have been given the right "to move and reside freely within the territory of the Member States"; to vote and to run for office in municipal elections where they reside, even though they are not citizens of the country in which the city is located; and to vote and stand as a candidate where they reside, regardless of their nationality, in the elections for the European Parliament. Conferral of these rights is not the only device the European Union has used to build links among the citizens of its member nations. The introduction of Euro coins and notes in fifteen of the twenty-seven member states is perhaps the most dramatic way in which European citizenship has become part of the daily lives of much (although not all) of the European Union's population. Commentators have suggested additional mechanisms for reinforcing European citizenship— for example, allowing citizens to draft initiatives that could be adopted in a Europe-wide vote.[9]

No meaningful regional consciousness, let alone a regional citizenship, now exists in American metropolitan areas. They would take time to develop even after a regional legislature was organized. Still, a regional citizenship is a worthwhile goal because it would help foster the kind of regional thinking needed to address metropolitan problems. As in Europe, a regional citizenship would not replace local citizenship but complement it. A regional identity would be one more item in the complex bundle of identities that people assume for themselves: people already are Americans as well as from their hometown, Red Sox fans as well as fans of the local high school team. Unlike many of these other aspects of identity, however, a regional citizenship would emphasize not sameness but difference. Indeed, the collection of the region's multiplicity into a common citizenship is likely to be subversive of the emphasis on sameness that advocates of local autonomy have long emphasized. The organization and functioning of the regional legislature is an appropriate vehicle for giving life to a concept of regional citizenship.

The Politics of Regional Institution Building

Some advocates of local power will insist that any regional institutional structure is unacceptable. Instead, they might say, each local government should simply be empowered to make its own decisions for its residents. But local government law never has allowed—and could not conceivably allow—individual cities to decide an issue simply because their residents care deeply about it. The local governments located in the same metropolitan area are so closely connected to each other that virtually every local decision has extraterritorial impact, and local decisions often affect residents' rights in a manner inconsistent with state or federal law. That is why federal, state, and special-purpose governments decide so many issues of importance to local residents. Neither local control nor centralized control accurately describes the status quo. The question is whether a better way to combine local and collective decision making can be designed. The judgment that it is better, of course, will depend not just on an analysis of its institutional structure but also on its ability to make progress on key regional issues.

Still, the question remains whether any regional institution, however cleverly constructed, is politically viable. Many people think that the answer to this question is "no." "The suburbs won't agree to the creation of a regional institution with real power," they say. In response, we want to point out that it is not the suburbs' decision. A state legislature could create the kind of institution we have been describing tomorrow if a majority of representatives from across the state agreed to do so. A majority vote by the state legislature, after all, is the way that special-purpose governments are now created. Of course, suburban residents are represented in the state legislature. They will—and they should—have a voice in the decision making. But there are many different kinds of suburbs, people within the same suburb disagree with each other, there are other voices as well, and unanimous consent is not the way democratic societies operate. If regionalism is to get off the ground, state legislatures have to stop requiring a referendum to set up regional institutions—particularly the kind of referendum that enables a minority, even a single jurisdiction, to veto the proposal. This kind of decision-making process dooms regional proposals from the outset. If a state legislature can create nonrepresentative, state-appointed regional authorities by majority vote, it should be able to create a democratically organized regional body in the same way.

The relevant political issue raised by the prospects for regionalism, then, involves an inquiry into state legislative politics. Can a legislative majority be constructed that would approve some kind of regional institution? No one thinks that the task will be easy. But it is also not impossible. Farmers, environmentalists, and Portland city leaders, each with their own agendas, formed the coalition that brought metropolitan government to Portland. The support of the business community, the split between rural Republicans and Republicans representing affluent suburbs, and the influence of a sponsor from a low-tax-capacity suburb created the state legislative coalition that enacted the Metropolitan Council and the Fiscal Disparities Act, which brought a limited form of regional government to Minneapolis-St. Paul. Myron Orfield's success in convincing the Minnesota legislature (if not the governor) to support further regional initiatives in Minneapolis-St. Paul came from representatives of hard-pressed, inner-ring suburbs, central cities, minorities, good-government groups, and church groups, among others. All of these efforts, it should be emphasized, focused on creating a different kind of institution than the one described above. The likelihood of building a political coalition, we have argued, will be affected by the organizational structure of the regional institution that is being pursued. More support for regionalism can be gained if it is seen as building a new form of decentralized power rather than as simply one more example of centralization.[10]

To change the popular understanding of regionalism in this way, it is important to begin the effort to establish a regional legislature by focusing on an issue—such as transportation or smart growth—that undeniably affects people across the region and over which they have little control. Another possibility would be to tackle a problem directly associated with one of the four futures just considered: affordability (the middle class city) or managing connections with other nations (the global city). Once a regional legislature is established, detailed work can then be done—state by state—to determine how to add related, but much more contentious, issues to the initial agenda. Consider, for example, two of the issues we have discussed in this book: housing and education. Local governments in America do not have the authority to decide their own housing policy. And they can do little to prevent their housing stock from deteriorating as people move farther and farther into the countryside. They lack the authority, as well as the necessary collective mechanism, to establish a growth boundary for their region. Restrictions on local power such as these need to be considered together with the state-granted authority to engage in exclusionary zoning to determine the best way to meet the housing needs of metropolitan residents. A sufficient number of regional legislators might well think that a combination of increases and decreases in local power would produce a better housing policy for more local residents. After all, a restriction on the authority to engage in exclusionary zoning would still leave most zoning decisions in the hands of local officials.

The same kind of analysis can be applied to education. Local control of education is a cherished ideal, but, as we have seen, state law controls much of educational policy. Moreover, the scandalous inequality in school funding does not enhance the power of poorly funded localities to improve the educational level of their schools. Of course, housing and education policy are complex issues, and it will take a lot of work to forge a perspective that does not instinctively defend the status quo. A regional legislature would enable metropolitan residents to do this work together—an option currently unavailable to them.

Establishing an institution that furthers the conception of regionalism requires an increase in local power over issues such as housing and education that counterbalances the decreases necessary to advance regional interests. And this requires the state to decentralize more of its own power to localities. Some people claim that the state simply will not agree to do so. This position, however, fails to recognize how much influence a region could have over state policy if it could overcome the intraregional conflict that exclusionary zoning and unequal school funding now cause. If popularly elected regional legislators could agree on a common position on housing or educational policy, they could become the vehicle for mobilizing political support in the state legislature to decentralize power from the state to the local level. Metropolitan areas make up 80 percent of the population of the country and a majority of the population of most states. More than half of 6.3 million people in Massachusetts live in the Massachusetts part of the Boston metropolitan area. Almost half of the population of California lives in the Los Angeles metropolitan region; adding only the San Francisco region brings the percentage to over two-thirds of the state. Metropolitan economies dominate not only state economies but the economy of the nation as a whole. The major hurdle impeding the decentralization of power is conflict within metropolitan regions, not between the metropolitan regions and the state. Local governments now rely on state-enacted legislation to gain power at the expense of their neighbors; they could instead rely on their neighbors to get the state to enact legislation in their common interest. State legislatures, one should recall, are made up of locally elected representatives.

Of course, state officials—like the governor—would have to agree to the legislation, and some state departments (say, the department of transportation) may oppose it. But state executives are not uniformly hostile to efforts to promote greater regional connections between localities. Governor Parris Glendening provided the leadership for "smart growth" in Maryland, and Governor Roy Barnes led the effort to create the Georgia Regional Transportation Authority. Nor are state officials always against promoting greater local power. Illinois granted its cities expansive home rule powers less than forty years ago, and Governor Deval Patrick of Massachusetts has made increased local fiscal power a centerpiece of his reform efforts. It is far too simplistic, therefore, to assert that leaders of centralized governments will always seek to hold on to power.[11] Some leaders believe in shifting power to decentralized units; some are against it but go along because they feel it is in their best interest; some may be powerless to stop it. Rural legislators might also embrace the metropolitan areas' efforts if they determined that doing so would better protect them from sprawl.

Even if there is enough political support to establish a regional legislature, countless important issues remain. One of them is the definition of the region. Like "Europe," the regional area is not self-defining. Because there are many other ways to define the region, and the definition of who is included in the region is political, as in Europe, it can change over time. In our view, however, the region should be defined at the outset, unlike the European Union, to be inclusive. It should accommodate as many of those affected by regional decisions as possible so that, like a growth boundary, the region can establish the parameters for people's decisions about how they should live together. Indeed, the simultaneous establishment of a growth boundary around the region, as defined, would help reinforce everyone's recognition that one can escape the region's problems only by quitting one's job and moving to another part of the country.

Another remaining issue is establishing the relationship between the effort to promote a regional city—whether through a revision of local government law or the creation of new institutions—and the goals of being a global city, a tourist city, and a middle class city. The future of the regional city, like the future of the central city considered alone, requires thinking about how to combine, or how to choose among, alternatives like these. The difference is that the thinking would be done on a larger scale—and with a focus more connected to the way the metropolitan areas have developed and will continue to grow.

Conclusion

Our review of the four futures illustrates how the current legal structure frames city decision making in the United States. As we suggested in the introduction to part III, current legal rules are not designed to enable cities, within state-defined limits, to pursue a vision of their future. There is too little city discretion on issues of major importance to local residents. At the same time, the state directs city decision making in ways that are not properly debated even at the state level. A second-guessing of local judgments—and a confidence in public authorities, state control, and privatization rather than in local democracy—seems to generate many of the legal rules that we have discussed in this book.

The legal structure that this process has produced has had a profound effect on city life. Cities, as we have emphasized, only have power to the extent they are given it by statutes and constitutional provisions adopted by the state government. Law therefore defines the extent to which cities can and cannot deal with the critical problems they face: housing shortages, inadequate schools, crumbling infrastructure, traffic congestion, global warming, crime—to name but a few. Law also defines the authority of other entities—state-created public authorities, state government agencies, nongovernmental institutions, private corporations—that play a role in dealing with same kinds of issues. Law thus creates the bureaucratic inefficiencies, dysfunctional agencies, regional fragmentation, and democratic deficits that make governance one of the major problems facing cities today. Law is involved too in the design of the built environment, either by regulating the size and location of housing and commercial life or by failing to regulate them, thereby empowering people to act in ways that otherwise would not be possible. Unleashing a different kind of urban age requires rethinking this structure from top to bottom. It does not have to be done overnight. It would be better if it were done step by step, state by state. But it's time—long past time—to start making sense of city power.

At this point, a reader might well ask: So what is the right legal structure for American cities in the twenty-first century? If we want to unleash a new urban age in the United States, how should we do it? These questions are likely to arise precisely because we have so consistently refused to respond to them. The reason for our refusal lies in our understanding of what the decentralization of power means. If there is to be a revision of local government law in the United States, the last thing one should want is a uniform model for how it is organized. One of the major advantages of having local democracy, as we have emphasized from the outset, is the experimentation that it allows in different places and in different contexts. There's no reason to believe that there's one right structure for local government law. There's no necessity that Boston, New York, Chicago, Atlanta, Denver, Seattle, and San Francisco have to be empowered and disempowered in the same way. Quite the contrary. It is important to enable the citizens of these cities to have a voice in their own future. And this requires them to have a voice in designing the kind of local government organization that they think best. As we have insisted throughout the book, this is not a call for local autonomy. State governments have a role to play in these decisions too.

Designing a workable structure that enables both a state and city role will not be easy. The revision of local government law is now largely in the hands of state legislatures. A way has to be found to give local governments a voice in this process. Experiments with creating new decision-making institutions—parallel to, but different from, those we imagined for regional decision making—will have to be devised. Many people outside of major cities do not understand the value of cities in American life, the need to strengthen their decision-making authority, and the implications of this agenda for virtually every urban problem. Local voices are necessary to bring these perspectives into state decision making. In making their voices heard, cities have to come up with a list of priorities much more sophisticated and worked out than "more money, please." And, for the state leadership to obtain local cooperation on matters of statewide concern, it needs a list of priorities and a way of implementing them more sophisticated than "do what I tell you." The multitude of possibilities that a process of rethinking of local government law can generate has the potential to do more than improve the organization of city life. It can enable city residents to learn from the progress and mistakes being made elsewhere.

Our book provides some basic guidelines for this undertaking. We have stressed that a revision of local government law should be based on substantive ideas about the kind of urban age that those designing the new legal structure want to bring about. To the extent they want to enable some or all of the four futures we have analyzed—or any other future that we have not discussed—the legal system should be structured to serve the goals they embrace. Even better, they should give cities themselves the ability to formulate innovative means of implementing any or all of them after debating the kind of urban future they find most desirable. We have also sought to make clear that the goal is not to delineate the functions that, in some Platonic sense, are statewide and those that are local, let alone to protect local autonomy. The task of finding a way to organize state-local relations is likely to be endless, as the participants respond to the impact of the changes that they have made and to other developments in American society. That's why finding a way to provide a regularized local voice in state decision making about local government law is so important.

We have also argued that a revision of local government requires addressing the problems now generated by the fragmentation of decision making about the critical urban issues discussed in this book. We refer not only to the geographic fragmentation of metropolitan areas into a multiplicity of local jurisdictions but the functional fragmentation created by assigning specific issues to uncoordinated government institutions. Over the course of the twentieth century, local governments have multiplied as metropolitan regions have grown and, equally important, more and more independent public authorities have been organized to deal with particular aspects of urban concern. As a result, the response to metropolitan development has been to allocate some issues to functionally specific institutions, others to state decision making, and the rest to fragmented local governments. The precise ways in which governmental power has been allocated to these different institutions would be hard to defend or even describe. But the result has been clear enough: a diminishment of local democracy. Local democratic governments, both in the central cities and the suburbs, have been overwhelmed by the impact of decisions made by other governments over which they have no control. Reversing this process requires taking into account the metropolitan nature of urban life. And this requires making regional cooperation an integral part of local decision making. We have argued that regional thinking and the revitalization of local democracy are not inconsistent with each other. Unleashing a new urban age involves both at once: empowering local democracy and recognizing the impact of local decisions on neighboring localities—and the larger world.

Institutional design, many people think, is a technical, even boring, task. It can be left to experts—perhaps even to their staff. This book outlines the opposite argument. We live in a structured world. Finding a way to alter this structure is a primary way in which we can enrich our individual and collective lives. This is the way we define what we mean by federalism, home rule, and local democracy. It is the way that we create the experience of cities and neighborhoods, and, thereby, the feel of everyday life. And, by helping to specify the physical, governmental, and social context in which much of America lives, it is one of the principal ways that we define who we are. It's not enough to say that cities are not making good choices and that they should make better ones. States often restrict the kinds of choices they can make. Too often, this basic fact is overlooked. It is no overstatement to say that empowering cities to better serve their population is one of the critical tasks of public policy.

Notes

PREFACE

1. For the New York Plan, see Nicolas Confessore and Diane Cardwell, "Hardest Part Lies Ahead for City's Traffic Plan," *New York Times*, July 21, 2007; for London's plan, see www.cclondon.com/, and Ken Livingstone, "Clear Up the Congestion-Pricing Gridlock," *New York Times*, July 2, 2007.

2. *New York Vehicle and Traffic Code*, §§1640, 1642; New York Constitution, Article 1X, §2.

3. *Automobile Club of N.Y. v. City of New York*, 1981 N.Y. Misc. LEXIS 3518 (Sup. Ct. N.Y. 1981); *New York State Public Employees Federation v. Albany*, 72 N.Y.2d 96 (1988).

4. Confessore and Cardwell, "Hardest Part."

5. NYC Department of Planning, *Population Division 2000 Census Summary*; www. nyc.gov/html/dcp/html/census/pop2000.shtml.

PART I. CITY STRUCTURES

1. Lewis Mumford, "What is a City?," reprinted from the *Architectural Record* (1937), in Richard T. LeGates and Frederic Stout, *The City Reader* (London: Routledge, 1996), 184; see also the opening sentence of Lewis Mumford, *The City in History: Its Origins, Its Transformations, and Its Prospects* (New York: Harcourt Brace Jovanovich, 1961), 1.

2. John Dillon, *Municipal Corporations*, 5th ed., vol. 1 (New York: Little, Brown, 1911), 448.

CHAPTER 1. CITY STRUCTURES AND URBAN THEORY

1. H. V. Savitch and Paul Kantor, *Cities in the International Marketplace: The Political Economy of Urban Development in North America and Western Europe* (Princeton: Princeton University Press, 2002), 30–31.

2. Robert A. Dahl, *Who Governs? Democracy and Power in an American City* (New Haven: Yale University Press, 1961).

3. Floyd Hunter, *Community Power Structure: A Study of Decision Makers* (Chapel Hill: University of North Carolina Press, 1953); Nelson W. Polsby, *Community Power and Political Theory: A Further Look at Problems and Inference* (New Haven: Yale University Press, 1980).

4. Paul Peterson, *City Limits* (Chicago: University of Chicago Press, 1981).

5. Peterson, *City Limits*, 4.

6. Peterson, *City Limits*, 222.

7. Clarence N. Stone, *Regime Politics: Governing Atlanta, 1946–1988* (Lawrence: University Press of Kansas, 1989).

8. Stone, *Regime Politics*, xi.

9. Richard DeLeon, *Left Coast City: Progressive Politics in San Francisco, 1975–1991* (Lawrence: University Press of Kansas, 1992).

10. Stone, *Regime Politics*, 233.

11. Manuel Castells, *The City and the Grassroots: A Cross-Cultural Theory of Urban Social Movements* (London: Edward Arnold, 1983), 319.

12. Harvey C. Molotch, "The City as a Growth Machine: Toward a Political Economy of Place," *American Journal of Sociology* 82 (1976): 226.

13. Guido Martinotti, "A City for Whom? Transients and Public Life in the Second-Generation Metropolis," in *The Urban Movement: Cosmopolitan Essays on the Late-20th-Century City,* ed. Robert Beauregard and Sophie Body-Gendrot, 1999).

14. Richard L. Florida, *The Rise of the Creative Class: And How It's Transforming Work, Leisure, Community, and Everyday Life* (New York: Basic Books, 2002).

15. Joel Kotkin, *The City: A Global History* (New York: Modern Library, 2005).

16. Savitch and Kantor, *Cities in the International Marketplace,* 31.

CHAPTER 2. CITY STRUCTURES AND LOCAL AUTONOMY

1. Sheryll Cashin, "Localism, Self-Interest, and the Tyranny of the Favored Quarter," *Georgetown Law Journal* 88 (2000): 1985, 1988–89.

2. See Richard Briffault, "Our Localism: Part I—The Structure of Local Government Law," *Columbia Law Review* 90 (1990): 1; Richard Briffault, "Our Localism: Part II—Localism and Legal Theory," *Columbia Law Review* 90 (1990): 346.

3. Todd Swanstrom, "What We Talk about When We Talk about Regionalism," *Journal of Urban Affairs* 23 (2001): 479–96 at 491.

4. Richard Briffault, "Our Localism, Part II," at 351–52, 415; Richard Briffault, "Our Localism: Part I," at 1–2.

5. For a description of this version of the home rule movement, see Jon C. Teaford, *The Unheralded Triumph: City Government in America, 1870–1900* (Baltimore: Johns Hopkins University Press, 1984); Howard Lee McBain, *The Law and Practice of Municipal Home Rule* (New York: Columbia University Press, 1916). For a general analysis of all of the versions of home rule described here, see David J. Barron, "Reclaiming Home Rule," *Harvard Law Review* 116 (2003): 2257.

6. A representative figure in this version of home rule was Frank Goodnow. See, for example, Frank J. Goodnow, "Municipal Home Rule," *Political Science Quarterly* 10 (1985): 1; Frank J. Goodnow, *Municipal Home Rule* (New York: Macmillan, 1897); Frank J. Goodnow, *City Government in the United States* (New York: Century, 1908).

7. See, for example, Richard T. Ely, *The Coming City* (New York: T. Y. Crowell & Company, 1902); Frederic Howe, *The City: The Hope of Democracy* (New York: C. Scribner's Sons, 1906); Delos F. Wilcox, *Great Cities in America: Their Problems and Their Government* (New York: Macmillan, 1910).

8. Robert A. Dahl, *Dilemmas of Pluralist Democracy: Autonomy vs. Control* (New Haven: Yale University Press, 1982), 96–107.

9. Exemplary cases invalidating federal legislation affecting local power include *National League of Cities v. Usery,* 426 U.S. 833 (1976); *New York v. United States,* 505 U.S. 144 (1992); and *Printz v. United States,* 521 U.S. 898 (1997). For a critique of this jurisprudence, see David J. Barron, "A Localist Critique of the New Federalism," *Duke Law Journal* 51 (2001), 377. The Supreme Court's strongest statement of the lack of a federal constitutional limit on state power over local governments was expressed in *Hunter v. Pittsburgh,* 207 U.S. 161 (1907).

10. "Treaty Establishing the European Community," Article 3b, O.J. (C340) (1997).

11. George A. Bermann, "Taking Subsidiarity Seriously," *Columbia Law Review* 94 (1994): 332, 339.

12. Bermann, "Taking Subsidiarity Seriously," 404.

13. Gerry Cross, "Subsidiarity and the Environment," *Year Book of European Law* 15 (1995): 107, 108.

14. Edward T. Swaine, "Subsidiarity and Self-Interest: Federalism at the European Court of Justice," *Harvard International Law Journal* 41 (2000): 1, 54.

15. *Report of the Metropolitan District Commission to the Massachusetts Legislature* (1896).

16. For example, "Advisory Commission on Intergovernmental Relations, Alternative Approaches to Governmental Reorganization in Metropolitan Areas" (1962); "Advisory Commission on Intergovernmental Relations, Governmental Functions and Processes: Local and Area-Wide" (1974).

17. David Rusk, *Baltimore Unbound: A Strategy for Regional Renewal* (Baltimore: Johns Hopkins University Press, 1996), 94. Emphasis in original.

18. Alexis de Tocqueville, *Democracy in America, Volume 1* (Cambridge, Mass.: Sever and Francis, 1863), 74–76.

19. Harvey Molotch, "Urban Deals in Comparative Perspective," in *Beyond the City Limits: Urban Policy and Economic Restructuring in Comparative Perspective,* ed. John Logan and Todd Swanstrom (Philadelphia: Temple University Press, 1990), 175, 176–77.

20. Isaac Martin, "Dawn of the Living Wage: The Diffusion of a Redistributive Municipal Policy," *Urban Affairs Review* 36 (2001): 470, 472.

21. Frederick Howe, *The City: The Hope of Democracy* (New York: Charles Scribner's Sons, 1906), 303.

PART II. SEVEN CITIES

1. The minority make-up of the cities differs. Boston's minority population is more diverse than that of Atlanta (predominantly black), San Francisco (predominantly Asian), or Denver (predominantly Hispanic); it is also more diverse than Seattle (which has the largest non-Hispanic white population of all seven cities).

2. Twenty-five percent of Boston's residents are foreign born, compared to 36% of New York's, 17% of Denver's, 6% of Atlanta's, and 11% of the nation as a whole.

3. Both San Francisco and Seattle have less poverty and more residents with higher education than does Boston (and San Francisco also has the highest percentage of foreign born of the seven cities).

4. There are number of different ways of defining the size of a metropolitan region in the United States: the Census Bureau's population figures for Boston range from 5,819,100 (the consolidated statistical metropolitan area) to 3,406,829 (the primary statistical area).

5. The job distribution within the seven metropolitan areas varies considerably: jobs in Atlanta are more dispersed—and in New York City less dispersed—throughout the region than in Boston. About a quarter of the Boston area's jobs are close to the central business district, and a little more than half are within ten miles of the city center. In Atlanta, the jobs are considerably more dispersed, with just over 10% within three miles of downtown and only about one-third within ten miles of it. By contrast, more than three quarters of all jobs in the New York City area are within ten miles of the city center, and nearly half are within three miles. Another way to get a sense of job distribution is to look at commuting patterns. In four of the seven metropolitan areas, including Boston, more residents commute from suburb to suburb than from a suburb to the city itself. Yet Boston still attracts a substantial commuter workforce: more commuters than residents work in Boston. Elsewhere, there is great variation in the extent to which the city workforce is comprised of suburban commuters or city residents. In New York, residents dominate the city's labor market, while in Atlanta suburbanites do.

6. Boston's overall decline, as a percentage of the region, was comparable to most of the other cities, although Seattle and San Francisco did better. The median family incomes in all of the cities except Seattle fell sharply as a percentage of their metropolitan areas' median family incomes from the 1950s to 2000 (in Seattle the decline was minor). As a group, they had 97.5% of metropolitan median family income in 1950 but had dropped to 76.5% in 2000. This decline demonstrates the impact of the suburbanization

of child-rearing, middle-class families on America's central cities. The decline was somewhat less severe when comparing city and regional median household incomes. (Single person households—yuppies as well as retirees—are counted for this figure but not for family income.) To be sure, it too declined in all seven cities. The decline for all cities combined was from 93% in 1950 to 77.5% in 2000.

7. Ten of the House districts are wholly within the city limits; the city shares the other seven districts with neighboring communities, casting a majority of the votes in all of them. Only two of the six Senate districts are entirely within the city, and the city casts a majority of the votes in only one of them; it casts a plurality of votes in the other three.

8. Except for San Francisco (3%), Boston has the lowest percentage of members of the House of Representatives of any of the cities, although Denver (16%), Atlanta (12%) and Seattle (12%) are roughly comparable. (New York has 42% of the state's representatives and Chicago 30%.) The figures also place Boston in the middle of the seven cities for the Senate, far short of New York (42%) and Chicago (31%). What is most unusual in Massachusetts is the shift of pattern of city-only and cross-border seats from the House of Representatives to the Senate. The other six cities largely maintained the pattern of representation they displayed in House seats in the state Senate.

9. Except for the current Speaker and his immediate predecessor, the leader of the House of Representatives has represented Boston for only ten years in the past century.

CHAPTER 3. HOME RULE

1. See, for example, *McCrory Corporation v. Fowler*, 570 A.2d 834 (Md. 1990).

2. See, for example, *Lilly v. City of Minneapolis*, 427 N.W.2d 107 (Minn. Ct. App. 1995).

3. *Marshal House, Inc. v. Rent Review and Grievance Board of Brookline*, 260 N.E.2d 200 (Mass. 1970) (rent control); *New Orleans Campaign for a Living Wage v. City of New Orleans*, 825 So. 2d 1098 (La. 2002) (Weimer, J. concurring) (living wage).

4. For the early history of Boston, see James Bugbee, *The City Government of Boston* (Baltimore: N. Murray, 1887); *Mass. Legislative Research Council, Municipal Home Rule* ("Massachusetts Senate Report," No. 950, 1965).

5. Thomas O'Connor, *The Hub: Boston Past and Present* (Boston: Northeastern University Press, 2001).

6. Edward L. Glaeser, *Reinventing Boston, 1640–2003* (Cambridge: Rappaport Institute for Greater Boston, JFK School of Government, Harvard University, 2003).

7. Thomas O'Connor, *Building a New Boston: Politics and Urban Renewal 1950–1970* (Boston: Northeastern University Press, 1993); Lawrence W. Kennedy, *Planning the City Upon a Hill: Boston since 1630* (Amherst: University of Massachusetts Press, 1992).

8. The Office of the City Clerk has printed a pamphlet that is the closest approximation of Boston's charter. It contains a five-paragraph preface that reveals just how total the state legislature's role has been in writing the charter. As if to underscore the point, the preface concludes: "Two useful works containing…many of the various statutes which are part of Boston's charter are 'Special Laws Relating to the City of Boston Enacted Prior to January 1, 1938,' and, 'City of Boston Code (1975),' both of which are out of print and available in libraries." Office of the City Clerk, Boston City Charter 1 (n.d.).

9. The charter amendment process under the Home Rule Amendment does provide a means by which Boston may reform its charter. It permits two-thirds of the city council to propose a change that voters can approve by referendum. If they do, the amendment becomes law. This procedure can be followed for limited changes to the charter; more substantial changes require use of the charter revision or adoption process. The requirement that amendments receive supermajority support on the city council makes the process relatively restrictive. The Colorado and Washington constitutions permit a simple majority of the city council to place a charter amendment on the ballot. The Georgia

home rule statute permits the city council to make charter amendments on its own without resort to a referendum.

10. Gabriel Metcalf, San Francisco Planning and Urban Research Association, *SPUR Newsletter 9*, "SPUR History: Forty Years of Citizen Planning for San Francisco" (January 1999).

11. *Board of Appeals v. Housing Appeals Commission*, 363 Mass. 339 (1973).

12. *Beard v. Town of Salisbury*, 392 N.E.2d 832 (Mass. 1979); *Marshal House, Inc. v. Rent Review & Grievance Board*, 260 N.E.2d 200 (Mass. 1970); *Bloom v. Worcester*, 293 N.E.2d 268 (Mass. 1973); *Greater Franklin Developers Association v. Town of Franklin*, 730 N.E.2d 900 (Mass. App. Ct. 2000).

13. Illinois Constitution, Article VIII; *Boytor v. City of Aurora*, 401 N.E.2d 1 (Ill. 1980).

14. Colorado Constitution, Article XX, §§ 1, 6; *Berman v. City of Denver*, 400 P.2d 434 (Colo. 1965).

15. California Const. art XI, §5; *Glendale v. Trondsen*, 308 P.2d 1 (Cal. 1957); *Law v. City of San Francisco*, 77 P.2d 1014 (1907).

16. New York Const. art XVI, §1; *New York State Clubs Ass'n v. City of New York*, 505 N.E.2d 915 (N.Y. 1987); *Vatore v. Comm'r of Consumer Affairs*, 634 N.E.2d 958 (N.Y. 1994); *Hertz Corp. v. City of New York*, 607 N.E.2d 784 (N.Y. 1992); *Council for Owner Occupied Housing v. Koch*, 61 N.Y.2d 942 (1984); *210 E. 68th Street Corp. v. City Rent Agency*, 34 N.Y.2d 560 (1974).

17. Washington Constitution, Article XI, § 11; *City of Atlanta v. McKinney*, 454 S.E.2d 517, 521 (Ga. 1995).

18. *1996 Georgia Laws* 1019 §§1–102(c); *City of Tacoma v. Taxpayers of Tacoma*, 743 P.2d 793 (Wash. 1987); *Heinsma v. City of Vancouver*, 29 P.3d 709 (Wash. 2001); *Peacock v. Georgia Mun. Ass'n*, 279 S.E.2d 434 (Ga. 1981).

19. *Powers v. Secretary of Administration*, 587 N.E.2d 744, 750 (Mass. 1922).

20. *Connors v. City of Boston*, 714 N.E.2d 335 (Mass. 1999).

21. *Anderson v. City of Boston*, 380 N.E.2d 628, 633 (Mass. 1978).

22. *Greater Boston Real Estate Board v. City of Boston*, 705 N.E.2d 256 (Mass. 1999).

23. Colorado Constitution, Article XX, § 6; *Fraternal Order of Police v. City of Denver*, 926 P.2d 582 (Colo. 1996); *Winslow Const. Co. v. City of Denver*, 960 P.2d 685 (Colo. 1998).

24. California Constitution, Article XI, § 5; *Bishop v. City of San Jose*, 460 P.2d 137, 141 (Cal. 1969); *Piledrivers' Local Union No. 2375 v. City of Santa Monica*, 198 Cal. Rptr. 731 (Cal. Ct. App. 1985); *Rees v. Layton*, 86 Cal. Rptr. 268 (Cal. Ct. App. 1970); *City of Glendale v. Trondsen*, 308 P.2d 1 (Cal. 1957).

25. Illinois Constitution, Article VII, § 61; *Scadron v. City of Des Plaines*, 606 N.E.2d 1154 (Ill. 1992).

26. In addition to the sources noted in chapter 2, see, for example, David Imbroscio, *Reconstructing City Politics: Alternative Economic Development and Urban Regimes* (Thousand Oaks, Calif.: Sage Publications, 1997), 148–50.

CHAPTER 4. REVENUE AND EXPENDITURES

1. *Ex parte Braun*, 74 P. 780, 782 (Cal. 1903) (quoting *United States v. New Orleans*, 98 U.S. 381, 393 [1878]).

2. John C. Parkhurst, "Article VII—Local Government," *Chicago Bar Record* 52 (1971): 94, 100.

3. *Massachusetts General Laws*, ch. 59, § 21(c).

4. Boston Redevelopment Authority, *Tax Exempt Property in Boston: Analysis of Types, Uses and Issues*, Report #562 (December 2002).

5. In 2003, Boston sought to increase this limit so that it could shield residents from the increasing tax burden spurred by a sharp upward trend in housing values. The state

agreed to this change only with conditions: it would allow Boston to tax commercial properties at higher rates for one year but, for the subsequent five years, the discrepancy would have to be reduced.

6. The resulting legislation—known as Chapter 121A—was passed by the state legislature to deal with blighted areas in the city. Private developments located in these areas were exempt from property taxation and special assessments for a period of fifteen years, with the time limit extended if the development provided certain amenities, such as affordable housing. At first, Chapter 121A could only be used for developments that were primarily residential. In an attempt to entice the Prudential Insurance Company to construct what is now the Prudential Center, Chapter 121A was amended in 1960 to include commercial developments. The construction of the Prudential Center is thought to have served Boston's economy well at the time that it was built.

7. Boston Redevelopment Authority, Insight Report, *Boston's Population Doubles— Every Day* (December 1996).

8. *Security Life & Accident Co. v. Temple*, 492 P.2d 63 (Colo. 1972).

9. *Emerson College v. City of Boston*, 462 N.E.2d 1098 (Mass. 1984).

10. Terri A. Sexton, Arthur O'Sullivan, and Steven Sheffrin, "Proposition 13: Unintended Effects and Feasible Reforms," *National Tax Journal* 52 (1999), 99, 107; *City & County of San Francisco v. Farrell*, 648 P.2d 935 (Cal. 1982).

11. *Russ Building Partnership v. City & County of San Francisco*, 234 Cal. Rptr. 1 (Cal. Ct. App. 1987).

12. *Endsley v. City of Chicago*, 745 N.E.2d 708 (Ill. App. Ct. 2001).

13. Alicia H. Munnell and Lynn E. Browne, *Massachusetts in the 1990s: The Role of State Government* (Boston: Federal Reserve Bank of Boston, 1990), 49–62, 154.

14. *Connors v. City of Boston*, 714 N.E.2d 335 (Mass. 1999).

15. *Schaefer v. City & County of Denver*, 973 P.2d 717 (Colo. Ct. App. 1998).

16. *Massachusetts General Laws*, ch. 29, §27C(a).

17. Under a 1966 act, the state also allows Boston to issue debt outside of the debt limit for specific purposes, such as construction and renovation.

18. In 1997, the state decided to discontinue its practice of funding cost of living increases for retired workers, adopting instead a local option statute enabling local pension boards to authorize increases. Boston accepted this option. But the legislation enabled local elected officials only to choose whether to make the initial commitment to award cost of living adjustments. All subsequent decisions would be made by the Retirement Board.

19. *Peters v. City of Springfield*, 311 N.E.2d 107 (Ill. 1974).

20. The only restraint on Denver's authority has traditionally been the language of the city charter. In November 2003, voters removed the guidelines for employee benefits from the city charter, allowing them to be set by ordinance. This change was designed to permit the mayor and council to accept, reject, or modify pay and benefit recommendations. Pay and benefits for the police and fire departments are different—they are set by collective bargaining processes that the Denver city charter makes mandatory.

CHAPTER 5. LAND USE AND DEVELOPMENT

1. For a review of the literature, see David J. Barron, "Reclaiming Home Rule," *Harvard Law Review* 116 (2003): 2255, 2267–70.

2. Lawrence W. Kennedy, *Planning the City upon a Hill: Boston since 1630* (Amherst: University of Massachusetts Press, 1992).

3. *Massachusetts General Laws* Ch. 40A; Cynthia M. Barr, *Boston Zoning: A Lawyer's Handbook*, 2nd ed. (Boston: Massachusetts Continuing Legal Education, 2003).

4. State law once allowed petitions for a zoning amendment to be brought only by property owners who would be affected by the proposed change. In 1993, in order to

increase community participation in Zoning Commission and Board of Appeal decisions, the state legislature amended the Enabling Act in 1993 to permit any Boston property owner or resident to petition the Zoning Commission for such an amendment. Although other Massachusetts cities can choose to adopt the zoning amendment process now in effect in Boston, only Boston is required to have it.

5. See Gregory Overstreet & Diane M. Kirchheim, "The Quest for the Best Test to Vest: Washington's Vested Rights Doctrine Beats the Rest," *Seattle University Law Review* 24 (2000): 1043; Roger D. Wayne, "Washington's Vested Rights Doctrine: How We Have Muddled a Simple Concept and How We Can Reclaim It," *Seattle University Law Review* 24 (2001): 851.

6. Jennifer T. Moulton and Bill Hornby, "Blueprint Denver Plan for the Future Melds Land Use, Transportation," *Denver Post,* March 17, 2002, E-1.

7. Barr, *Boston Zoning.*

8. The city does receive payments in lieu of taxes from Massport, but this is substantially less than the city would receive were the land taxable.

9. Stapleton/Denver development: www.stapletondenver.com/.

10. *Massachusetts General Laws,* ch. 81A; Massachusetts Turnpike Authority, "Memorandum of Understanding between Massachusetts Turnpike Authority and the City of Boston, Acting by and through the Boston Redevelopment Authority" (1997).

11. Richard Briffault, "A Government for Our Time? Business Improvement Districts and Urban Governance," *Columbia Law Review* 99 (1999): 365.

12. *Massachusetts General Laws,* ch. 40B.

13. City of Boston, *Leading the Way II: A Report on Boston's Housing Strategy FY2004— FY2007* (May 2004).

14. City of Boston, *Leading the Way II;* Boston Redevelopment Authority, *Residential Land Use in Boston,* Report #592 (February 2004); New York City Housing Authority website: www.nyc.gov/html/nycha/html/home/home.shtml; Chicago Housing Authority website: www.thecha.org/index.html.

15. David W. Chen, "One Housing Woe Gives Way to Another," *New York Times,* December 21, 2003, sec. 1, at 49; Dennis Hevesi, "Transforming the City's Housing: Act 2," *New York Times,* May 2, 2004, sec. 11, at 1.

16. Barr, *Boston Zoning;* John Avault and Geoff Lewis, Boston Redevelopment Authority, *Survey of Linkage Programs in Other U.S. Cities with Comparisons to Boston* (May 2000); Boston Redevelopment Authority, *The Boston Economy,* Report #589 (October 2003).

17. *Bonan v. City of Boston,* 496 N.E.2d 640 (Mass. 1986).

18. National Housing Conference, "Inclusionary Zoning: Lessons Learned in Massachusetts," *National Housing Conference Housing Policy Review* 2, no. 1(January 2002).

19. Nick Brunick, Lauren Goldberg, and Susannah Levine, "Large Cities and Inclusionary Zoning," (Business and Professional People for the Public Interest, November 2003).

20. Jane Schukoske, "Housing Linkage: Regulating Development Impact on Housing Costs," *Iowa Law Review* 76 (1991): 1011.

21. *Marshal House v. Rent Review and Grievance Board of Brookline,* 260 N.E.2d 200 (Mass. 1970).

22. City of Boston, *Leading the Way: Boston's Housing Strategy FY 2001—2003 Completion Report* (October 2003); Boston Foundation, *The Greater Boston Housing Report Card 2003: An Assessment of Progress on Housing in the Greater Boston Area* (April 2004), 24.

23. *Greater Boston Real Estate Board v. City of Boston,* 705 N.E.2d 256 (Mass. 1999).

24. *Town of Telluride v. Lot Thirty-Four Venture, L.L.C.,* 3 P.3d 30 (Colo. 2000).

25. Boston Redevelopment Authority, *The Boston Economy.*

26. The median housing price in San Francisco topped $650,000 in 2003, and the median price for the Bay Area was $545,000—18% higher than the previous year.

27. City of Boston website: www.cityofboston.gov/.

28. City of Chicago website: egov.cityofchicago.org/.

29. Department of Housing, Preservation and Development, City of New York, *Home-Works Homeownership Program* (2004).

CHAPTER 6. EDUCATION

1. San Francisco manages 114 schools with nearly 60,000 students, Denver 144 schools with more than 72,000 students, Seattle about 130 schools with 47,000 students, and Atlanta 102 schools with 55,000 students.

2. African Americans constitute 48.8% of the school population and 25.3% of the city population, Hispanics constitute 26.9% of the school population and 14.4% of the city population, and Asians 8.9% of the school population and 7.6% of the city population. The Boston teaching staff is 61% non-Hispanic white and 26% African American.

3. San Francisco's school population is more than 40% Asian and 20% Hispanic, while Atlanta's is approximately 90% African American. Seattle has the largest non-Hispanic white population with 40%; no other city had a non-Hispanic white population in excess of 20%.

4. Boston has fewer English learners than Denver (it is just over 25%), but its percentage is higher than found in New York City (13.5%), Chicago (14%), and Seattle (11.7%). Atlanta has the lowest percentage: 2.5%.

5. The comparison between cities on this dimension is difficult because different school districts have different criteria for defining who qualifies as a special education student. The percentage of students receiving special education in New York City public schools is 14.0%, in Seattle 12.6%, Chicago 12.3%, San Francisco 11.9%, Denver 11.0%, and Atlanta 7.4%.

6. *1991 Massachusetts Acts* 108 § 7(a).

7. Concern about the limited role given to Seattle's city government led to the city's adoption of the Families and Education Levy in 1990. The ordinance authorizes a special city property tax "grounded in the notion that school success for all students does not lie solely with the Seattle Public Schools—it is the responsibility of all of Seattle's citizens." The city has used this authority to raise nearly $140 million over the last fifteen years. A seven-member oversight committee (composed of three citizens, the mayor, the city council president, the district superintendent, and a school board member) controls the distribution of the funds. City of Seattle, *Families and Education Levy: Progress Report* (2003).

8. Changes include adopting a uniform reading and math curriculum for all but the top two hundred high-performing schools, announcing the end of "social promotions" for third graders who perform poorly on standardized tests, breaking up a number of large, struggling high schools into smaller ones, revamping the high school admissions process, and shaking up the city schools' bureaucracy.

9. *Serrano v. Priest*, 557 P.2d 929 (Cal. 1976).

10. *San Antonio Independent School District v. Rodriguez*, 411 U.S. 1 (1973).

11. *McDuffy v. Secretary of Executive Office of Education*, 615 N.E.2d 516 (Mass. 1993).

12. *Hancock v. Commissioner of Education*, 822 N.E.2d 1134 (Mass. 2005).

13. Boston Foundation, *Creativity and Innovation: A Bridge to the Future, A Summary of the Boston Indicators Report 2002*, § 4.5.2 (2002).

14. The percentage of African American students in private schools, at approximately 28%, is also closer to the citywide population—considerably smaller than the public school figure of 48.5%. The private school population is less than 10% Hispanic (Boston's public schools are almost 28% Hispanic) and Asians make up 3% of private schools (and 9% of public school students).

15. SchoolChoiceInfo.org, "Education Tax Credits and Deductions," www.schoolchoice info.org/; *Owens v. Colorado Congress of Parents, Teachers & Students,* 92 P.3d 933 (Colo. 2003).

16. Joseph M. O'Keefe, "What Research Tells Us About the Contribution of Sectarian Schools," *University of Detroit Mercy Law Review* 78 (2001): 425.

17. The demographics of Boston's charter schools are quite different from those of the Boston public school system as a whole. African American students predominate in charter schools—more than 70% of charter school students are African American, while only 13.7% are Hispanic and Asian. Non-Hispanic white students, who enroll in charter schools at about the same rate as they do in public schools, are concentrated in very few schools. Special education students in Boston account for almost 20% of the student population in the public schools, but in the charter schools they account for around 10%. In the Boston public schools 73.6% of all students are eligible for free or reduced lunch programs, but only 53.6% of charter school students are. The most striking statistic is that, according to one report, although nearly 25% of students in Boston's public schools are learning English, not a single student in Boston's charter schools is similarly categorized.

18. Karen Hawley Miles, *Rethinking School Spending: A Case Study of Boston* (Cambridge: Harvard Graduate School of Education, National Center for Educational Leadership, 1993).

19. Rosanne Tung, Monique Ouimette, and Jay Feldman, Center for Collaborative Education, *How Are Boston Pilot School Students Faring? Student Demographics, Engagement, and Performance 1998—2003* (March 2004).

20. Clarence Stone, *Building Civic Capacity: The Politics of Reforming Urban Schools* (Lawrence: University Press of Kansas, 2001).

21. For the racial composition of Boston's schools, see Chungmei Lei, *Racial Segregation and Educational Outcomes in Metropolitan Boston* (Cambridge: The Civil Rights Project, Harvard University, April 2004). For racial preferences in New York, see Tamar Lewin, "Public Schools Confronting Issue of Racial Preferences," *New York Times,* November 29, 1998, sec. 1, at 11. For racial preferences in Chicago, see Ana Beatriz Cholo, "City's Selective Schools Urged to Be More Open; Consider Abilities as Well as Test Scores, Panel Recommends," *Chicago Tribune,* March 1, 2005, C-1. The Supreme Court decision is *Parents Involved in Community Schools v. Seattle School District,* 127 S. Ct. 2738 (2007). The Court of Appeals decision in Boston is *Wessman v. Gittens,* 160 F.3d 790 (1st Cir. 1998).

22. *Parents Involved in Community Schools v. Seattle School District.*

PART III. CITY FUTURES

1. See generally, Urban Age website: http://www.urban-age.net/.

CHAPTER 7. THE GLOBAL CITY

1. John Friedmann, "The World Cities Hypothesis," in *World Cities in a World-System,* by Paul L. Knox and Peter J. Taylor (Cambridge: Cambridge University Press, 1995), 317.

2. Saskia Sassen, *The Global City,* 2nd ed. (Princeton: Princeton University Press, 2001), 3–4.

3. This hierarchical image has led to criticism of the world cities literature on the grounds that it concentrates on a small set of wealthy urban centers, rather than on the cities that have been hurt by global economic integration or on those that are located in countries on the periphery of this transformative process. Arthur S. Alderson & Jason Beckfield, "Power and Position in the World City System," *American Journal of Sociology* 109 (January 2004): 811; J. V. Beaverstock, R. G. Smith, and P. J. Taylor, "A Roster of World Cities," *Cities* 16 (1999): 445.

4. Friedmann, "World Cities Hypothesis," 317.

5. Arjun Apadurai, "Deep Democracy: Urban Governmentality and the Horizon of Politics," *Public Culture* 14 (2002), 21, 24; Saskia Sassen, Introduction to *Global Networks: Linked Cities,* ed. Saskia Sassen (New York: Routledge, 2002).

6. Robert Beauregard, "Theorizing the Global-Local Connection," in Knox and Taylor, *World Cities in a World-System.*

7. Drum Major Institute for Public Policy, "Saving Our Middle Class" (April 2007), www.drummajorinstitute.org/.

8. *Maready v. City of Winston-Salem,* 467 S.E.2d 615 (1996).

9. *Kelo v. City of New London,* 546 U.S. 807 (2005); for an analysis of post-Kelo legislation, see www.american.com/archive/2007/june-0607/life-after-kelo.

10. Boston Redevelopment Authority, press release, "Seeking World Class Architecture for New Downtown Building, City Releases 115 Winthrop Square RFP," (May 30, 2006), www.cityofboston.gov/bra/press/PressDisplay.asp?pressID=312.

11. Peter Marcuse and Ronald van Kemper, *Globalizing Cities: A New Spatial Order?* (Oxford: Blackwell, 2000).

12. Susan Clarke and Gary Gaile, "Local Politics in a Global Era: Thinking Locally, Acting Globally," in Globalization and the Changing U.S. City, *Annals of the American Academy of Political and Social Science* 551 (1997): 28; David Audretsch, "The Innovative Advantage of U.S. Cities," in *Innovation and Competitive Cities in the Global Economy,* by James Simmie (Oxford: Brookes University, School of Planning, 2001), 72–78.

13. *Code of Ordinances, City of Atlanta, Georgia,* Sec. 16–18P.028; David Pendered, "City Pushing New Zoning: Everything in Walking Distance," *Atlanta Journal-Constitution,* February 25, 2002, 1-B; *City of Seattle Legislation,* Ordinance Number 122054.

14. Savannah Blackwell, "The Real Welfare Problem in San Francisco: Giving Away the Store," *San Francisco Bay Guardian,* June 23, 2004, at www.sfbg.com (last visited, May 17, 2005). The Boston Redevelopment Authority has itself recently made a point of courting the life sciences industry; www.lifetechboston.com.

15. For an analysis of city international relations efforts, see Sydney Leavens, "When Cities Take Up Diplomacy: The Function of Municipal International Relations Departments in Five U.S. Cities" (unpublished manuscript 2007).

16. *530 U.S. 363* (2000).

17. David Keeling, "Transport and the World City Paradigm," in Knox and Taylor, *World Cities in a World-System.*

18. Andy Newman, "Cargo Ships Leaving Red Hook? Maybe Not So Fast," *New York Times,* August 5, 2007.

19. New York City Economic Development Corporation: www.nycedc.com/Web/About Us/WhatWeDo/WhatWeDo.htm.

20. This section relies heavily on an excellent paper by Sameer Dhond, "Municipal Broadband Law and Policy in the United States" (unpublished paper, 2007).

21. Richard Hoffman, "When It Comes to Broadband, U.S. Plays Follow the Leader," *Information Week,* February 15, 2007.

22. Stephen Graham, "Communication Grids: Cities and Infrastructure," in Sassen, *Global Networks and Linked Cities.*

23. Muni Wireless, "The Voice of Public Broadband," www.muniwireless.com/.

24. *Lincoln Electrical Systems v. Nebraska Public Service Commission,* 655 N.W.2d 363 (Neb. 2003) found that there was municipal home rule power, but cities were later forbidden by the state legislature to implement broadband. States that prohibit municipal broadband include Nebraska, Arkansas, and Nevada; states that bar retail services include Washington, Utah, and Wisconsin; states imposing financial and procedural requirements include Florida, Tennessee, and South Carolina; states forbidding cross-subsidization include Iowa, South Carolina, and Virginia; states requiring a private provider include

Pennsylvania and Michigan; states requiring a referendum include Colorado, Oregon, and Florida.

25. *541 U.S. 125* (2004).

26. Sassen, *Global City,* 338–39.

27. City of Johannesburg, South Africa: www.joburg.org.za/joburg_2030/.

28. See Gerald Frug, *City Making: Building Communities without Building Walls* (Princeton: Princeton University Press, 1999).

29. Our discussion of immigration is based on a superb analysis of subject by Rick Su, *The Immigrant City* (forthcoming). On metropolitan immigration, see Sam Roberts, "Minorities Now Form Majority in One-Third of Most-Populous Metropolitan Counties," *New York Times,* August 9, 2007; on the value of immigration to cities, see Paul S. Grogan and Tony Proscio, *Comeback Cities: A Blueprint for Urban Neighborhood Revival* (Boulder: Westview, 2000); the Hazleton case is *Lozano v. City of Hazleton,* 2007 U.S. District Lexis 54320 (Dist. Ct. Pa. July 26, 2007).

30. These suggestions are made by Su, *Immigrant City.*

31. For statistics on the foreign-born population in the United States, see *Census 2000 Brief:* "The Foreign-Born Population: 2000" (December 2003); for an analysis of resident alien voting, see Jamin Raskin, "Legal Aliens, Local Citizens: The Historical, Constitutional and Theoretical Meanings of Alien Suffrage," *University of Pennsylvania Law Review* 141 (1993): 1391. On the European Union, see http://ec.europa.eu/justice_home/unit/elections/reports/index_en.htm.

CHAPTER 8. THE TOURIST CITY

1. Dennis Judd and Susan Fainstein, eds., *The Tourist City* (New Haven: Yale University Press, 1999).

2. Johan Hannigan, *Fantasy City: Pleasure and Profit in the Postmodern Metropolis* (London: Routledge, 1998); Dennis Judd, "Constructing the Tourist Bubble," in Judd and Fainstein, *Tourist City.*

3. Craig Horowitz, "Stadium of Dreams," *New York Magazine,* June 14, 2004.

4. Terry Nichols Clark, ed., *The City as an Entertainment Machine* (Amsterdam: Elsevier/JAI, 2004). For a related critique of this distinction, see Judd and Fainstein, *Tourist City,* 270.

5. Clark County, Nevada, website: www.co.clark.nv.us/Public_communications/About_clark_county.htm.

6. Barbara Land and Myrick Land, *A Short History of Las Vegas,* 2nd ed. (Reno: University of Nevada Press, 2004).

7. For Chicago, see *Chicago Convention and Tourism Bureau,* "Dedicated Busway Now Open at McCormack Place," www.choosechicago.com/media, www.transitchicago.com/; for Boston, see www.mbta.com; for Portland, see www.trimet.org/about/index.htm.

8. *City of Philadelphia v. Schweiker,* 858 A.2d 75 (2004). For a case upholding a city's taxing authority on private garages that competed with public garages, see *City of Pittsburgh v. Alco Parking Corporation,* 417 U.S. 329 (1974).

9. The quotation is from www.nycgovparks.org/sub_about/about_parks.html. See dnr.state.il.us/lands/Landmgt/PARKS/R2/region2.htm; www.parks.wa.gov/parks/regnps.asp; www.mass.gov/dcr/forparks.htm.

10. www.mass.gov/der/hatch_events.htm.

11. The fact that Boston's hotel tax is one of the few non-property-tax revenue sources that the city has makes it hard for the city to dedicate a portion of it to a particular program rather than to support the general budget. For a general analysis of these issues, see the Boston Foundation, *Funding for Cultural Organizations in Boston and Nine Other Metropolitan Areas* (2003).

12. New York City Department of Cultural Affairs website: www.nyc.gov/html/dcla/html/home/home.shtml; San Francisco Grants for the Arts website: www.sfgfta.org/grants_html/hist.html; www.sfgfta.org/grants_html/grants_visual_arts.htm; City of Boston Arts, Tourism and Special Events website:www.cityofboston.gov/arts/bcc_recipients_05.asp.

13. Christina Pazzanese, "Globewatch: Buck Stops Passing," *Boston Globe,* July 9, 2006.

14. Cruise Lines International Association website: www.cruising.org/press/overview%202006/2.cfm; Port of San Francisco website: www.sfport.com/site/port_index.asp?id=30555; www.bryantstreetpier.com/media.html.

15. For the Newark budget, see https://index.ci.newark.nj.us/dsweb/Get/Document-139488/I.+Overview_R1.pdf; Peter Eisenger, "The Politics of Bread and Circuses," *Urban Affairs Review* 35 (2000): 329.

16. This argument runs though many of the essays in Michael Sorkin, ed., *Variations on a Theme Park: The New American City and the End of Public Space* (New York: Hill and Wang, 1992).

17. Richard Foglesong, *Married to the Mouse: Walt Disney World and Orlando* (New Haven: Yale University Press, 2001); see also Richard Foglesong, "Walt Disney World and Orlando: Deregulation as a Strategy for Tourism," in Judd and Fainstein, *Tourist City,* 89.

18. Themed Entertainment Association/Economic Research Associates (TEA/ERA) Theme Park Attendance Report: www.connectingindustry.com/pdfs/TEA-ERAAttendance06.pdf.

19. Canary Wharf Group website: www.canarywharf.com/mainFrm1.asp.

20. Growth of the festival marketplace is chronicled in Bernard Frieden and Lynne Sagalyn, *Downtown, Inc.: How America Rebuilds Cities* (Cambridge: MIT Press, 1994); Judd and Fainstein, *Tourist City;* and Hannigan, *Fantasy City.*

21. Matt Viser, "Detroit Betting Heavily on Casinos," *Boston Globe,* August 5, 2007.

22. MGM Mirage website: www.mgmmirage.com/companyoverview.asp#.

23. Dennis Judd and Dick Simpson, "Reconstructing the Local State: The Role of External Constraints in Building Urban Tourism," *American Behavioral Scientist* 46 (April 2003): 8.

24. Heywood Sanders, "Space Available: The Realities of Convention Centers as Economic Development Strategy," *Brookings Institution Metropolitan Policy Program* (January 2005).

25. Eisenger, "Politics of Bread and Circuses," 329.

26. Mandy Rafool, *Playing the Stadium Game: Financing Professional Sports Facilities in the '90s* (Denver: National Conference of State Legislatures, 1997); Eisenger, "Politics of Bread and Circuses," 316.

27. Judd and Fainstein, *Tourist City;* Hannigan, *Fantasy City;* Sorkin, *Variations on a Theme Park.*

28. Christine Spolar, "Barcelona Shows What Olympics Can Mean," *Chicago Tribune,* August 22, 2007.

29. City of London website: www.london2012.com/.

30. World Expo 2010 Shanghai, China, website: www.expo2010china.com/expo/expoenglish/index.html.

31. Judd and Fainstein, *Tourist City,* 272.

32. Bruce Ehrlich and Peter Dreier, "The New Boston Discovers the Old Tourism and the Struggle for a Livable City," in Judd and Fainstein, *Tourist City,* 177.

33. An Act Establishing the Boston Landmarks Commission, Acts 1975, Chapter 772.

CHAPTER 9. THE MIDDLE CLASS CITY

1. Barry Bluestone and Mary Huff Stevenson, *The Boston Renaissance: Race, Space, and Economic Change in an American Metropolis* (New York: Russell Sage Foundation, 2000), 1–22; Jason C. Booza, Jackie Cutsinger, and George Galster, Brookings Institution

Metropolitan Policy Program, *Where Did They Go? The Decline of Middle-Income Neighborhoods in Metropolitan America* (June 2006).

2. Janny Scott, "Cities Shed Middle Class, and Are Richer and Poorer for It," *New York Times*, July 23, 2006 (quoting Edward Glaeser).

3. Booza et al., "Where Did They Go?" 23.

4. For a classic analysis of class, see Paul Fussell, *Class* (New York: Summit Books, 1984).

5. See, e.g., Brookings Institution Center on Urban and Metropolitan Policy, *Growing the Middle Class: Connecting All Miami-Dade Residents to Economic Opportunity* (June 2004), 8.

6. Budget Options for New York City: www.ibo.nyc.ny.us/iboreports/options.pdf.

7. *Mendoza v. State of California*, 37 Cal. Rptr. 3d 505 (Court of Appeal, 2nd District, 2007).

8. Jonathan Kozol, *Savage Inequalities: Children in America's Schools* (New York: Crown, 1991); Stephen D. Sugarman and Frank R. Kemerer, *School Choice and Social Controversy: Politics, Policy, and Law* (Washington, D.C.: Brookings Institution, 1999), 14–17.

9. Joel Kotkin, *The City: A Global History* (New York: Modern Library, 2005).

10. Education Commission of the States, "Charter School Caps," mb2.ecs.org/reports/Report.aspx?id=80.

11. Remarks of U.S. Secretary of Education Margaret Spellings at the 2007 National Charter Schools Conference: www.ed.gov/news/pressreleases/2007/04/04272007a.html.

12. Pietro Nivola, *Laws of the Landscape: How Policies Shape Cities in Europe and America* (Washington, D.C.: Brookings Institution, 1999), 22–24.

13. For ideas about how to do this (albeit on the state level), see William H. Simon, "Social-Republican Property," *UCLA Law Review* 38 (1991): 1335.

14. *American Financial Services Ass'n v. City of Oakland*, 104 P. 3d 813, 833 (Ca. 2005) (George, C. J., dissenting).

15. Darin M. Dalmat, "Bringing Economic Justice Closer to Home: The Legal Viability of Local Minimum Wages Laws under Home Rule," *Columbia Journal of Law and Social Problems* 93 (2005); *New Orleans Campaign for a Living Wage v. City of New Orleans*, 825 So.2d 1098 (2002).

16. *New Mexicans for Free Enterprise v. City of Santa Fe*, 126 P.3d 1149 (2005).

17. Ellen Perlman, "Residency Laws: Placing City Limits on Public Employees," *Governing Magazine* (May 1995); *Gusewelle v. City of Wood River*, 374 F. 3d 569 (7th Cir. 2004); *NYC Administrative Code*, § 12–120 (2005); *Residency Requirement Ord. 1976 c. 9, City of Boston Code* § 5–5.3 (2005); *McDonald v. Menino*, 1997 WL 106955 (D. Mass 1997); Andrea Estes, "Most Workers Free from City Rule," *Boston Globe*, April 19, 2004. The U.S. Supreme Court case is *McCarthy v. Philadelphia Civil Service Commission*, 424 U.S. 679 (1976); the California case, *Ector v. City of Torrance*, 514 P.2d 433 (1973), was modified by a new provision of the California Constitution, Article XI, section 10.

18. On San Diego, see "San Diego Defeats Wal-Mart Superstore Ban," *Associated Press*, July 10, 2007; the California case is *Hernandez v. City of Hanford*, 159 P.3d 33 (Sup. Ct. Cal. 2007).

19. Queens West Development Corporation/Empire State Development website: www.queenswest.org/home.html. For a look at one small-scale industrial site, see David Gonzalez, "In Place of Smokestacks, Makers of Dumplings and Doors," *New York Times*, September 10, 2007.

20. City of New York, *Protecting and Growing New York City's Industrial Job Base* (January 2005).

21. This discussion is based on Emily Thatcher-Renshaw, "Industrial Job Retention in Boston: The Back Streets Initiative" (unpublished paper, 2005).

22. U.S. Small Business Administration, "The Small Business Economy" (2005); Citizens Budget Commission and the Federal Reserve Bank of New York, *What Firms Value Most: Encouraging Small Business Success in New York City and Northern New Jersey* (2004); Brookings Institution Center on Urban and Metropolitan Policy, *Growing the Middle Class,* 8; Paul Grogan and Tony Proscio, *Comeback Cities: A Blueprint for Urban Neighborhood Revival* (Boulder: Westview Press, 2000).

23. Center for an Urban Future, *A World of Opportunity* (February 2007), 11.

24. Michael Porter, "The Competitive Advantage of the Inner City," *Harvard Business Review,* May 1, 1995; Initiative for a Competitive Inner City, *State of the Inner City Economies: Small Businesses in the Inner City* (October 2005).

25. City and County of San Francisco website: www.sfgov.org/site/moed_page.asp?id=33310; New York City Economic Development Corporate website: www.nycedc.com/WorldTradeCenter/GrantsInfo/LibertyBondProgram.html; Denver Office of Economic Development website: www.milehigh.com/business/financing.

CHAPTER 10. THE REGIONAL CITY

1. Peter Calthorpe and William Fulton, *The Regional City* (Washington, D.C.: Island Press, 2001).

2. David Barron and Gerald Frug, "Defensive Localism: A View from the Field," *Journal of Law and Politics* 11 (Spring–Summer 2005): 261; David Barron, Gerald Frug, and Rick Su, *Dispelling The Myth of Home Rule: Local Power in Greater Boston* (Cambridge: Rappaport Institute for Greater Boston, 2004).

3. Stephen McGoldrick, "Interlocal Collaboration," *Metropolitan Area Planning Council Initiatives* 34 (2003).

4. *Mass. General Laws,* Chapter 40B.

5. Anthony Downs, *New Visions for Metropolitan America* (Washington, D.C.: Brookings Institution, 1994), 170.

6. For a more extended discussion of these ideas, see Gerald Frug, "Beyond Regional Government," *Harvard Law Review* 115 (2002): 1763.

7. *Reynolds v. Sims,* 377 U.S. 533 (1964); *Avery v. Midland County,* 390 U.S. 474 (1968).

8. Simon Hix, *The Political System of the European Union* (New York: St. Martin's, 1999); Helen Wallace and William Wallace, *Policy-Making in the European Union,* 5th ed. (Oxford: Oxford University Press, 2005).

9. *Treaty Establishing the European Community,* articles 17–18; Jurgen Habermas, *The Inclusion of the Other: Studies in Political Theory* (Cambridge: MIT Press, 1998); Joseph Weiler, *The Constitution of Europe* (Cambridge: Cambridge University Press, 1999).

10. Margaret Weir, "Coalition Building for Regionalism," in Bruce Katz *Reflections on Regionalism,* 127 (Washington, D.C.: Brookings Institution Press, 2000); Myron Orfield, *Metropolitics; A Regional Agenda for Community and Stability* (Washington, D.C.: Brookings Institution Press, 1997).

11. Rob Gurwitt, "The State vs. Sprawl," *Governing* (January 1999); Arthur Nelson, "New Kid in Town: The Georgia Regional Transportation Authority and Its Role in Managing Growth in Metropolitan Georgia," *Wake Forest Law Review* 35 (2000): 625.

About the Authors

Gerald E. Frug is the Louis D. Brandeis Professor of Law at Harvard Law School. Educated at the University of California at Berkeley and Harvard Law School, he worked as a Special Assistant to the Chairman of the Equal Employment Opportunity Commission, in Washington, D.C., and as Health Services Administrator of the City of New York before he began teaching in 1974 at the University of Pennsylvania Law School. He joined the Harvard faculty in 1981. Professor Frug's specialty is local government law, a subject he has taught for more than twenty-five years. He has published dozens of articles on the topic and is the author, among other works, of a casebook, *Local Government Law* (4th edition, 2006, with David Barron and Richard T. Ford), *Dispelling the Myth of Home Rule* (2004, with David Barron and Rick Su), and *City Making: Building Communities without Building Walls* (Princeton University Press, 1999).

David J. Barron is a Professor of Law at Harvard Law School. A graduate of Harvard College and Harvard Law School, he was a law clerk to Judge Stephen Reinhardt of the United States Court of Appeals for the Ninth Circuit and Justice John Paul Stevens of the Supreme Court of the United States. Prior to teaching, he served as an attorney-adviser in the Office of Legal Counsel in the United States Department of Justice. Professor Barron's research and writing focuses on local government law, constitutional law, and the separation of powers. He has published widely on these topics, and his articles have appeared in the *Harvard Law Review,* the *Stanford Law Review,* and the *Yale Law Journal.* He is also the author of a casebook, *Local Government Law* (4th edition, 2006, with Gerald Frug and Richard T. Ford), and a study of local power in the greater Boston area, *Dispelling the Myth of Home Rule* (2004, with Gerald Frug and Rick Su).

Index

administrative city model, 37, 38
agency, 12–14, 15, 17, 21, 23–30, 141
airports. *See under* transportation
annexation, 38, 46, 105
arts and cultural programs, 172–73, 181
Atlanta, 5, 10, 90, 232; business-friendly
regime in, 21; characteristics of, 54, 55–57,
237nn1–2, 237n5, 238n8; charter of, 64,
65, 102, 104; employment policies in, 94;
as global city, 151–52, 161; home rule in,
69, 72; land use policies in, 101–2, 104, 109,
110, 111, 151–52; school system in, 122,
125, 131, 133, 135, 136, 242n1, 242nn3–5;
special legislation and, 93; sports in, 180,
182; taxes in, 78, 79, 83, 84, 85, 86; as tourist
city, 180, 182
autonomy, local: city-building compared to,
6, 31, 52, 232; dangers of, 42; debate about,
14, 17, 30, 31, 34–35, 52; education and,
122–23; equity and, 48; federalism and, 44,
45; fiscal autonomy, 75, 76, 87; home rule
and, 31–34, 36, 61, 207, 214; interlocal relations and, 14, 39–40; limits on, 6, 30, 34–35,
38–39, 76, 99, 123, 143; and regionalism,
214, 221, 225. *See also* home rule

Beijing, 154, 182
borders. *See* boundaries
borrowing powers and limits, 62, 66, 67, 68, 69,
72, 73, 95–96, 108, 148, 171
Boston, 1, 4, 5, 53, 232; affordable housing
in, 82, 112–14, 119; arts and cultural programs in, 172; bonds and debt limits in,
95, 96, 240n17; and business improvement
districts, 110–11; characteristics of, 54,
55–57, 161, 237nn1–6, 238n8; charter of,
62, 64–66, 71, 73, 238nn8–9; charter, parochial, and private schools in, 128–30, 131,
132, 136, 194, 242n14, 243n17; community
support for schools in, 136–37; convention
centers in, 180; defensive localism in, 207–8,
212; development strategies of, 82, 83, 98,
103, 109, 110–11, 119, 150, 151, 166, 178,
179, 201–2, 240n6, 244n14; elections in,
63, 162; employment policies in, 94, 95, 96,

97–98, 199, 201; expenditures in, 62, 93, 94,
95, 96, 97–98; federally controlled land in,
172; fees in, 88, 89–90; fiscal constraints on,
78–79, 82, 89–90, 91, 93, 95, 96, 109, 150,
166, 211–12; fragmented control over public
land in, 172, 173–74; as global city, 150,
151, 161, 166; historical attractions in, 170,
173–74, 184; historic preservation in, 184;
home rule in, 38, 53, 61, 64–66, 73, 74, 93,
96, 100, 109, 111, 112, 124, 208; inclusionary
zoning in, 114–15; interdistrict schooling
in, 133–34; land use in, 82, 100–101, 102,
103–4, 105, 107, 109, 113–15, 151, 202;
limitations on home rule in, 66–67, 69–70,
74, 76, 84, 109, 112, 135, 162, 211–12; linkage programs in, 113–14; magnet schools
and tracking in, 138–39; mayoral control
over schools, 123–24, 191, 192, 194; as
metropolitan center, 55, 82, 228; as middle-
class city, 188, 189, 191, 194, 199, 201–2;
middle-class housing in, 118–19; parks in,
172; pilot schools in, 135–36; planning powers in, 103–5; police and fire services in, 93;
pre–home rule powers of, 61–64; property
taxes in, 76, 78–80, 82, 83, 91, 107, 150, 166,
172, 188, 189, 239n5, 240n6; and public
authorities, 98, 103–4, 105, 106–7, 112–13,
155, 157, 170, 172, 174, 180; as regional
city, 82, 207–8, 211–12, 219, 222, 228; and
regional government, 46, 222; rent control
in, 116–17; residency requirements in, 199;
school choice program in, 139; school committee in, 71, 123–24; school enrichment
programs in, 134–35; school system in, generally, 71, 93, 123, 125, 191, 194; segregation
in, 129, 161; small businesses in, 201–2; state
aid in, 76, 90–91; state control over, 9–10,
58–59, 61–64, 71, 73, 74, 78, 89–90, 91, 93,
94, 95, 97, 100–101, 102, 104, 107, 112, 123,
150, 172, 180, 184, 188, 199; state-controlled
property in, 105, 106–7, 172, 180; student
demographics in, 122, 129, 133, 138, 242n2,
242n4, 242n14, 243n17; and suburbs, 1,
55, 133–34, 219; taxes in, 76, 78–80, 82, 83,
84–85, 86–87, 91, 150, 166, 172, 188, 189,